Centennials

ALEX HILL

Centennials

The 12 Habits of Great, Enduring Organisations

Cornerstone Press

10 9 8 7 6 5 4 3 2 1

Cornerstone Press
20 Vauxhall Bridge Road
London SW1V 2SA

Cornerstone Press is part of the Penguin Random House group of companies whose addresses can be found at global.penguinrandomhouse.com

First published by Cornerstone Press in 2023

www.penguin.co.uk

A CIP catalogue record for this book is available from the British Library

ISBN 9781847942807 (Hardback)
ISBN 9781847942814 (Trade paperback)

Typeset in 11.2/15 pt Minion Pro Regular
by Integra Software Services Pvt. Ltd, Pondicherry.

Printed and bound in Great Britain by Clays Ltd, Elcograf S.p.A.

The authorised representative in the EEA is Penguin Random House Ireland, Morrison Chambers, 32 Nassau Street, Dublin D02 YH68

www.greenpenguin.co.uk

For
Lois, Dylan, Aurelia and Pheonix
My family

Centennial /sen-ten'yəl/
adjective

Lasting a hundred years
One hundred years old

Contents

CONTENTS

Centennials

Prologue

THE THEORY OF EVERYTHING

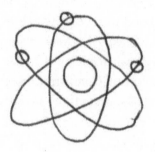

Stable core, disruptive edge

1.

When, ten years into my career, I made the move from being an engineer and manager at the TI Group to being a researcher and teacher at the University of Oxford, I was immediately struck by how fundamentally different the mindsets of the two organisations were. At TI it was all about the short term: hitting daily sales targets, achieving monthly budgets. At Oxford it was about the long term: conducting research over several years, working on ideas that might bear fruit only many years later, and preparing students for the future. While I was at TI, the short-term approach seemed to make sense. After all, I reasoned, if you don't survive the short term, you won't make it to the long term. But my Oxford experience started to make me doubt the wisdom of this view. Over time I came to realise that, if applied as a driving principle, the short term can actually destroy the long term: attention is diverted from the important to the immediately visible, sales get brought forward, investment gets cut – all in the name of hitting a particular target. The short term may be necessary, I concluded, but it's no guarantee of ultimate survival and may indeed conspire against it. TI's fate rather proved the truth of my insight: it failed and was bought by the Smiths Group.

A decade later, in 2012, I found myself working with UK Sport, the funding body for the British Olympic teams, who had recently enjoyed their best performance ever at a summer Games (they finished third with sixty-five medals) and were seeking to build on this success. On learning that they had looked at various arts organisations for inspiration, I contacted the Royal Academy of Music, the Royal College of Art and the Royal Shakespeare Company and discovered that they too had the long-term view of success that I had encountered at Oxford. Like Oxford, they had been around for a long time. Intrigued, I started – in tandem with four other researchers – to look at other organisations with long pedigrees, from educational establishments such as the University of Cambridge (founded in 1209) and Eton College (1440) to sports organisations that ranged from New Zealand's All Blacks (1884) to the Lawn Tennis Association (1888), and from such manufacturers as Morgan cars (1909) and Rolls-Royce engines (1904) to Moorfields Eye Hospital (1805), the Royal Marines (1664) and the BBC (1922).

I soon discovered that all these organisations – which I came to refer to as 'the Centennials' – shared the same mindset: they set themselves ambitious long-term goals and refuse to be deflected by short-term gains in their pursuit of them. Their philosophy was that, while it was necessary to keep a constant eye on the ground immediately in front of them, their focus should always be on the horizon.

2.

There was an analogy here, I thought, with the discovery of the atom. First posited by the Greek philosopher Democritus back in the fifth century BCE, it became a key focus of the work of a series of outstanding scientists who shared the single goal of unravelling its secrets.[1] The English chemist John Dalton laid the foundations of modern atomic theory in 1808, with his method for calculating the weight of different atoms and his embryonic periodic table.[2] A fellow chemist, Michael Faraday, then accidentally discovered that atoms were not the smallest particles, though it took the work of the English physicist John Thomson sixty years later to narrow in on what would later be called electrons.[3] At the end of the century Marie and Pierre Curie, along with Henri Becquerel, refined the picture further with their discovery of radioactivity.[4] Their former student Ernest Rutherford, who had also worked with John Thomson and was now working with the German physicist Hans Geiger, then made the breakthrough discovery after years of toil that there was a strong positive charge in the centre of the atom (later to be called the nucleus) and created the model of the atom that we recognise today.[5] All these scientists, in other words, were united by a common aim, they each devoted years of their lives to fostering it, and their communal work on it ultimately stretched across the centuries.

The analogy with the Centennials goes a little further. Rutherford discovered that atoms exist in different states. If they're too large or too small, they will be volatile and will either latch on to other atoms or become radioactive and start to decay. The 'classic atom' of Rutherford's model has, by contrast, a stable nucleus at its centre, and electrons that move around it, just as the planets orbit the Sun. Part of it, in other words, is unchanging; part of it is constantly on the move.

So, I have discovered, it is with the Centennials. The people who work with and for them are constantly on the move, coming up with fresh discoveries, swapping ideas. They are the electrons of the organisation. But at the heart of each Centennial is a stable nucleus of values developed over time and passed by one long-serving generation to the next; of goals that are constant and unwavering; and of a culture that values the past just as it looks to the future. If change becomes necessary, this nucleus embraces it, but it does so carefully and slowly.

In short, the Centennials have both a stable core and a disruptive edge, and they preserve a careful balance between the two. In the neat formulation of Paul Thompson, the vice-chancellor of the Royal College of Art, they're 'radically traditional'.[6] Out of this balance emerges the energy that propels them forward and a stability that ensures that no one loses sight of what each Centennial is there to achieve or forgets what has led to success in the past.

It's a balance that is sadly lacking among many non-Centennial enterprises today. An obsession with the here and now, with short-term results, and with immediate shareholder value has come to dominate strategic thinking to the exclusion of almost everything else. This obsession has exacted a price. Essentially, as companies have become more short-term, so their life expectancy has fallen. When the Standard & Poor's index was set up in 1957 to track the financial performance of the 500 most valuable companies in the US (the S&P 500), the lives of most organisations were measured in decades. Since the 1980s, when shareholder value became the dominant mantra, their expectation of survival has fallen fivefold to the point where the average life of an S&P company is now only fifteen years.

Some argue that shorter business life cycles are all to the good. When a company that has fallen from favour dies, the argument goes, its resources are freed up for more effective exploitation by another concern. The problem with this point of view is that it neglects the friction and wastage that corporate death involves.[7] It also fails to recognise that the long-term success of any economy or society relies on the stability of its core organisations and institutions, and that if everyone is solely focused on the here and now then the long-term questions and challenges that societies face – such as climate change, poverty, immigration, health and education – are less likely to be addressed.[8] If everything is constantly booming and busting then nothing will last and, eventually, everything will collapse.

3.

Over the years, various studies have sought to pinpoint what creates long-term success. Some, such as *In Search of Excellence* (1982), *Built to Last* (1994) and *Good to Great* (2001), have done so by analysing what successful companies do and extracting from the analysis general truths that can be widely applied.[9] *In Search of Excellence* argued that we should 'stick to our knitting'. *Built to Last* warned of the dangers of focusing too much on profit. *Good to Great* promoted the notion of the Level 5 leader. Other studies – such as *The Four Principles of Enduring Success* (2007) and *Three Rules for Making a Company Truly Great* (2013) – have crunched vast quantities of data about a wide range of organisations to extract general truths.[10]

Both methodologies have had their share of critics. Those who have reservations about the *In Search of Excellence* school argue that the subsequent decline of many of the companies held up as exemplars (Hewlett-Packard, Kodak, Motorola and so on) shows how difficult it is to embody these qualities and retain performance in these areas.[11] Those who criticise the *Four Principles* and *Three Rules* schools argue that the business truths they promote (for example, the *Four Principles*' 'exploit before you explore' and the *Three Rules*' 'get better before you get cheaper') are too generic and vague to have real practical application. As one CEO said to me: 'We all want to get better, before we get cheaper, but how do you do that? And we all want to exploit before we explore, but what does that really mean? How should we do it? And when should we switch?'

It's perhaps because case studies based on companies have proved problematic that some people who have studied the conundrum of business longevity have turned away from businesses altogether and looked to see what we can learn from success in other fields. *Moneyball* (2003), *Outliers* (2008) and *Rebel Ideas* (2019) are just three examples of books that look at such spheres of activity as the arts, education, science and sports for inspiration.[12] But this approach, too, has its problems. It tends to be more anecdotal than analytical. It doesn't offer comparative analysis. It's therefore sometimes difficult to know whether the success described was a one-off phenomenon, or a process that can be replicated elsewhere.

In this book, I've sought to take account of the undoubted strengths of each approach, while offering what I hope is a fresh perspective through my focus on seven of the Centennials I have studied over the years; organisations that have each been in existence (if not now precisely in their original form) for more than 100 years and that have regularly outperformed their peers over that time.[13]

> Eton College (founded in 1440), which has educated many of Britain's leading figures, including, over the past 300 years, twenty prime ministers.
>
> The Royal Academy of Music (1822), which has produced some of Britain's finest musicians.

The Royal College of Art (1837), responsible for producing world-class artists and designers.

The Royal Shakespeare Company (1879), arguably the world's pre-eminent theatre organisation.

British Cycling (1896), which has won fifty medals at the last four Olympic Games.

The All Blacks (1884), arguably the most successful sports team of all time.

Nasa (1915), which has dominated space exploration since the 1960s.

I and my fellow researchers studied each Centennial in minute detail. Where possible, we spent a year with each one to experience from the inside how it functioned. We then formulated a set of general principles that all seven collectively appeared to embody. After that, we spent five years sharing these principles with dozens of organisations and thousands of people across the world, inviting them to test them, critique them and retest them. And we looked for additional insights to a vast range of organisations, both successful and unsuccessful, whose stories helped clarify our thinking.

Some readers might object that the Centennials don't face the immediate challenges that their own organisations do. The Centennials don't have shareholders to keep happy. They are not required to hit profit targets as small businesses and FTSE 100 giants alike have to do. To that extent, such readers might think, the strategies and skills they have developed may be interesting to read about, but are not applicable in a conventional business setting. These objections, however, ignore the underlying goals that all organisations have to achieve if they are to survive. The Royal Academy of Music would not have flourished for 200 years if it was not economically viable or if it failed to win new 'customers' in the form of students. The Royal Shakespeare Company similarly would have collapsed if its finances were unsound or it failed to connect with consumers. Nasa may be funded via the US federal budget, but such funding would not be forthcoming if it didn't meet targets and deliver technological breakthroughs.

The Centennials, in other words, have much to teach all of us.

Part 1: Stable core

Purpose

Habit 1

BUILD YOUR NORTH STAR

In it for a long time, not a good time

1.

Saturday, 25 July 1981. Waikato, New Zealand. The South African rugby team were preparing for their second match on their tour of New Zealand. The stakes were high. 'It was a big game,' Pat Bennett, the Waikato captain, recalls. 'And the first time a New Zealand rugby match had been broadcast live, around the world. So we knew we had to win.'[1]

Meanwhile, a 300-strong group of protesters, deeply unhappy that a New Zealand team was preparing to take on a team from apartheid South Africa, had gathered outside the stadium in Hamilton. As the match started, they proceeded to kick down a fence and invade the pitch. The crowd hurled bottles at them. The police tried to remove them. But, with arms linked, they stood their ground. 'The whole world's watching! The whole world's watching!' they chanted. Concerned that more protesters were on their way, the police ultimately decided to cancel the match.[2]

Over the next few weeks, further protests against the South African tour took place. Each scheduled match was disrupted. Demonstrators gathered in front of government buildings and blocked roads. 'It was the biggest uprising in New Zealand's history,' John Minto, one of the protesters, remembers. 'A watershed moment when the country stood up for what it believed, and took their place on the world stage. I can remember my dad arguing with my mum at the time, saying, "I don't understand what all the fuss is about, it's only a game." And my mum saying, "No, it's not. It's our national sport. It represents us – our values, and our beliefs. And I don't believe apartheid's right!"'[3]

As arguments flew back and forth and the debate raged, the New Zealand national side – the All Blacks – listened attentively. At the end of the tour, even though only 5 per cent of the population had protested, and even though rugby fans had not been among the demonstrators, the team took the decision not to play South Africa again until the apartheid regime had been dismantled. The ban lasted eleven years. In 1995, the newly elected president of South Africa, Nelson Mandela, visited New Zealand and offered his thanks for the stance people had taken. 'You elected to brave the batons,' he told them, 'and pronounce that New Zealand could not be free when other human beings were being subjected to a legalised and cruel system of racial domination.'[4] When they stopped that match at Hamilton, he said, 'we cheered and rattled the prison doors in celebration. It was like the dawn of a new era as the sun came out.'

The people of New Zealand have enjoyed an extraordinary relationship with rugby – and have used it to represent their society, its values and beliefs on the world stage – ever since the national team's second international tour, in 1905. Then, as New Zealand prepared for 'Dominion status' within the British empire, the country's prime minister asked the All Blacks to make it one of their goals to promote New Zealand values and trading links abroad.[5] Arguably, the link between country and game goes back well before that. Before the first European settlers arrived in 1642, the indigenous Māori people were playing a rugby-like game called *ki-o-rahi*. When the first New Zealand team toured Britain in 1888, twenty-one of their twenty-six players were Māori.[6] Women became part of the national rugby story in 1915 (though the first official women's league was not established until 1980). It truly is a national sport.

Many have detected a direct link between the 'national character' and success at the national game. 'Imagine in the 1800s,' Richie McCaw, the former All Blacks captain, says, 'getting on a boat not knowing where you are going . . . and [having to make] your own way. That's going to make you pretty tough, and I guess, if you have that sort of outlook it's going to get passed down through the generations.'[7] The journalist Peter Bills talks of 'an unwillingness to accept defeat', an ability to 'dig deep and stay calm in adversity', a talent for 'making coherent decisions while all around you is chaos' that he believes characterises the average New Zealander and argues how these qualities lead the individual to sacrifice 'personal concerns or causes to the mantra of helping your mates'.[8] Then there's the traditional Māori *haka* that is performed before each match that further fosters a sense of teamship and a desire to achieve.[9] It's no wonder that not only have the national side been astonishingly successful over the past century and more, winning 77 per cent of their 620 games and scoring twice as many points as their opponents, but that more and more New Zealanders have taken up the sport.[10] It's an expression of who they are, and what they want to become.

Which is why the decision taken by the national side in 1981 after the apartheid demonstrations seems in hindsight the obvious one for them to have taken. As upholders and ambassadors of New Zealand's values, the All Blacks felt they had to take a stand. They didn't see themselves simply as a sports team or even as the national sports team. They viewed themselves as part of the society from which they were drawn, and they accepted the obligations that go with that world view.

2.

For most businesses, turnover and profit are everything. Centennials don't think this way. They look at the whole of society, and every possibility, and ask themselves: How can we shape how society thinks, and behaves, not only today, but for the next twenty to thirty years? How can we ensure that the next generation of money and talent, and the one after that, will want to work with us? As Catherine Mallyon, the executive director of the Royal Shakespeare Company, put it to me: 'If you don't positively shape society then, at some point, it will stop supporting you. And, at some point, it will stop wanting to work with you. And then suddenly, before you know it, all your money and talent will start to go elsewhere.'[11]

This mindset explains why, for organisations that have stood the test of time, there is always a higher purpose that guides everything else. The All Blacks, for example, want to win matches, but their higher purpose is to raise New Zealand's national profile. British Cycling wants to create world-beating competitors but its higher purpose is to improve the UK's health. Nasa launches space missions, but its ambition is to increase our understanding of the universe and our place within it. The Royal College of Art's ultimate goal is to transform the world through art and design.[12] A long-term philosophy underpins them all.

This may all sound very idealistic, but there's a strongly practical rationale for it. All these organisations know that if they don't have a super goal that involves positively shaping the society of the future, at some point all the money and talent will go elsewhere. It's a mindset resisted by most conventional businesses, and by all that focus purely on the short term because, on the surface, it appears to ignore everyday realities. As one CEO put it to me: 'It's easy to shape society if you're a public company, serving public needs. But we're a business, not a charity, and our world is much more competitive than theirs. We've got competitors who are after our people and our customers, and investors who want us to make a profit today not tomorrow, so we don't have the luxury of time, and we can't look twenty years ahead, as we have problems we have to fix today.' The problem with that world view, though, is that it carries no guarantee for survival beyond today.

The short-termism of contemporary businesses has often been commented on, as is the fact that most enterprises are very short-lived.[13] While, for example, the 500 largest companies in the US – the S&P 500 – may collectively have increased their market value fivefold over the past forty years, their average lifespan is – at fifteen years – five times shorter than that of their predecessors.[14] The popular assumption is that this reflects the volatile nature and fierce competitiveness of the current commercial environment. However, it's interesting to note that not all organisations follow this short-lived pattern, and that there are still a number on the index, such as Colgate, Con Edison, Corning, Hartford,

Levi Strauss, Kellogg's, Nordstrom and State Street, whose roots go back a century or more. These vigorous survivors cover very different markets: from dental care to energy, insurance to clothing, fibre optics to food, retail to financial services. What they have in common, though, is a guiding purpose – a north star – that has helped carry them through the last 100 years and more.

Colgate wants to help 'create a healthier future for people and their pets'; Con Edison aspires to help 'develop a cleaner and more resilient society'; Levi Strauss sets out to make 'better clothes that can be worn for longer'; Kellogg's seeks to help 'feed and nurture the world'.[15] All have set up additional enterprises that serve to further their ambition. Colgate, for example, has funded Colgate University in New York since 1890, the Colgate Women's Games since 1975, and the Starlight Children's Foundation since 1990. The Levi Strauss Foundation, founded in 1952, invests more than $10 million each year in environmental and social projects that help it achieve its long-term purpose of 'better clothes that can be worn for longer' – such as its 'water reduction' and 'better cotton' initiatives, and its ongoing education and health programmes in its own and its suppliers' factories.

'It's an important pillar for us as a company,' Chip Bergh, the Levi Strauss CEO, explains. 'It's an important pillar from an innovation standpoint, but it also goes all the way back to our values as a company. This company's been around for 162 years, going back to our founder, Levi Strauss; the man, the myth, the legend himself. We invented blue jeans about 142 years ago. He was an entrepreneur – I like to think about us as the original Silicon Valley start-up. He, from the very beginning, was very big into giving back and making sure that the company always operated with principle and doing the right thing. As a result of that, sustainability in the broadest definition of the word – not just environmental sustainability, but social sustainability and everything else – is part of the fabric of this company . . . The company, every year, funds [the Levi Strauss] foundation with a percentage of the profits that we make . . . The more successful we are as a company, the more earnings or profits we deliver, the more we're able to give to the Levi Strauss Foundation, and then give back to the communities. It is a big part of who we are as a company . . . It's something that we're really proud of. It is part of our ethos. It is helpful in attracting and retaining talent, there's no question about it. Especially today where young people are looking for companies that align with their personal values. That's just the kind of company we are. We didn't change it to attract Millennials; that's who we've been since the inception of this company.'[16]

Equally, the W. K. Kellogg Foundation, founded in 1930, invests more than $100 million each year in education and health programmes, such as its dentist, doctor and nurse fellowships, agriculture research, and its ongoing support of various schools and universities around the world as it seeks to develop future scientists and leaders who will help 'feed and nurture the world' (the foundation is, for example, one of the largest donors to California State, Michigan State and Northwestern universities in the US, and Kellogg College at Oxford University in the UK). 'Our central theme is action,' Russell Mawby, the foundation's CEO for more than twenty-five years, explains, 'taking the best of what's known from various disciplines . . . to tackle significant societal concerns.'[17] And because the foundation is also the largest shareholder of the Kellogg Company, and owns 35 per cent of its shares, it can also help govern and guide its actions. Equally, Con Edison's and State Street's foundations offer grants of more than $10 million each year to other organisations who can help them achieve their cause – to 'develop a cleaner and more resilient society' and 'create better outcomes for the world's investors and the people they serve' – and they also encourage staff to work on volunteer programmes and serve on the boards of charitable organisations.[18]

In the short term all these businesses might have been better off using the funds they diverted to social projects to hit profit targets. In the longer term, the sacrifice of their super goal this would have entailed would have involved an internal cultural shift that would have undermined and, possibly, destroyed them. There's a degree of trade-off here. Most of the companies on the index that are more than 100 years old achieve annual sales of less than $10 billion and make a profit of between 5 and 15 per cent each year. They are, on average, 10 per cent smaller and 20 per cent less profitable than the 200 companies on the index that are less than fifty years old. To that extent, they don't tend to enjoy the booms the younger companies experience.[19] But then they don't suffer the busts either and the appalling waste those busts entail. Dominic Barton, a researcher at McKinsey Global Institute who has analysed the long-term financial performance of 615 publicly traded US companies from 2001 to 2016, acknowledges that it's difficult to measure precisely what the cost of short-termism is. But when it comes to assessing the benefits of a longer-term perspective, he concludes: 'If all public US companies had created jobs at the scale of the long-term-focused organisations in our sample, the country would have generated at least 5 million more jobs from 2001 and 2015 – and an additional $1 trillion in GDP growth (equivalent to an average of 0.8 percentage points of GDP growth per year).'[20]

3.

Sony's mixed fortunes over the years offers a casebook example of the benefits that accrue from having a higher purpose and the dangers of losing sight of it. Back in 1946 its founders, the Japanese engineers Masaru Ibuka and Akio Morita, had a bold ambition.[21] Japan had just emerged from defeat in the Second World War and, as Morita recalled later: 'Suddenly our world was very different.' 'The Emperor,' he went on, 'who until now had never spoken directly to his people, told us the immediate future would be grim. He said that we could "pave the way for a grand peace for all generations to come", but we had to do it "by enduring the unendurable and suffering what is insufferable". He urged Japan to look ahead. "Unite your total strength to be devoted to the construction of the future," he said. And he challenged the nation to "keep pace with the progress of the world". I knew my duty was to go back to my station and do what would be required of me.'[22] When Morita and Ibuka opened their first factory – in a burnt-out Tokyo suburb – they announced to their workers: 'Today, our company has made its first start, and, with superior technology, and a spirit of unity, we will grow. And, as we do, we will contribute to Japanese society, and help restore its rightful place in the world.'

Their choice of company name – Sony – was a carefully calculated one. By giving a Japanese twist to the English word 'sound', they sought to demonstrate their ambition to sell Japanese products all round the world. They simultaneously expressed a determination to restore a sense of national pride. And they also sought to make their staff part of their ambition. 'The emphasis on people must be genuine and sometimes very bold and daring,' Morita explained, 'and it can even be quite risky. But in the long run – and I emphasise this – no matter how good or successful you are or how clever or crafty, your business and its future are in the hands of the people you hire. To put it a bit more dramatically, the fate of your business is actually in the hands of the youngest recruit on the staff.' 'We did not draft you,' he told new employees when they started. 'This is not the army, so that means you have voluntarily chosen Sony. This is your responsibility, and normally if you join this company we expect you to stay for the next twenty or thirty years.'[23]

Each night the founders would eat dinner with a different group of people from across the company to discover what ideas they had, and how they thought they could change the world. They also moved people between jobs, every two to three years, to give them new things to do and provide new challenges. And, every few years, they came up with a new product that changed people's experience of the world, whether it was the TR-63 radio in the 1950s, the Trinitron TV in the 1960s, the Walkman in the 1970s and the CDP-101 compact disc player in the 1980s. With the success of each new product, Japan's pride received a boost. It became a forward-looking, cutting-edge society. And its economy grew thirtyfold, leapfrogging from being the ninth to the second largest economy in the world – just behind America.[24]

But then, in 1995, the two Sony founders stepped down and the company's vision and ambition changed. Under its new leader, Nobuyuki Idei – an economist rather than an engineer – the focus moved from innovation and a desire to enhance people's lives to an obsession with maximising revenue and minimising costs. At first the strategy seemed to work. Over a three-year period, as 30,000 people were let go (a sixth of the workforce), revenues grew by a quarter and profits increased sixfold. But then decline set in. 'The problem was', the journalist Brent Schlender explained, 'that most of its growth had come from selling its old products into new markets – particularly Europe. But there had been very little innovation in its core markets. So it struggled to compete with Apple's iPods and Samsung's flatscreen TVs when they came out.'[25]

As sales continued to fall, Idei stepped down and an American, Howard Stringer, took his place. He cut another 10,000 jobs and focused on selling Sony's existing products into new markets in Asia. Again, there was a short-term gain: sales bounded back by a quarter and profits rose to more than $3 billion – the highest they'd ever been. But it was only temporary. On 14 May 2009, Sony announced the largest loss in its sixty-year history. It proceeded to lose another $8 billion over the next four years. The company had lost its sense of purpose, and the lack of innovation that came as a result of this soon took its toll.

4.

The relentless pursuit of short-term profit at the expense of a wider vision is baked into the DNA of the vast majority of present-day organisations. But that hasn't always been the case. Throughout the eighteenth, nineteenth and much of the twentieth centuries, successful companies had a very different philosophy, based on the establishment of long-term family enterprises. In his account of the economic history of New England, Peter Temin describes how families would borrow money from the bank only as was necessary to ensure their company's survival from one generation to the next. Most of the people who worked for that company would have a job there for the next forty or fifty years.[26] The one significant economic development in this period was the rise of a stock market that could supply extra capital to help launch or expand an enterprise – an innovation with roots in medieval Venice and beyond, now built on by such families as the Dukes, du Ponts, Fords and Rockefellers.[27] The stock market proved volatile, crashing spectacularly at times – most notoriously in 1929 – but most individual businesses survived and kept going.

Then the Nasdaq appeared in the early 1970s and suddenly everything changed. For the first time in history company shares could be traded electronically. Short-term opportunism became that much easier. Speculation became more attractive. The number of stockbrokers rose exponentially, as did the number of people who held shares. By the early 1990s a fifth of the US population were shareholders and more than 100 million shares were being traded each day on the US stock exchanges. The average tenure of a share fell to less than two years (by 2020 it was less than six months).[28]

With the rise of share dealing came the notion of shareholder value. First mooted in the 1950s, it started to become a mantra in the 1970s, in part thanks to the advocacy of the economist Milton Friedman, who argued that 'the social responsibility of business is to increase its profits – and nothing else'.[29] At one level, it was very successful. Over the following thirty years, as companies focused increasingly on making money to keep their shareholders happy, their market value increased fourteenfold.

Simultaneously, however, their average life expectancy fell by half.[30] As the story of Sony illustrates, there is a price to be paid for pursuing sales and profit at the expense of everything else. In the short term, maximising revenue may pay off. It will certainly keep shareholders happy. In the medium to long term, however, the strategies required to achieve this – cutting costs, selling old products into new markets – stifle innovation and build in looming obsolescence. In fact, there seems to be a rule that the faster a company grows, the quicker it can lose control of its destiny. Consider the long list of companies that enjoyed their best trading years shortly before going under. BlackBerry, General Motors, Hewlett-Packard and Lucent all reported their highest sales and profits ever two years before they collapsed. In the case of Nokia it was three years, for Motorola it was four years, for Chrysler five years and Texaco six years before they got into trouble. The list goes on. Their short-term success before their ultimate collapse shows that it wasn't market conditions that brought them down. It was the decisions that they took.

5.

With that in mind, it's interesting to consider the story of another Sony-type company: Apple. There are so many parallels between the two. Apple, like Sony, was started by people obsessed with the technological potential of what the company could do. Masaru Ibuka and Akio Morita were engineers. Apple's founding fathers in 1976 – Steve Jobs, Steve Wozniak and Ronald Wayne – were friends who all loved technology, and who had previously worked together at Atari and Hewlett-Packard. Ibuka and Morita wanted to build a new future and transform Japan's standing in the world. Jobs, Wozniak and Wayne wanted to democratise computing – or, as Jobs put it: 'We wanted to make a simple computer that everyone could use.'[31]

Sony innovated continuously throughout its early years. Apple created a new personal computer market, bringing out the Apple I in 1976 and then the Apple II in 1977. Sony stopped innovating and summoned the money men. Apple hit a five-year spell when effectively all they were doing was manufacturing tweaked versions of existing products, and then as their market share fell fourfold, to less than 6 per cent, employed a money man, John Sculley, to turn things round. Sony faltered. Apple hit bad times.[32]

'At the time,' as the journalist Owen Linzmayer explains, 'Sculley was working at Pepsi and had become famous for inventing the Pepsi Challenge – where people were asked to taste a glass of Coca-Cola and Pepsi on TV, and say which one they preferred which, of course, was always Pepsi!'[33] 'Do you want to sell sugared water for the rest of your life?' Jobs asked him. 'Or do you want to come with me and change the world?' 'I want to change the world!' Sculley replied. But that wasn't really Sculley's ambition. He wanted to focus on money. He took a pay rise to join Apple and within three years was the highest paid CEO in Silicon Valley. He kicked Jobs out over a fundamental difference of opinion over future strategy. 'Jobs thought they should kill off their old products and focus on the Macintosh to move forward,' Walter Isaacson, who wrote Jobs' biography, explained. 'But Sculley thought they should try to make as much money as they could from what they already had.'[34] As with the new brooms at Sony, Sculley started looking for ways to cut costs and achieved success accordingly (sales increased fourfold and profits eightfold over the next eight years). His successor in 1993, Michael Spindler, continued his approach and saw sales grow another 50 per cent over a three-year period. But then, as at Sony, the inevitable decline occurred, and, as at Sony, it happened very quickly indeed. Sales suddenly dropped by a third between 1995 and 1997 and the company lost nearly $2 billion. As Apple desperately flailed around to save itself, it bought NeXT, the company that Jobs had set up after he had been fired, and then rehired Jobs himself.

The myth has grown up that Jobs' return to Apple signalled an immediate transformation in its fortunes. That's not actually the case. In fact, the early years were unspectacular, largely because Jobs put in place the kind of strategies more associated with a traditional company than a mould-breaking one. He streamlined product lines from fifteen to three. And while it's true that he launched the iMac, with its multi-coloured variants, this was arguably more 'business as usual' than cutting-edge innovation. It wasn't until Jobs launched the iPod in 2001 that Apple really started to experience a cultural sea change. It may have taken a couple of years for the new device to catch on, but when it did sales rocketed. By 2007 the company was shipping 50 million iPods a year.

It's worth considering, in this context, the language of Steve Jobs' speech to a packed San Francisco theatre in the same year as he announced the launch of a new product:

> Every once in a while a revolutionary product comes along that changes everything. Apple's been very fortunate. It's been able to introduce a few of these products into the world. In 1984, we introduced the Macintosh . . . it changed the whole computer industry. In 2001, we introduced the first iPod . . . it changed the entire music industry. Well, today, we're introducing three revolutionary products of this class. The first one is a wide-screen iPod with touch controls. The second is a revolutionary mobile phone. And the third is a breakthrough internet communications device . . . These are not three separate devices. This is one device. And we are calling it iPhone.[35]

'Revolutionary' three times; 'change' three times. It might be tempting to assume that Apple's success stemmed simply from an ability to innovate. But that would be telling only half the story. It was Jobs' driving ambition to change people's experience of the world that was the driver that created innovatory change. 'We knew we had to keep innovating,' Scott Forstall, the software engineer who led the development of the iPhone and iPad, explained,[36] 'to keep moving forward and bring out a new product before the old one died. So, even before the iPod took off, we were looking for the next one and had started playing around with different ideas, as we knew it normally takes four years to develop a product, two years to get people to like it, and then – if you're lucky – it might sell well for another four to eight years. So you've normally got a ten- to fifteen-year window to bring out a new product, before the old one dies.' By 2021, worldwide ownership of an iPhone had exceeded the 1 billion mark.[37]

6.

Every year, for the last twenty years, *Fortune* magazine has undertaken a survey of more than 3,000 people to establish which companies they admire, and why. What they've discovered is that those that garner the greatest praise are not the biggest ones with the highest sales, or the most profitable ones. Rather, it's the organisations that shape society positively, and have shown that they can do this over a number of years.[38] 'If the companies we most admire were the most profitable ones then Visa and Mastercard would always be at the top of the list – as they make nearly 50 per cent profit each year – but they aren't!' one of the researchers explained. 'And if they were the biggest ones, then Walmart would be at the top of the list too – as they have sales of over $500 billion each year – but they aren't there either!' Instead, the four companies that are always at the top of the list, and have been in the top ten every year for the last ten years, are: Amazon, which has changed how we buy and sell products; Apple, which has changed how we interact with the world; Google, which has changed how we find and use information; and Starbucks, which has changed how we hang out together. In each case, these companies' super goals are accompanied by a range of supporting aims. So Amazon's mantra is affordability, convenience and choice; Apple's is design, innovation and simplicity; Google's is availability, democracy and usability; and Starbucks' is belonging, connection and community. But they don't stop there. Having established their values they then work out how to design these values into everything they do.[39]

Take Starbucks, for example: a simple business model and a product that is pretty easy to deliver. How can you take something so basic and ordinary as coffee and find a way to make it extraordinary? That was the question going around in Howard Schultz's head when he came back from visiting the espresso bars of northern Italy in 1996, as he sought a way to reproduce their café culture – with its strong sense of belonging, connection and community – in North America, and transform the small group of six coffee shops he'd been working in for the last two years in Seattle into a worldwide venture. 'From the beginning,' Schultz explained, 'I wanted us to be a different kind of company. One that not only celebrated coffee and the rich tradition, but also brought a feeling of connection. Our mission was to inspire and nurture the human spirit – one person, one cup, and one neighbourhood at a time.'[40] Starbucks took its name from a character in *Moby-Dick* who personified reason and goodness.[41]

Schultz clearly wasn't just in it for the money. He wanted to build a business that could transform a whole community and leave a legacy. 'The day my father died of lung cancer in January 1988 was the saddest of my life,' he recalled. 'He had no savings, no pension. More important, he had never attained fulfilment and dignity from work he found meaningful. As a kid, I never had any idea that I would one day head a company. But I knew in my heart that if I was ever in a position where I could make a difference, I wouldn't leave people behind.'[42]

This sense of higher purpose guided everything Starbucks did under Schultz's direction – from how it treated its suppliers and the staff in its shops, to the experience it created for its customers and the neighbourhood where the stores were based. And the company forensically analysed everything it did to make sure that helped it achieve its purpose. 'The Starbucks sensation', a researcher at the Corporate Design Foundation explained, 'is driven not just by the quality of its products but by the entire atmosphere surrounding the purchase of coffee: the openness of its store space, the beauty of its packaging, friendly and knowledgeable service, interesting menu boards, the shape of its counter, the quality of lighting, the texture of the walls, the cleanliness of the floorboards. What Starbucks recognised long before its imitators was that the art of retailing coffee went way beyond product. The details of the total experience mattered.'[43] 'We can't let the coffee down,' Jim Donald, who took over from Orin Smith as the Starbucks CEO in

2005, explained. 'Day in, day out we have to consistently execute on the details.'[44]

But it wasn't just the customer that was important to Schultz. He wanted to ensure that Starbucks had a positive impact on the wider society. 'My quest has never been just about winning or making money,' he said. 'It has also been about building a great, enduring company, which has always meant trying to strike a balance between profit and social conscience.'[45] This is why he set up the Starbucks Foundation in 1997. It was initially to help reduce the coffee chain's environmental impact through handing over leftover coffee grounds for composting; today the foundation seeks to 'strengthen communities across the world'. It's why reusable coffee cups were introduced in 2008. And it's why the chain introduced fair trade products in 2000, and invested in the communities that grew their coffee, from Mexico to Indonesia.[46]

People loved Starbucks' larger sense of purpose and the business expanded accordingly, from being a local business with six stores in 1987, to a national one with 1,300 stores in 1997, to an international one with 15,000 stores in forty-three countries in 2007.

But then it lost its way. 'Obsessed with growth, we took our eye off operations and became distracted from the core of our business,' Schultz explained. The overwhelming sense of belonging, connection and community was lost. 'No single bad decision or tactic or person was to blame,' Schultz continued. 'The damage was slow and quiet, incremental, like a single loose thread that unravels a sweater inch by inch.' Sales started to fall. More than 100 US stores had to be closed. 'We lost our soul,' Schultz admitted.[47]

The great turnaround began at 5.30 p.m. on 26 February 2008, when Starbucks closed all of its 7,100 US stores so that it could spend three hours retraining staff (at a cost of just over $6 million in lost sales). A sign was put on each Starbucks front door that read: 'We're taking time to perfect our espresso. Great espresso requires practice. That's why we're dedicating ourselves to honing our craft.' 'It is not about the company or about the brand,' Schultz told his employees in a short video at the beginning of the training session. 'It is not about anyone but you. You decide whether or not it is good enough, and you have my complete support and, most importantly, my faith and belief in you. Let's measure our actions by that perfect shot of espresso.' 'It was a galvan-ising event,' Schultz recalled later, 'a stake in the ground that helped re-establish some of the emotional attachment and trust we had squan-dered during our years of focusing on hypergrowth.[48]

Some companies faced with the reversal of fortunes that Starbucks was experiencing would have looked to save costs by cutting their com-mitment to non-core projects. Starbucks didn't. Indeed it redoubled its efforts. The foundation remained open. From 2010 regular donations were made to food banks. Other new initiatives included offering free online college degrees to staff (from 2014), discounted gym member-ships (2018), banning single-use plastic straws (2020) and setting up a $100 million fund to donate $10 million per year to help develop local businesses and $2 million a year to help coffee-growing communities (2020).[49] In immediate terms, Starbucks' bottom line suffered; the com-pany recorded its first ever loss in 2013. But then its strategy started to pay off. Consumers re-engaged with its purpose and fell back in love with its product. Starbucks' sales doubled over the next eight years. In 2021 the company recorded sales of $29 billion and profits of $5 billion from 33,000 stores in eighty-four countries around the world.

7.

It's important to bear in mind that establishing an overarching goal for an enterprise is not sufficient in itself. Too many companies lavish atten-tion on creating a mission statement that they then wholly fail to live up to. Only when vision becomes an integral part of an organisation's DNA – what it thinks and how it behaves – does transformative change follow.

It's a mindset that lies at the heart of what Schultz has done at Star-bucks. And it sits at the core of each of the Centennials. The All Blacks, for example, seek to embody equality, humility and tenacity; at Nasa, it's ambition, exploration and safety; at the Royal College of Art, it's art-istry, community and creativity; and at the Royal Shakespeare Com-pany, it's ambition, inclusion and integrity. 'If you want to shape society and change how it thinks and behaves,' Steve Tew, the former All Blacks CEO, said to me, 'then you need to change how you think and behave first. So you model the beliefs and behaviours you're trying to shape.

And the best way to do that is to work out how to embed them into the rituals and routines of daily life.'[50]

The All Blacks and New Zealand Rugby offer a textbook example of this. To live up to their equality goal, for example, they decided to focus on increasing their racial and gender diversity, bringing in more players of Māori or Pacific Islands heritage descent (half the 2011 World Cup squad) and giving more support to their women's team (a female became overall player of the year for the first time in 2018). Humility has been served by taking it in turns to clean the changing rooms. Tenacity is achieved by forensically reviewing every training session and every match, to learn lessons and to strive to be better.[51] In a similar way, at the Royal College of Art, students are asked to work on projects across departments to serve artistry, community and creativity, and the Royal Shakespeare Company develops roles for visually and physically impaired actors to foster ambition, inclusion and integrity.[52]

Finally, it's essential that what the organisation offers to the wider community ultimately serves and develops its vision. Take Tesla, for example, which has set itself the goal of moving the world towards more sustainable sources of energy. It recognises, of course, that it is not going to achieve that in a single bound. But each element of what Tesla has to offer is a step in that direction, whether it involves batteries, chargers, solar panels, trucks or cars.[53]

The history of Tesla's car production nicely illustrates the incremental way in which the company is heading towards its ultimate super goal. The first Teslas were never going to change the world: they were too expensive for most people (they were also not that profitable). The lessons Tesla learnt from their development and production, though, were invaluable and set the company on a course first to develop smaller, less expensive cars that more people could buy, and ultimately (it is hoped) very small, very cheap cars that everyone can purchase. Those wealthy individuals who bought the first Teslas were therefore helping push a business model the aim of which is ultimately more democratic than its original model and that, of course, stands to profit from the mass market it is seeking to reach. And because Tesla has been true to its vision, it has won trust and support. People know what it stands for, they understand the message, and they believe that Tesla is sincere in its desire to live up to it. That support will remain in place for as long as Tesla lives up to it. In the process it will guarantee future success.[54]

The dangers of a mismatch between stated goal and actual product are well illustrated by the problems experienced by Facebook. On the one hand, the tech giant claims to have an ambition to 'give people the power to build community and bring the world closer together to share ideas, offer support and make a difference' via Facebook, Instagram and WhatsApp.[55] On the other, its primary focus on making money brings its goals into question, particularly in the light of its failure to address the problem of the spread of hate on the internet. Is it really trying to shape society positively? Or is it interested only in making a profit? And can it ignore the potential problems it might face if the 'difference' it makes is not positive, and the thoughts and behaviours it disseminates don't positively shape society? In the short term, this dissonance is survivable, just as it was for Sony and Apple, who were able to prosper for several years after they lost sight of their founding goals. The fact is that Facebook is currently very profitable: its revenues and profits increased fortyfold in the ten years from 2010 to 2020 and it usually makes between 30 and 40 per cent profit each year. That makes it, along with Visa and Mastercard, one of the most successful companies in the world – certainly, in terms purely of profit margin, far ahead of Apple and Google, who usually make around 20 per cent each year. But then Apple and Google are reinvesting in lots of new products in such areas as health and education.[56] Facebook is living on existing success. Given the experience of other companies that have been there, this recipe for success should be a cause for concern for Facebook.

As Tesla's approach shows, while each step taken has to serve an ultimate goal, that individual step doesn't in itself have to be a world-changing one. Take Levi Strauss, for example. Serving its super goal of creating 'better clothes that can be used for longer', there have been – and continue to be – a whole host of smaller, more local initiatives. The company gave some of its first profits to an orphanage in 1853; it introduced a policy of welcoming and supporting workers with HIV/Aids in 1983; it started working with CARE Cambodia in 2010 to improve conditions in its factories; and it launched a repair and recycle service in 2020. In much the same way, while Colgate fulfils most of its super goal through the products it sells, it supports this through smaller, targeted ventures: offering free dental care for thousands of children each year via its mobile dental vans, for example, and operating school workshops. Both Levi Strauss and Colgate also match the money that any of their staff choose to give to a non-profit organisation of their choice up to $2,000.[57]

When goals, values and outputs align, the results are transformative. They're also readily apparent. Everyone who worked in and with the Centennials I studied understood precisely what they were seeking to achieve and how they were planning to get there, and they could list the ambitions involved. They also regard the time they spend working with or at the Centennials, whether as actors, artists, astronauts, athletes, coaches, designers, directors, engineers, scientists, students or teachers, as a key moment in their lives: the moment when they create real impact and shape society.

By contrast, companies that claim one thing and do another can be dispiriting places to work. 'To be honest, I've struggled ever since I left,' one former Centennial told me. 'The people I now work with are more focused on making money than shaping society. I tell them that we need to look beyond our current customers to the whole of society, and think about how we can shape them for years to come, but they're not interested. They're too focused on trying to make money today from what we already have, and they don't really care about the future.'

A true sign of a great organisation is that people outside it want to know how it ticks. 'I've always loved Nasa,' one CEO said to me; 'what they stand for, and what they do. From achieving the impossible, with the first Moon landing, to promoting racial and gender diversity with the mathematicians that were shown in the *Hidden Figures* story. They've always been such a fascination, and such an inspiration for me! That's why we've all got Nasa T-shirts in my family, and proudly wear them, to show how much we love them!' 'I can't believe you've spent time with British Cycling!' another CEO exclaimed. 'Who did you speak to? What are they like? What do they do?' Such organisations may sometimes get criticised – and Centennials such as the All Blacks, Nasa, Eton College and the Royal Shakespeare Company have all been attacked by the media at some point – but there's ultimately a real love for them and desire to know more about them.

8.

In summary, the Centennials seek to shape society positively by:

Establishing and clearly stating a purpose – or north star – that embodies the beliefs and behaviours that they want to create in society

Asking their suppliers, staff, customers and communities to help foster and sustain this purpose

Analysing everything they do, and how they do it, to ensure it helps them meet and serve their purpose

Making sufficient money to survive and fulfil their purpose, but not being obsessed with profit for its own sake

Regularly going back to their purpose to check it's right and they're still on track

Never straying from their long-term purpose to meet a short-term goal.

Habit 2

DO IT FOR THE KIDS' KIDS

Will your grandchildren's grandchildren want to work with you?

1.

It was a cloudy afternoon on 18 October 2009 at the Nasa research centre in California. Four engineers – two men and two women – were staring at a computer screen and trying to work out what to do next.

'What's happening?' one engineer asked. 'I can't really see.'

'I think we're stuck,' the other one replied.

On the other side of the screen was a pit filled with dust. Sitting on top of the pit was a machine that resembled a prehistoric robot – with a bucket at the top, a tractor wheel at the bottom and a conveyor belt on the side. The belt was theoretically supposed to pick up the dust and deposit it in the bucket, and the tractor wheel was then supposed to move the machine so that the bucket could be tipped out elsewhere. Unfortunately, the wheel wasn't working and the machine was stuck.

These engineers weren't the only ones grappling with malfunctioning equipment. Their machine was, in fact, just one of many competing in the Nasa Regolith Excavation Challenge, an annual technical tournament for university students across the US. With a prize worth half a million dollars it attracts hundreds of competitors each year.[1]

'It's a tough challenge,' a Nasa engineer explained. 'Each team has to build a machine that's less than four foot wide and weighs less than 200lb, so it's small enough to be sent to the Moon; that's quick enough that it can move over 300lb of dust in less than thirty minutes; and is nimble enough that it can be operated from a distance using a remote-controlled camera – where there's a two-second delay between the control and the machine, just like there would be if it was being used on the Moon.' These combined challenges had been sufficient to defeat every team that had tried to overcome them for more than three years. For its part, this latest attempt had become mired in a specific problem that the Nasa engineers had seen before. Dust had got trapped in the wheel; it could only be dislodged if the student's robot was able to move backwards and forwards in short, sharp movements; and the robot didn't appear to have the capability to do this.

The students took a deep breath and tried again. This time the machine moved. Indeed, over the course of the next twenty minutes, it went on to move 600lb of dust.

The students duly found themselves the recipients of the $500,000 prize.

The annual Nasa competition may sound as though it's staged just for fun. But it has two very serious purposes. The first is perhaps the obvious one: by effectively crowdsourcing challenges, it is able to draw on very bright minds to solve them. Over the past twenty years, in fact, Nasa has offered prize money of up to $2 million to those able to do everything from produce a device that can convert carbon dioxide into sugar, to green aircraft that can fly 200 miles in two hours on just a gallon of fuel, to a solar battery that can operate on the Moon at temperatures of minus 200 degrees Centigrade.

The second equally important aim is to inspire students to want to become involved in technological innovation when they graduate. Nor does Nasa stop at college students. 'It's about inspiring and developing kids too,' says an engineer, 'as we want them to fall in love with science when they're young, and study it as they grow older, so they can help us solve the problems we'll need to solve, and will want to work with us.'

Hence the reason for Nasa's decision to provide online resources for students and parents alike, set up school laboratories, fund science apprenticeships and internships, organise science roadshows and much else besides.[2]

The results speak for themselves. The number of applications to be an astronaut have quadrupled over the past twenty years, from 3,000 in 2000 to more than 12,000 in 2020. Not just that, but the talent pool has become more diverse too. Nasa recruited its first non-military astronaut in the 1960s. The first female astronaut was taken on in the 1970s, and the first non-white astronaut in the 1980s. Of the twenty astronauts who have joined in the past ten years, half have been women, a third weren't from the military and a fifth weren't white.[3]

2.

Engaging with colleagues of the future is something that most organisations don't do. They assume that all the necessary preparation for the world of work will be carried out by schools and universities, and that people will duly be on tap when they're required. That is not how the Centennials tick. They know that if they don't get people's attention when they're young, arouse their enthusiasm and help them develop appropriate skills, then when it comes to choosing a job, the talent won't exist or will go elsewhere.

'Some of the most important work we do is with schools,' Catherine Mallyon, the executive director of the Royal Shakespeare Company, explains to me. 'It keeps us alive and relevant to the world. If kids don't want to work in the arts, and don't want to work with us, then it's only a matter of time before we'll die.[4] Hence the reason why the RSC, like Nasa, has in place a whole range of outreach programmes with schools and universities. Obviously, it wants to share what it does with the wider world. But initiatives such as those involving summer programmes for students and teachers, online acting, directing and production workshops, and funding for apprenticeships and internships are also designed to engage the best of the next generation and persuade them to consider a career in the arts.[5] In the same way the All Blacks have developed Rippa Rugby, which can be played by kids from the age of four, and British Cycling holds lots of competitions each year to help promote its sport.[6]

There's obviously a degree of idealism in all this. But it's hard-headed common sense too. Organisations that fail to take a long-term view of future talent all too often find that when they need it, it's not there. Or, as Dave Brailsford, the former British Cycling performance director, puts it: 'A child's head can be turned any moment. If you're not there to help turn it and guide it, then, before you know it, all the talent has gone elsewhere.'[7]

The world of cricket offers a textbook example of this. Between 1975 and 1995 the West Indies Test cricket team won thirty-four of their thirty-eight matches. This was followed by a disastrous decade during which they won only a third of their matches, suffering their worst defeat of all time on 6 November 2005 when they lost the first Test against Australia in Brisbane by nearly 400 runs. The easy explanation for this is that they were unlucky in their players in that decade; the talent simply wasn't there. But closer inspection reveals something more fundamental: the ecosystem that generated new players had been disrupted, and the team's fortunes suffered accordingly.

The West Indies has a long tradition of cricket-playing in many of its islands. Viv Richards, who joined the national side in 1974, has described how he started playing the game with his two brothers almost as soon as he could walk. 'I loved those knockabouts with my father,' Richards remembers. 'He was a sporting hero of mine. After all, he did play a lot of cricket for Antigua, which did make him something of a local star and he often brought home his bats for us to play with.'[8] Soon Richards was playing cricket for the local team – on bumpy pitches, pitted with hoof marks – and with friends at the beach, with a tennis ball on the wet sand. 'I didn't realise it at the time, but I was getting the best training I could.'

As an adult, Richards experienced ups and downs in his early cricketing career. What transformed it, giving him both the technical and mental skills he needed, was a long spell in England, first at the Alf Gover cricket school and then as a county player alongside many other West Indian players who were rising through the game in much the same way – figures such as Gordon Greenidge (7,000 runs between 1974 and 1991), Desmond Haynes (7,000 runs between 1978 and 1994) and Malcolm Marshall (300 wickets between 1978 and 1991).[9] Richards, in other words, benefited from a cricketing environment that encouraged children to play in the first place, and then offered growing players the opportunity to build their skills.

Then things changed. The English cricket board, frustrated by the national team's lack of success against the West Indies, decided to halve the number of overseas players who could play for English counties from two to one, while almost simultaneously other countries made a move to pick up the best of West Indian talent and adapt them to their own national sports. US baseball teams started taking the region's sharp batsmen, US basketball teams began taking their tall bowlers. Many athletes who had initially considered cricket moved to other sports: Patrick Ewing joined the NBA; Usain Bolt became a sprinter.[10] Almost at a stroke the talent pipeline that had served the West Indies so well for so many years had been cut – and the national team paid the price.

The Jamaican athletics team, meanwhile, were experiencing mirror-image fortunes. For many years, Jamaican athletes who showed potential tended to seek athletics scholarships abroad – particularly in the US. That started to change in the late 1990s and early 2000s when Jamaican coaches set up two local running clubs: Maximising Velocity and Power in 1999 and Racers Track Club in 2004.[11] The breakthrough came with the arrival of Asafa Powell – an athlete who hadn't previously performed so well that US universities wanted him but in whom the Jamaican coaches could see great potential – and the moment in 2005 when he vindicated his compatriots' faith in him by breaking the men's 100 metres world record. His example inspired others. In 2004, there were just five Jamaican-trained athletes at that year's Olympics. In 2008 there were twelve. The medal haul rose from five to eleven, with Jamaican athletes finishing first, second and third in the women's 100 metres final. Thirteen years later, in 2021, the Jamaican women's team achieved the distinction of winning gold, silver and bronze in an Olympic event – twice.

3.

We tend to assume that a career is something most people decide comparatively late in the day – while they're at secondary school or university. In fact, the roots of career choice reach down into our earliest years.

Back in 1980 researchers from Chicago University decided to study the development of 120 successful people – forty artists, forty athletes and forty scientists who had, respectively, shown their work in a major exhibition, competed at a major event, or won a major prize – by interviewing them, their parents and their teachers at length to try to understand how they'd developed, and what, if any, had been the defining moments for them.[12] 'We expected there to be a pattern,' Benjamin Bloom, the lead researcher, later explained, 'but we didn't expect it to be at clear as it was.'

Essentially, the researchers discovered, people go through four distinct phases in their acquisition of life skills, regardless of their background or any natural ability they may possess.

The first stage – 'purposeful play' – normally starts when a child is four to five years old, when they are introduced to an activity by a 'passionate parent' (or sibling or grandparent) who plays with them and encourages them to experiment with activities that may range from sport to music to painting and drawing. From an adult point of view, there is a serious purpose behind the activities the children are being encouraged to try out, but the main emphasis is on having fun. Essentially, the child is being offered the opportunity to try lots of different things so that he or she can decide which ones appeal. Psychologists often call this a 'sampling' period.[13]

Three to five years later, if the child is still enjoying the activity or activities they tried earlier in their lives, then their development starts to move to the next stage – 'playful practice'. This is the point where, as a rule, the 'passionate parent' will find them a 'nurturing teacher' to give them some formal training for perhaps two or three hours a week. More structure is now introduced to the child's activities, but the emphasis is – or should be – still on having fun.

The third stage – 'serious practice' – starts three to five years later when the child is ten to fifteen years old. Now the 'nurturing teacher' gives way to the 'demanding teacher', who takes their student back to basics and then starts building them up again. Training sessions become more intense and lengthier (five to ten hours a week). And the student is now expected to practise on their own, away from the training sessions. Even at this stage, though, it's not unusual to encounter people who move from one activity to another, or who nurture other interests via playful practice at the same time as they focus on their core passion.

Assuming that this core passion is sustained, then the student will move on to the fourth and final stage – 'serious performance' – when they are aged between thirteen and twenty. Now training doubles to around ten to twenty hours a week. The student will probably compete against others in competitions. He or she may well have other hobbies, but these receive relatively little attention, certainly in comparison to the main interest. By the time the student is anywhere between sixteen and twenty, what was once something they played with is on its way to becoming a profession and a way of life.[14]

These stages are not fortuitous. They actually map the way in which our mental capacity develops.[15] Neuroscientists suggest that our brain quadruples in size during the first four years of life, and then, as we start to learn, undergoes a tripling of blood levels as new nodules and connections are created. It then stays relatively static for six years until we reach the age of ten when it falls by a third, but we're still developing twice as fast from ten to sixteen as at any later point in our lives.

Since our passions are easier to ignite, and our skills are easier to develop, when our brains are hyper-developing – from the age of four to sixteen – it follows that this is the time to instil early enthusiasm and build early ability. If they're not triggered and nurtured then, the child will either fail to develop them or will find other things to occupy their time. This doesn't mean that passions and skills can't be developed later in life: the brain is like a muscle and responds to new stimulus and mental exercise. But the fact remains that the surest way to acquire the talent of the future is to spot, encourage and nurture it at an early stage. Organisations that assume that others will do this for them are taking a big gamble. They may be lucky. But they may equally find that the talent goes elsewhere or simply isn't there when they need it.[16]

4.

The dangers of leaving early intervention and encouragement to others, and assuming that they will supply the people required, is clearly shown in the computer science arena. At present, there are insufficient computer science graduates to meet demand. The gap is particularly wide among female graduates.[17] Both deficiencies are having a serious impact. A lack of graduates in general suggests a future capacity problem when it comes to innovating and tackling new challenges. A lack of female graduates skews the technological world, because it results in an environment created by men for men, where, for example, mobile phones are often too big for women to hold easily and comfortably, where Alexa struggles to interpret female voices, and where the AI involved in the development of medicines and driverless cars is potentially dangerous for half the population because it has not been designed to take them into account.[18]

It wasn't always like this. There were female codebreakers at Bletchley Park in the 1940s, and female Nasa scientists in the 1960s. By 1985 half of all students graduating with a computer science degree from an American university were women. But the advent of the personal computer brought about a seismic change. 'The turning point came in 1984,' Jane Margolis, an education researcher at UCLA, explains, 'when people first started buying personal computers for their sons, and not their daughters, and put them in their sons' bedrooms so their daughters couldn't get to them.'[19] And because the boys enjoyed playing with their computers at home, they also set up clubs so they could play with them at school. Suddenly computers were a boy thing, not a girl thing, and all the girl talent went elsewhere. As Margolis points out, it also didn't help that so many early computer games and films were so clearly directed at boys.[20] Between 1985 and 1990 the number of female computer science undergraduates more than halved in the US from 15,000 to 7,000. The situation has not really improved since then. The number of women studying science may have gone up in absolute terms, but in relative terms they still lag a long way behind men. More work in, say, healthcare than in computers.[21]

The point for employers in the computing industries is that if they become involved with the next generation of computing scientists only when those people are at undergraduate level, it's already too late. According to Shalini Kesar, a researcher at Southern Utah University, 'the turning point seems to come when they're thirteen. Before that, half of them say they'd like to work in computers. Five years later only a tenth of them decide to study computer science at university.'[22] It's precisely because this tendency has become so firmly entrenched that Nasa, among others, works hard to create early interest and enthusiasm among young women. That the strategy has to be sustained over the long term is shown by the fact that across Nasa as a whole only a third of astronauts and a quarter of engineers and scientists are women.[23] This strategy has ultimately paid dividends because 50 per cent of the astronauts Nasa has recruited over the past decade, and 50 per cent of the engineers and scientists it has taken on in the past five years, have been women. It's worth noting, by comparison, that across the US only a fifth of engineers and scientists are women. It's a situation that remains unchanged from twenty years ago.[24]

When contemplating future talent, it's also important to recognise that getting access to it doesn't simply involve nurturing round pegs for existing round holes. The fact is that in many areas of life we simply don't know what the world will look like in, say, twenty years' time. The Organisation for Economic Co-operation and Development (OECD) and World Economic Forum have recently predicted that over the next two decades a sixth of jobs will disappear in their current form and half will change significantly.[25] If that seems unrealistic or alarmist, it's worth bearing in mind that between 1980 and 2000 the number of farming jobs in the US fell by a half, and that in the following twenty years, the number of manufacturing jobs fell by a quarter as industries moved operations abroad or automated them.[26] Now it's the turn of services. Soon it will be the turn of technology. What we need for the future, therefore, are not people who can do jobs as they are but people with a portfolio of skills who have the mental agility to find new solutions to old and new problems and challenges.[27]

What that means in practice is that employers in any given sector need not only to consider what skills they want to draw on that are immediately relevant to the tasks at hand but what skills may aid them in the future. The Centennials are very used to this way of thinking.

The All Blacks know they need physiotherapists, but they also know they need to find cutting-edge nutritionists and psychologists. British Cycling knows that within the mix of skills it requires are sleep experts. Nasa recruits geologists and doctors. The Royal College of Art seeks data scientists and health experts. Identifying future talent for core tasks is essential. But identifying future talent for future possibilities is equally important.

There's another reason for looking for the staff of the future now. Many sectors are prone to homophily – the tendency to seek out people who are alike. Research has consistently shown, however, that innovation and groupthink don't go together. The best ideas come from teams that have different perspectives, ask different questions, and look at things in different ways from one another. Only by making contact with and nurturing the future talent pool now will it be broad enough to give the diversity that creativity so depends on. Again, the Centennials point the way here. Thanks to outreach programmes, half of the All Blacks' players are now Māori or of Polynesian descent; two-fifths of Nasa astronauts do not come from the military; two-thirds of Royal College of Art students come from overseas.[28]

5.

Some non-Centennial companies have woken up to this need to develop the right talent and the risks involved in leaving the task solely to educational institutions. Apple and Microsoft have developed lessons, guides and apps for students. The BBC holds annual writing competitions. Penguin Random House sets up libraries in schools to help children develop the skills they need, and has created programmes for future talent.[29] Kellogg's, Nordstrom and Starbucks have established internships. All know that if they don't act now, then at some point their talent pool will dry up.[30]

Inevitably there will be those who regard such activities as a waste of time and money, particularly when there are more immediately pressing issues to address – such as how to make a profit this year. But as the problems in computer science demonstrate, this is a very short-sighted view that will get such individuals into trouble later on. It also ignores some immediate benefits that accrue simply from making the effort to connect with young people: learning how the next generation of customers and staff tick, getting them to comment on new products and new ideas, and spotting early on the cultural shifts that occur with every generation.[31]

A number of agile smaller businesses have cottoned on to the advantages of early outreach. For them, it's a way to acquire an edge in acquiring talented people who might otherwise opt for employment at a larger, better-known concern. It also reduces the risk of hiring the wrong person and simultaneously raises the organisation's profile.[32] 'Offering work placements for kids at school has not only raised our profile in the local community, but has encouraged more of them to apply for a job with us too,' says the director of a small housebuilding business.[33] 'And if they do a great job in their placement, then we normally just keep them on.' The owner of a small restaurant explains how giving free meals as prizes at two local schools has not only provided helpful publicity for the enterprise but has also generated a steady stream of part-time workers too.[34]

It doesn't take much to create an effective outreach programme. Placements, challenges and prizes are both effective and easy to organise. Apprenticeships, graduate schemes and internships don't have to be conceived on a grand scale for them to yield results. All such schemes cut both ways too. They help young people learn what is needed and they show businesses what young people want and expect.

Few disciplines highlight the dangers of failing to open up early lines of communication more clearly than the computing industry. Research has shown that many highly qualified and talented women abandon careers in computing science because they don't want to 'work for long hours in dark rooms', they don't want to 'have to go for a drink after work' and they don't see 'many other women in senior roles, [so] they don't know who to talk to, or how they can progress'.[35] In other words, there's a failure among those at the top to understand – and to want to understand – what motivates many in their potential talent pool. The resulting wastage is appalling. Tarika Barrett, the CEO of Girls Who Code, has observed that 'even if a woman decides to study computer science at university, only a third of them will decide to work for a tech company when they graduate. Only a half of them will stay there for more than one year after they arrive.'[36] Five years ago only a fifth of the engineers at Apple, Facebook and Google were women. Even today it's only a quarter.[37] The computing sector is therefore drawing on only a proportion of the talent out there, not all of it.

Early outreach would help correct this damaging anomaly. More generally, early outreach creates the experts and leaders of the future.

6.

In summary, to stay alive and relevant to the world, Centennials engage the next generation, by:

Working out the problems they think they'll face in the next twenty to thirty years, and the skills they will need to solve them

Visiting schools and universities, and sharing videos online, showing kids and students what problems they face and what skills they need

Creating 'fun' challenges for kids to solve from the age of four to fifteen, and 'serious' ones from the age of ten to twenty-five

Using summer programmes and online games and tutorials to help kids learn and teachers teach the skills they need

Using work placements, apprenticeships, internships and graduate programmes to encourage people to work with them

Asking kids and students to help them redesign their workplaces

Working with as many different kids as they can, to help them develop the skills they need.

Stewardship

Stewardship

Habit 3

HAVE STRONG ROOTS

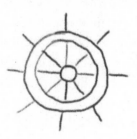

No second first times

1.

When new students arrive at Eton College they are allocated to a house. For the next five years they will constantly criss-cross the school campus on their way to different lessons, activities and assemblies, but the house will always be the centre of their existence – their home – to which they and fifty other boys will continually return each day to eat, drink and hang out. They will spend a fifth of each term in class, studying. But they will spend most of the rest of their time in their house, relaxing, social-ising and learning from those around them.[1]

Presiding over the house is a triumvirate of adults: the house master, a 'dame' who looks after students' wellbeing, and a tutor who keeps an eye on their academic performance. But it's the house master who has the ultimate responsibility. He is the one who makes sure that students get their homework done, and who advises them on which societies to join and which pastimes to pursue. He, in other words, oversees the pastoral care that is so essential for their development.

This is why the role is such an important one, and why becoming a house master is no minor undertaking. Each person who is selected for the post will live in the house full-time with their family. They will constantly be on call. What's more they will serve in the role for thirteen years. The chances are that the new arrival at the school will still have the same house master when they complete their A level studies and leave half a decade later. 'In one sense it seems a crazy thing to do,' Jonnie Noakes, Eton's director of teaching and learning, explains to me, 'because house masters can't go in too young – they need to have a certain amount of experience. But if you're asking them to stay in for thirteen years, that's the middle of their career. The reason why we do that is that the house system is really the central aspect of the education that they get – in social skills, character education and so on. It's where values are passed on, not just by the staff but by the older students – and the house masters are, if you like, the overseers of that process. So it's absolutely essential that they aren't just on their way through to somewhere else, but that they understand the environment that they work in, and that they are fully signed up to and willing to hand on the values of that community. They are the people who oversee and guard the community values.'[2]

Over the years Eton has been criticised for its perceived social elitism. Some of its alumni have pursued controversial careers and lives. But it's worth remembering that in the past 600 years the school has produced some extraordinary people – from actors and athletes to religious leaders, scientists and novelists – who have collectively shaped for the better how society thinks and behaves.[3] It's also a more diverse community than you might expect. Many of Eton's annual intake do indeed come from the wealthier sections of society, but that's not true of all. A quarter of students receive financial support from the school to help pay their fees, at a cost to the school of more than £2 million per year. In the long term, the school is hoping to become 'needs blind' and move to a point where education is free to all parents and carers who are at a financial disadvantage.[4] 'I've met such a diverse group of people at Eton,' one student says to me. 'We're all from such different places, and do such different things. One of my friends is a former refugee from Lebanon, and another is the son of a lord. One's an English rugby player and another is a concert pianist. But we all get along and hang out together, as no background or talent is ranked higher than any other.'⁵

Eton's ambition far transcends a desire simply to excel in academic league tables. According to the school's former head master Tony Little, it's providing the broadest education possible that matters, not ticking exam boxes. Consequently, seeking to ensure that it attracts as diverse a range of students as possible is not a peripheral goal but a central one. It wants children from very different backgrounds who will mix together and pursue a wide range of interests (the school's curriculum embraces forty subjects and fifty clubs and societies). The house masters are central to this ambition. They shape the living ethos of the school, encouraging students to become hard-working, confident, enthusiastic and tolerant individuals who will go on to shape society positively.

They're also there for the long haul. Each house master must have at least twenty years' experience before they take on the role. They must then fulfil that role for more than a decade. It's worth noting that such extended service commitments tally very closely with the cycle of being a parent or operating in a caring profession such as medicine. Nurturing, inculcating values, educating the next generation are all processes that take and need time.

2.

Many organisations would regard such a strategy as unwise. People who stay in the same job for a long time may offer continuity, they would argue, but a desire for continuity can all too easily turn into hostility to necessary change and innovation.

They have a point. 'Innovate or die!' is an important mantra for every organisation. If you don't keep moving forward and adapting to a changing world, then you'll be left behind. To that extent, every organisation needs 'disruptive experts' who, like teenagers, question and challenge everything they are told to do. But the very fact that they're 'disruptive' means that they also need guiding. Innovative thought often comes at the cost of an understanding of context or implication. Disruption may well lead to innovation. Unguided, though, it can cause organisations to forget who they are and why and how they became successful. At worst it can lead to their collapse.

Enron offers a cautionary tale here, as the energy conglomerate's CEO Jeffrey Skilling was arguably the ultimate disrupter. Skilling arrived at the company just five years after it had been founded, with a Harvard MBA (he had been top of his class) and a McKinsey pedigree (he had been the youngest partner in the consulting firm's history). As soon as he arrived, he started to shake things up. First, he set up a 'talent management programme', based on the McKinsey model that involved hiring hundreds of MBA students each year, straight out of school, and getting them to rethink every aspect of the old Enron business model. Then he introduced a 'rank-and-yank' management process, drawing on feedback from customers, deputies, managers and peers, that resulted in the top 10 per cent of staff being promoted each year and the bottom 25 per cent being fired.[6] 'I don't want people sitting in the same place, getting bored,' Skilling explained. 'Fluid movement is critical for our company. And the type of people we hire enforces that.'[7] To create a 'war for talent' between its different businesses – another McKinsey idea – salaries and titles were awarded according to the individual involved, not the position they held, and poaching was openly encouraged. (When Enron set up its new broadband business in 2000, it moved over fifty of its 'top 100 performers' from elsewhere in the business in less than a week.)[8] To incentivise staff to set up new businesses, bonuses were linked to share price and earnings. Skilling's own role changed every couple of years.

Amid all this internal change, Skilling transformed the company into an exciting new business that was continually launching new products and moving into new markets. For a while the formula seemed to work. Sales doubled in the five years after Skilling took over, and then increased tenfold in the five years after that.[9] The press loved what Skilling was doing. *Business Week* said he was one of US's 'top managers'. *Fortune* claimed that Enron was the country's 'most innovative company'. 'Imagine a country-club dinner dance,' one of its reporters wrote, 'with a bunch of old fogeys and their wives shuffling around halfheartedly to the not-so-stirring sounds of Guy Lombardo and his All-Tuxedo Orchestra. Suddenly young Elvis comes crashing through the skylight, complete with gold-lamé suit, shiny guitar, and gyrating hips ... In the staid world of regulated utilities and energy companies, Enron is that gate-crashing Elvis.'[10]

But all this disruption came at a price. 'It created a culture of chaos,' one of its directors later explained, 'where everyone was always looking for the next thing and wouldn't work on a project unless it delivered something tangible in the first six months, so they could bag their bonus, grab their promotion and move on.'[11] With no respect paid to long-serving, reliable staff – indeed such people were frowned upon – there was no collective memory to guide the new people and new ideas that were coming through. And as the old ways of doing business were jettisoned and individual ambition took over, Enron became rudderless, and started to move faster and faster in the wrong direction. In 2002, twelve years after Skilling had joined the company, it famously crashed and burnt after one dubious venture too many: the energy giant had taken to booking future profits as current earnings – standard practice on more stable oil and gas projects but a high-risk strategy nonetheless. In the aftermath, Skilling – once the darling of the business world – was fined $45 million and sentenced to twenty-four years in prison, the second longest sentence ever handed out to a white-collar criminal.

3.

Centennials strike a careful balance between what might be termed the 'disruptive experts' essential for innovation and change, who are always questioning, challenging and trying to move things forward, and the 'stable stewards', who preserve what is best about the organisation's culture and stop it lurching off track.

Their disruptive experts account for a third to two-thirds of their staff. To ensure that they're always at the top of their game, they may well be moved around or be spread across a range of projects. British Cycling's nutritionists, psychologists and scientists, for example, work simultaneously with two other Olympic teams. Nasa's biologists, engineers and meteorologists all work on at least three programmes at once, some of which may well be with outside organisations. (This is discussed later in Habit 7).

The stable stewards typically account for a quarter in larger organisations where teams contain between fifty and seventy people. (The other tenth to a half are 'effective executers' who get things done). They work for the organisation full-time, and they are spread throughout it. For every long-serving All Blacks CEO there will be a long-serving coach and probably a long-serving player too. The Royal Academy of Music looks for a principal, department heads and music tutors who will serve the institution for many years. Such stable stewards are invariably self-effacing and humble, more concerned about what they might have missed than with what they've achieved. Their focus is less on the here and now than on the legacy they'll leave behind. As Catherine Mallyon, the executive director at the Royal Shakespeare Company, described her position to me: 'Taking on this role was like being handed a precious vase, and asked to walk across an ice rink. My job is to carefully carry it, keep it safe, and gently pass it on to the next person. And that's a feeling you never forget.'[12]

In recent years businesses have underplayed the importance of such people. They're constantly on the lookout for the new, particularly at the very highest levels of management – among CEOs. Two decades ago the average CEO of a top-500 company in the US stayed in post for at least ten years. These days it's five. The reason for this is closely bound to the emphasis that's been placed on trying to increase profit and shareholder value. CEOs are better remunerated and incentivised to achieve these goals than ever before and, as a result, their salaries have increased twentyfold in the past forty years to an average of $19 million each year – a figure that's 300 times higher than the average salary of the people they manage.[13] But the pressure on them to deliver has grown exponentially too. And since many of them fail to hit the ambitious targets set, their time at the top is curtailed accordingly. More than 1,600 US CEOs lost their job in 2019, a figure that has also doubled in the last twenty years.[14]

Those who defend the new status quo point out that the market values of the businesses these CEOs lead have increased twentyfold in the last four decades. The ends, they argue, justify the means.[15] But if you look a little closer, this correlation between high pay and a rapidly revolving door on the one hand, and profit and shareholder value on the other, is more apparent than real.

Every year, Harvard University examines the performance of the CEOs of the 1,200 largest companies in the world, meticulously scrutinising how their firms have performed on a whole range of measures (profits, customer service, carbon footprint and so on).[16] If received wisdom is to be believed, you'd expect the highest performing companies to be the ones that are always swapping their CEOs in and out to maximise their innovation and guard against complacency and underperformance. But Harvard has demonstrated the opposite. It has found that 80 per cent of the top 100 CEOs it identifies each year were promoted from within the organisation, and 80 per cent have also been in their current post for at least ten years.

And when it comes to the very best of the best – the six CEOs who have appeared on the list every year for the past six years – then what is most striking is that, first, their average tenure is well over a decade, and, second, that all but one of them either founded or rose through the ranks of the company they now run. There's certainly movement within the highest echelon – around a third of the top leaders Harvard identifies change each year as some retire, or resign, or are edged out because their performance has slipped – but the continuity displayed is nevertheless very apparent. The names and figures speak for themselves: Jeff Bezos at Amazon (in post for twenty-six years), Renato Alves Vale at CCR (twenty-three years), Paolo Rocca at Tenaris (twenty years), James Taiclet at American Tower (nineteen years) and Pablo Isla at Inditex (seventeen years).

Conversely, the data suggests that the shorter the tenure of individual CEOs, the shorter the life of the company they head.[17] Some might argue that this is because less successful companies need to get rid of underperforming CEOs (and indeed most struggling businesses go through at least three CEOs before they finally fall). But the reality is that when many CEOs leave it's the lack of continuity in itself that proves undermining. And when many are in post, it's all too often their focus on career and remuneration rather than on the interests of the company that weakens the underpinning of that company. They regard their role as being that of a disruptive expert who will move on rather than a stable steward who will certainly preside over change where it is needed, but who also ensures necessary continuity.

There's an interesting parallel here from the world of sport. On 6 October 2007 New Zealand crashed out of rugby's World Cup, losing 20–18 in the quarter-final against France. The match represents the only occasion the team have failed to make the semi-final and still stands as their worst ever World Cup performance.[18]

In the post-mortem that followed many theories were put forward to explain why the team should have performed so badly. Some argued that they'd been arrogant and complacent, too readily convinced that they would easily beat France because they had already beaten them twice that year. Some felt they'd selected the wrong players and had rested too many before the game, so fielding a team on the day that wasn't fully match fit. Others said they'd used the wrong tactics, focusing too much on scoring tries rather than taking easy penalties.

But after two months of debate and discussion the All Blacks reached a different conclusion. The reason they had lost, they decided, was that they lacked the stable stewardship to guide the team and know what to do when the pressure was on. For the previous twenty years, just like most other World Cup teams, they had changed their coach every four years, at the beginning of each World Cup cycle. And if they felt a particular coach wasn't working before then, they would replace him after only two years. Now, they realised, this strategy wasn't working. If you change your leader every four years then you fail to build a collective memory. You lose out on applying lessons you've learnt from one World Cup in the next, and you leave yourself with insufficient time to build up all the knowledge you require.

Given the disaster of the France match, the All Blacks must have been tempted to sack their coach. They didn't. They stuck with him. And what followed was a period widely regarded as a golden age of New Zealand rugby.

In the decade before the 2007 World Cup, the All Blacks won 80 per cent of their matches – no mean feat. But in the decade after it they won 90 per cent, scored twice as many points as their opponents, and became the first country to win back-to-back World Cups, in 2011 and

2015. The coach, Graham Henry, stayed in post for eight years, from 2003 to 2011. He then handed over to Steve Hansen, who'd been his assistant coach throughout that time. Hansen in turn stayed in post for another seven years, from 2012 until 2019.[19]

The New Zealand model is not one that that many countries' national teams follow. But those that do certainly tend to be the most successful. The world of rugby offers plenty of examples here. When coaches have been part of the coaching team for at least six years, the teams they run are the ones that win the World Cup. And the most successful teams are generally ones where a quarter of the players have been in place for at least eight years. Inevitably, stable stewardship and stable team membership tend to go hand in hand. Fresh talent is always needed, but world-beating success demands continuity too.[20]

4.

Any organisation that wants to stabilise its stewardship needs to address three key questions: Who do we have who has the knowledge and influence to be a stable steward? How do we keep them? And how do we bring on the stewards of tomorrow?

The most important thing to remember here is that not all stewards will sit at the top of the organisation. In fact, the most important ones will probably occupy positions two to three levels down. They won't necessarily be managers or senior experts. Instead, they will be highly capable people who possess a deep understanding of what the organisation does, how it operates, and what its fundamental beliefs and behaviours are. The chances are that they are people who don't crave promotion because they're doing the job they want to do and know they already have the influence they need. They are the house masters at Eton, the coaches and senior athletes at the All Blacks and British Cycling, the directors and senior experts at Nasa and the Royal Shakespeare Company, and the heads of department at the Royal Academy of Music and Royal College of Art. Within a company, they might well be anyone from a long-standing member of a department to the receptionist on the front desk who greets everyone in the morning and sets the tone for each day.

All the data suggests that at any given moment around a quarter of the staff of an organisation need to be stable stewards. They are that organisation's parents or, in army terms, the sergeants – the non-commissioned officers who have been promoted through the ranks, not appointed from outside. Interestingly, the whole concept of stewardship is deeply embedded in the British Army, and in many other successful fighting forces around the world. British Army sergeants are its backbone. They have served for a decade or so and they account for roughly a quarter of army personnel: seventy in a battalion of 300, twenty in a platoon of fifty, and one in a squad of five.[21]

With the right stable stewards in place, how do you ensure they stay for the next ten years? The parent analogy points the way here. Parents devote years to bringing up their children, not because they're hoping for remuneration or promotion but because they feel they are doing something that is worthwhile. That sense of purpose is their key motivating force. At the same time, they know that their role will constantly change as their children develop and that every day will bring a fresh challenge or obstacle to be overcome.

In the same way, stewards need to be confident that their jobs matter and that they will constantly evolve. An Eton house master, for example, will work with dozens of experts every year, either in the form of new members of staff or outside speakers. The cohort of pupils for whom they have responsibility is constantly changing too, as new ones arrive and the eighteen-year-olds leave. The basic role may remain the same. The people, the challenges and the ideas are constantly changing. And although the house master works long hours during term time – from seven in the morning to eleven at night – he will have school holidays (which account for a third of the year) in which to recharge his batteries, pursue other interests and, of course, prepare for the next term.

The picture for an All Blacks coach is not dissimilar. Again, they will work with outside experts from all parts of the world, both from within and outside sport. They'll experience continuity with players who have been with the team for a while, and the stimulus of change with fresh talent. They will work astonishingly hard during the playing season, but they have six months to recover and pursue interests elsewhere.

The same is also true of Nasa scientists, Royal College of Art tutors and Royal Shakespeare Company directors.

Many organisations might baulk at such an approach to steward management. They would argue that building flexibility rather than narrow focus into a role is inefficient; that bringing in outside expertise to help stimulate and inspire their stewards is impractical; and that giving people regular breaks is financially unworkable. But this is a false way of thinking. Lack of flexibility leads to boredom. A lack of interest in keeping people engaged ultimately leads to a reduction in creativity and productivity. And keeping a tight rein on time-keeping leads to burn-out and stress.

Besides there are many ways for an organisation to keep its stewards stimulated in a way that for the Centennials is second nature: temporary secondment to another project; allowing a break in the everyday routine by giving someone the time to work on something else that they feel passionate about; giving them flexibility rather than micromanaging them. All these approaches can make the difference between retaining and enthusing a valuable and long-serving member of staff and losing them.

Ideally, the most senior stewards will already be in place, and all that is required is to identify them and make sure that their role is shaped in such a way as to continue to engage them. Inevitably, though, it will occasionally be necessary to seek new blood from outside (just as 20 per cent of Harvard's top 100 CEOs came from other companies). The search, however, has to be undertaken with considerable care. For a steward to be high-performing, they need to have demonstrated stamina and ability elsewhere. That's why, for example, when the Royal College of Art was looking for a new vice-chancellor in 2009, it appointed Paul Thompson. An academic, curator and researcher, he had directed the Smithsonian Design Museum in New York for eight years and been director of the Design Museum in London for eighteen years, in which role he had partnered with the Royal College of Art on a number of projects. He may have technically been an outsider, but he knew the field and he also had prior knowledge of his new institution.[22]

Ultimately, of course, every stewardship will come to an end, and when it does it's important there's new talent waiting in the wings. Eton usually has at least two executive leaders and four house masters on hand at any given moment (and will normally need to fill roles for half that number). The Royal College of Art generally has one senior officer and four programme heads ready to come through. It's a similar picture across the range of Centennials. The average steward will serve for somewhere between ten and fifteen years, and there will be at least one person lined up who could take their place.

And since 20 per cent of those new stewards will come from outside, it's essential to be on the constant hunt for candidates for the roles that periodically need filling. 'We're always looking out for new talent to guide us,' says Thompson of the Royal College of Art. 'But we don't sit around waiting for them to turn up. We shake the trees and see what happens.'[23]

'It took them five years to persuade me to come,' says Zowie Broach, the head of its fashion programme, 'as I was too busy running my own fashion label and didn't want to teach. But then I came, and I love it now I'm here.'[24] Eton's current head of drama also describes how he was contacted 'out of the blue' when he was working with the Royal Shakespeare Company. 'I'd never considered teaching before,' he confesses. 'But they saw something in me that I didn't see in myself, and the opportunity to build a department, to leave a legacy, to impact so many lives, was too hard to resist!'[25]

5.

In summary, Centennials capitalise on the stable stewards who will help guide them forward, by:

Dividing their organisation into communities of 50 to 70 people

Making a quarter of each of these communities stable stewards

Ensuing that their stewards have important and interesting roles, so that they will want to stay in post for at least ten years

Guaranteeing continuity by having at least two years' worth of future stewards waiting in the wings at any given moment

Drawing on the organisation for 80 per cent of its future stewards, and bringing in 20 per cent from outside, as necessary.

Habit 4

MIND THE GAP

Grandparents are as cool as teens

1.

It was the final of the 2015 Rugby World Cup and the All Blacks were playing Australia. With just fifteen minutes to go, they were eighteen points up and seemed to be in complete control. But then their full-back was sent to the sin-bin, and things started to fall apart. In a worryingly short space of time, Australia scored fourteen points and seemed very much in the game. The All Blacks needed to make a swift choice. Should they stick with the tactics that had brought them this far, or should they try something different?

'What do you think?' Dan Carter, the All Blacks fly-half, asked his captain, Richie McCaw. 'Should we kick long and play for territory? Or should we kick short and hope they turn over the ball?' 'Kick short,' McCaw told Carter. 'They won't be expecting that; it will change the flow of the game.' The All Blacks changed their tactics, went back on the attack, and were soon piling the pressure back on the Australian side. When the final whistle blew, the New Zealanders were seventeen points ahead and became the first rugby team in history to win two World Cups in a row.

The All Blacks had performed a sudden change of tactics and, in doing so, managed to secure the match. But that change in tactics was not some arbitrary decision that was desperately arrived at when all else failed. It was something that had been developed over time and done very successfully before – most recently in the semi-final against South Africa the previous week and in the group game against France in the last World Cup four years earlier. In other words, it was part of a suite of tactics that the team had honed and that they could trot out very efficiently when the need arose.

There are arguably two reasons why they were able to do this so effortlessly. The first was that the team had the right mix of fresh new talent and long-serving experience. McCaw himself was playing in his fourth World Cup and had been with the team for more than a decade (as indeed had a quarter of his teammates). A quarter were on their second World Cup. And half were fresh talent playing in their first World Cup. In other words, as well as young talent, there were the stable stewards in place who could draw on their long collective memory and guide the team forward.

The second factor is related but subtly different. In establishing a world-beating team with players at different stages of their careers, the All Blacks ensured that bubbling under the surface would be the captains of the future who would learn from the current captain and then pass on their experience to the next. McCaw himself had learnt from Tana Umaga and would then pass his knowledge on to Kieran Read, who was playing in the final that day in what was his second World Cup. Read, who assumed the captaincy the following year, would in time pass the baton on to Sam Cane (also in the final that day in what, for him, was his first World Cup). Cane's captaincy came in 2020 after his second World Cup.

When McCaw claimed victory against Australia on that extraordinary day in 2015, the All Blacks already knew the answer to the tricky question: 'Who comes next?'

2.

Organisations often pay lip service to what they call 'succession planning' but they rarely give it much attention in practice. As a rule, when changes occur at the top, the previous regime wants to move on to its next challenge as soon as possible, and the new incumbent is keen to clear out the old guard and bring in their own people. Even simple hand-overs can be pretty perfunctory: a recent study in the US, for example, showed that only a third of serving CEOs stayed on after their successor was appointed.

But here's the problem. Since two-thirds of the new appointees covered by that same US study came from outside the organisation, there's bound to have been a sharp dislocation in leadership. And that dislocation will have brought with it huge risk. Such risk might be palatable in those cases where a company is in crisis and requires fundamental transformation. But where the company has previously been stable or thriving, such disruption threatens to have an entirely negative effect.[2]

With this in mind it's worth considering another cautionary tale, again drawn from the world of sport – this time from football. If the All Blacks demonstrate the wisdom of the calculated handover, then Manchester United's disastrous run in the early 2000s shows the inherent risks in an abrupt dismissal.

Under manager Alex Ferguson, Manchester United had had an extraordinary run of success. A competitive and driven man, Ferguson arrived at the club in 1986 and would go on to achieve dazzling results through his forensic attitude to solving problems and his willingness, when he first joined, to spend weeks talking to people about their experiences to find out what had worked and what hadn't. ('We spoke to Fergie more times in the first five days than we'd spoken to [Ron] Atkinson, the previous manager, in the last five years,' one coach later recalled.)[3]

Some of the changes Ferguson made were simple, practical ones. He improved the team's diet, for example (emphasising the benefits of por-ridge and vegetables). He made them train harder, abandoning his pre-decessor's more casual approach to start times and arriving at the club promptly at 9.30 every morning. He sought to instil greater team pride and coherence by insisting that players wear a jacket and tie to matches.

But his reforms also went much deeper. In his determination to secure future talent, he doubled the number of coaches working with the youth team players and tripled the number of scouts to help find and bring in new talent from other clubs too. And as he did this the players improved and their performance did too. 'The demands of players are different at United,' he explained. 'The expectations are higher, and the scrutiny is greater. And you need a special type of player, with a special type of character, if you want to succeed.'[4]

He was careful, though, not to throw out the baby with the bathwater. Resisting the temptation many leaders often have to start from scratch, he retained a quarter of the old players, and kept them on to help guide the new ones through – players such as Bryan Robson, who played for the club from 1981 to 1994, and Mark Hughes, who was there for fifteen years until 1995. Ferguson also instituted a careful system of overlapping stewardship, looking for stars of the future who would not only shine themselves but provide the necessary continuity that would help the club continue to thrive. Thus, for example, he signed Ryan Giggs in 1987 when he was only fourteen and who then stayed with the club for more than a quarter of a century; Gary Neville played for nineteen years between 1992 and 2011; and Roy Keane stayed for twelve years until 2005. Beyond these individuals, he created another generation of stewards that included Darren Fletcher (2003–15) and Wayne Rooney (2004–17). Four generations of stewards in a period of twenty years, all overlapping with one another and passing on their knowledge, expertise and team spirit on to the next contingent. This constant lacquering and layering of leadership, with a five- to ten-year handover between one generation and the next, led to an increase in collective knowledge and Manchester United experience among the players and their coaches from 100 years in 1986, to 150 in 1992, 200 in 1999 and 300 in 2010.[5]

The success of the Ferguson approach was soon reflected in the team's list of wins. Before his arrival, United had not won the league in the previous two decades, and although they didn't win it in the first six years that he was there, they then won it thirteen times between 1993 and 2013, and came second or third in every other year.

Then Alex Ferguson stepped down, and David Moyes took his place. Moyes proceeded to undo almost everything that Ferguson had put in place. He fired three of the club's coaches, regarding their approach as too old-fashioned, and in the process lost twenty-nine years of United coaching experience at a single stroke – fifty-six years if you also include

Ferguson's twenty-seven. In their place he put men with whom he had worked at his previous club, Everton, but who had never worked with United before. (Everton had not been particularly successful under their stewardship – they had lost half their matches and had never come higher than fifth in the league – so beyond a desire to surround himself with familiar faces, it's hard to see why Moyes thought this strategy would succeed.)[6]

There were mass exoduses elsewhere too. Moyes dispensed with the services of half the existing squad, losing forty years of United experience in the process. Most of the stewards he kept on – four players with ten years' experience apiece – felt unhappy in the new environment and would leave over the next twelve months. Overall, the collective 'United experience' within the club fell by half – from 300 to 150 years – in less than three years.[7]

Turmoil off the pitch was accompanied by failure on it. In the first year of Moyes' reign as manager, United lost two-thirds of their matches, and ended up seventh in the league – their worst performance in more than two decades. On 20 April 2014 they lost 2–0 to Everton. It was the final straw. Two days later, Moyes was fired. Over the next eight years, four more managers would try, and fail, to restore United to its former glory but the damage was done – the cuts had been made and the experience had gone.

'The problem with Moyes', a coach would say later, 'is that he thought he was leading a turnaround. But he wasn't. The team had just won the league five times in the last seven years. He wasn't there to turn it around and fix it. He was there to help it sustain its success!' Unfortunately, the one person who didn't realise this was David Moyes. It's a picture that is all too familiar to organisations in so many different sectors.

3.

Manchester United, founded in 1878, is technically a centennial organisation. But its massive miscalculations in the years after Ferguson left show how even the most successful organisations can stumble when they lose sight of the strategies that made them successful in the first place. The wiser and more consistent of them avoid this trap, carefully building up a multi-generational organisation involving three or even four generations of talent: grandparents, parents, teenagers.

According to Jonnie Noakes, director of teaching and learning at Eton: 'We always expect a new house master to join the school at least four years before they take over, and we announce the new one two years before the old one steps down, so people aren't surprised when they see them shadowing them, in key moments, at key events. The old one always stays in the school for at least two years after they take over to offer advice and support.'[8] It's a similar pattern elsewhere. At Nasa, around a quarter of the seventeen astronauts on the Artemis programme in 2021 had ten years' experience and were on their third mission; a quarter had been in post for more than five years and were on their second mission; the remaining half were new recruits and talents of the future. Interestingly, the proportions here are identical to those in other Centennials. They are to be found, for example, among the athletes in the 2020 British Cycling squad and the cast and crew of the Royal Shakespeare Company's *Matilda* production in 2022.

It's actually possible to arrive at a mathematical rule to plan succession and nurture talent. Essentially, a successful group of five will normally require a minimum of twenty years' collective experience to help sustain its success. An organisation of fifty will require a collective experience of more than 200 years – hence the reason why, when Manchester United's collective experience fell under the 150 mark, they struggled to stage a comeback.[9]

Neurological evidence supports the wisdom of the Centennials' practical approach. Research suggests that right-brain thinking – which involves creativity and problem-solving – is something that develops slowly over time. It might not take 10,000 hours for every person to master every task in every situation, as some writers claim. But it is certainly the case that most tasks – particularly complex, challenging ones – take at least ten years to master.[10] Over that period, as the individual becomes more proficient, more blood starts to flow to the right-hand side of their brain as they try to complete whatever particular task or skill it is that they have taken on or sought to acquire.[11] Their physical ability develops. So, too, does their mental ability. And physical and mental abilities come to reinforce each other, creating a virtuous circle.

There have seemingly been some outstanding exceptions to this ten-year rule. The mathematician, philosopher and scientist Blaise Pascal, the mathematician Srinivasa Ramanujan and the composer Wolfgang Amadeus Mozart are just three examples of child prodigies who achieved extraordinary things at a very early age. Even these geniuses, though, acquired true mastery only after exhaustive effort over many years. Mozart was eight years old when he wrote his first symphony. But his finest works did not start to appear until at least a decade later. Albert Einstein may have been only twenty-six when he published his theory of relativity, but by then he had been studying science for more than half his life. As for most talented authors, CEOs, entrepreneurs and Nobel Prize winners, they generally have to wait until they are in their forties or fifties before they achieve true mastery.[12]

The benefits that accrue from that critical decade of experience are nicely illustrated by a study that was done back in 1987 of a group of inexperienced medical students and a group of experienced doctors who had been practising for at least five years. All were asked to analyse thirty-two patient cases via their medical cards and a short description of their symptoms, and were then asked to recommend a suitable course of treatment. 'We tried to make the situation as realistic as possible,' Pie Hobus, one of the lead researchers, explained, adding that, as so often in real life, some of the information supplied was useless and some key details were missing. Each volunteer was given a minute to examine the evidence and a minute to work out their recommendations.[13] They were then asked to precisely explain how they had come to form their final views.

The researchers had rightly assumed that the doctors' diagnostic abilities would be better than those of the students, who were, after all, still at medical college. What they hadn't expected was that the doctors would be twice as accurate. They were much better at sifting the important from the unimportant. They knew how to reconcile seemingly conflicting evidence. They understood how and when to make often very difficult assumptions. In short, they forcefully demonstrated why acquired, collective experience is so important. Their example also shows why organisations that fail to have mechanisms in place to ensure that such experience and wisdom is handed from one generation to the next are living on borrowed time.

4.

Most organisations, as I have said, are very poor at identifying the next generation of leaders and ensuring that they are given the time to grow into their future role. They also rarely ensure that they receive proper mentorship from those currently in post and that there is a seamless flow from the old cohort to the new.

This can be a particular problem when the leader currently in place is a larger-than-life character or an inspirational founder. So dominant are they, so unthinkable is the organisation without them, that the issue of succession planning seemingly never arises in people's minds. The designer Christian Dior offers a case in point. So closely associated was he with the fashion house he founded in 1946 and with the 'New Look' he established shortly afterwards that when he suddenly died from a heart attack in 1957, no plans for his successor had been made. In a panic Jacques Rouët, his business partner, tried to close the company. When the fashion industry and others resisted (at this point Dior was responsible for 5 per cent of France's exports), Rouët put himself in charge of day-to-day operations and made Yves Saint Laurent artistic director. A period of turmoil ensued. Saint Laurent, who was only twenty-one at the time and had been with the company for just two years, was called up for military service four years later, and Marc Bohan – also a relatively new arrival – had quickly to take his place. The company survived (though it would go bankrupt in 1978), but, arguably, amid the chaos it lost its leading edge. And it's only under the stable stewardship of Bernard Arnault over the last thirty-nine years that it has regained it.[14]

Clearly, provision has to be made for an organisational structure that will facilitate the smooth handing over of leadership roles. But there are other considerations to bear in mind. First, it's essential to identify what recurrent decisions any new leader will need to take that are critical to the success of the organisation, and then ensure not only that the steward in line to take on this responsibility has the ability to make those decisions but also the training to know how to. Some of the decisions that will face them – such as pitching for new work, performing at a high-profile event, or managing an important meeting – are predictable. Others – managing a toxic team member, responding to an unexpected crisis, working with a suffocating stakeholder – may emerge suddenly but will almost certainly have cropped up before in some form or other. It's therefore entirely possible to prepare future leaders for the vast majority of challenges they will face.

Second, it's critical to identify a successor four or so years before the current incumbent steps down. As mentioned earlier, all too often these days organisations are prone to be attracted by the lure of the new and novel. In the US over the past twenty years, the number of new CEOs joining from other companies (as opposed to being promoted from within) has doubled.[15] The notion adopted by so many companies, according to one recruitment consultancy, is that it makes sense to 'bring in a new perspective, with a different set of ideas, to shake things up'.[16] The fact, though, that the number of leaders from outside should have doubled over precisely the same period that the life of the average US company has halved should be sufficient to suggest that the strategy isn't working. It's also a dangerously self-perpetuating approach. Lacking a thorough knowledge of the organisation they're taking over, the new leader proves a disappointment. He or she is therefore quickly replaced by another outsider who inevitably proves an equal disappointment. Disruption becomes a constant, and the company suffers as a result.

Key leaders such as Andy Jassy at Amazon, or Satya Nadella at Microsoft, or Tim Cook at Apple were all long-serving company employees who had worked closely with the previous CEO before they themselves took over – Jassy having worked with Jeff Bezos for fifteen years, Nadella with Steve Ballmer for four years, Cook with Steve Jobs for thirteen years. That continuity and the careful way in which handing the baton from one generation to the next was dealt with was crucial to each company's stability and continuing success.

Finally, there needs to be a proper handover period and process. This is something that has always been rare and is becoming rarer. As the revolving door of CEOs spins faster, few stay around long enough to guide the next incumbent. Unfortunately, all this adds to the instability among senior leaders that is now so ubiquitous. With no one around to explain company culture, and talk through challenges and opportunities, the learning curve becomes steeper and the chances of failure that much higher. New senior leaders are increasingly flying blind, and they and the organisations they run suffer accordingly.[17]

By contrast, those organisations and institutions that build in a proper handover period display greater robustness as a consequence. Harvard's recent study of the world's best CEOs shows that 90 per cent were supported for at least a year by the previous incumbent before they assumed full responsibility for the role themselves. In the same way, Arthur Levinson, chair at Apple, stayed on to support Tim Cook, while Eric Schmidt remained at Google to support Sundar Pichai.

It makes all the difference.

5.

In summary, Centennials carefully manage their handovers, so nothing gets lost along the way, by:

Maintaining at least three generations of leaders at all times, in every community

Maintaining twenty years' collective experience in a team of five, and 200 years in a community of fifty

Identifying a new steward four years before they are promoted, and giving them as much experience and responsibility as possible in that time

Promoting from within 80 per cent of the time, and bringing in outsiders 20 per cent of the time

Giving the old steward an important and interesting job to do after the new one steps up, so they will want to stay on and support them for at least two years.

Openness

Habit 5

PERFORM IN PUBLIC

Strangers are the best audience

1.

In 2008 three US psychologists asked 220 people to solve a murder mystery.[1] Each participant was provided with a map of the crime scene, a newspaper account of what had happened, and transcripts of interviews with three suspects. All were then asked to say who they thought the guilty person was.

'Participants were presented with the murder mystery task,' Katherine Phillips, the lead researcher, explains, 'and given twenty minutes to make an individual decision as to which of three individuals was the most likely suspect and write a brief explanation for their choice.'[2] After that they were divided into fours, given a further twenty minutes to discuss the case with other members of their group, and, at the end of it all, asked to deliver a consensus view. Each group comprised people who already knew each other. However, to shake things up a little, half the groups were introduced to a 'stranger' at the end of their allotted discussion time, with whom they proceeded to deliberate for a further quarter of an hour.

'When the newcomer joined the group,' Phillips continues, 'the old-timers were told: "X's [the newcomer's] last task took a little longer to complete. X is from XYZ [group]. To help bring X up to date, why don't you all tell her who you initially identified on your sheet as the murderer and then X will tell you who she thinks did it. You still have fifteen minutes for discussion."'[3]

The results were revealing. Left to their individual devices, two-fifths of the insiders in the study got the answer right (slightly better than the one-in-three odds that simply guessing would have involved). That level of accuracy remained unchanged following group discussion. However, when a stranger was added to the group the accuracy rate doubled to four-fifths.

Video recordings of the various group discussions soon revealed the reason why. Groups made up of people who knew each other quickly settled for an answer they could all accept. Groups to whom a stranger was added scrutinised the evidence more carefully. The stranger knew no more than they did and possessed no greater expertise. However, the presence of an outside voice broke up the easy tendency to settle for groupthink, forcing people to look at the documents more carefully, consider different angles and possibilities, and so come up with a more thought-through conclusion. 'Performance gains did not result from the ideas or contributions of the newcomer per se,' Phillips adds. 'Rather, it was the old-timers' reaction to the newcomer's presence that [improved their] performance.'[4]

The murder mystery findings are no one-off. Dozens of studies over the past two decades have revealed very similar results. Almost without exception, groups perform better when strangers are present.[5] 'They are more likely to share information and communicate openly when they deal with a task that requires collaboration,' the psychologist Hong Bui concluded after reviewing the findings from thirty-five previous studies.[6] 'They deliberate longer, discuss more information, and make fewer factual errors,' according to psychologist Samuel Sommers, after he had observed how 200 jurors made decisions in different types of groups. 'Moreover, if inaccuracies were made, then they were more likely to be corrected too.'[7] The psychologist Charles Bond concluded after reviewing the findings from another 241 studies that 'the mere presence of [a stranger] suffices to influence an individual's physiology and performance'. It creates a drive and desire to perform better – to show them what you can do.[8]

There is an important corollary. When people are challenged, they experience slight stress, and that stress stimulates the front area of the brain – the cerebral cortex – that is responsible for consciousness and reason. The result is clearer and better thinking. However, if that challenge becomes so intense that it appears to resemble a threat, the amygdala is stimulated and the result is a sense of unfocused panic. If a discussion is to be profitable, then, it's vitally important that an outside voice is allowed to express opinions, and that that outside voice is not so aggressive or overbearing that it comes to undermine or silence others. When the right balance of challenge and support is achieved it creates what psychologists term 'peak performance', or 'flow', whereby everyone in the group feels engaged and is stimulated to achieve to the very best of their abilities.[9]

'You are on that knife-edge of challenge,' the psychologist Susan Perry explains, 'and that is different for every person . . . that knife-edge of too hard or too easy.'[10] 'It happens when you're sufficiently challenged to stay engaged in a task, but not so frustrated by your inability to accomplish the task that you become anxious and quit. You forget yourself, time changes or stops for you, and you feel part of something larger than yourself.' She continued: 'Something is coming through you – it's you – it's your brain, but different parts are firing. It's not left brain or right brain, it's the whole brain, and the upper and the subconscious and sometimes the unconscious.' Or as the neuroscientist, musician and surgeon Charles Limb simply put it: 'I think those are times when you really feel like you're alive.'[11]

When the wrong balance is struck, the result is stress and dysfunction, poor decision-making and team disharmony. Contrarians are valuable, but they require careful handling. Simply engaging someone who prides themselves on 'thinking outside the box' is a recipe for disaster. It's much better to find what might be termed an 'adjacent stranger' – someone who is far enough removed from the task in hand that they can offer a fresh perspective, but not so far that they simply prove too disruptive.

2.

A story from the Nasa archives illustrates not just the value of 'strangers' but the importance of utilising their skills and insights in the right way.

On 27 March 1977 a KLM Boeing 747 was taking off from Tenerife airport when it hit a Pan Am Boeing 747 that was on the runway preparing for take-off. In the ensuing explosion and fireball nearly 600 people died; only sixty survived. It remains the deadliest accident in aviation history. As the cockpit voice recorder later revealed, the Pan Am flight's first officer, Robert Bragg, spotted the Dutch plane's lights as it accelerated through the fog and screamed to the captain, Victor Grubbs, who tried to steer his plane off the runway. But it was too late. 'There he is!' Grubbs yelled. 'Look at him! Goddam, that son of a bitch is coming!'[12] Two minutes later, both planes went up in flames.

In the aftermath of the tragedy, the Spanish government brought together seventy experts from across the airline industry to scrutinise what had gone wrong that day and to make some recommendations.[13] They duly spent fifteen months listening to hours of audio flight recordings, checking and cross-checking witness statements, and looking at detailed weather reports of that day. Their fifty-page report concluded that the Pan Am pilot had misinterpreted the instructions he had been given, and that the KLM pilot had not realised there was a plane sitting in his flight path. It therefore recommended that in future one language – English – should serve as the common language for the aviation industry and that there should be an agreed list of standard words and phrases employed by both pilots and air traffic control. 'The accident was not due to a single cause,' the report concluded. 'The misunderstanding arose from generally used procedures, terminologies and habit-patterns. The unfortunate coincidence of the misunderstanding with a number of other factors has nevertheless resulted in a fatal accident.'[14]

The report contained a lot of common sense. But it was also in some ways very limited. It might have explained the specifics of the Tenerife disaster and made some useful recommendations. What it didn't do was acknowledge that the incident, appalling though it was, was not a one-off. There would be sixty other fatal accidents that year. And the number of deaths in airline disasters would continue to be a serious blot on the industry's reputation. In the 1950s, around 9,000 people perished in accidents involving commercial aircraft. In the 1970s that figure rose to more than 18,000. An increase in the overall volume of flights helped explain the increase in fatalities. But the figure was nonetheless worryingly high. Ensuring that English became the lingua franca of the airline industry might help cut the numbers slightly, but it wasn't an overall solution.

Aware that the aviation industry had had at least thirty years to get its own house in order, the US government now moved in. It could, of course, have opted to commission yet another report by more commercial flight experts. It didn't. Instead, it decided to bring in experts from a very different, if related, sector: space exploration. Nasa did not fly conventional commercial aircraft or have to negotiate the complex logistics of civilian airports. But it understood the technology of flight, it appreciated the pressures that pilots were under, and it dealt with risk and safety on a daily basis. As Albert Frink, a former Pan Am captain, put it: 'The timing appeared appropriate for an exchange of ideas and information . . . to facilitate these activities, and, accordingly, a Nasa–industry workshop devoted to resource management on the flight deck was organised.'[15] Captain Robert Crump, a former United Airlines pilot, said: 'We were interested in having a neutral organisation, specifically, Nasa, do this research in establishing standards for resource management.'[16]

The team Nasa put together was a very carefully balanced one, comprising a mix of fifty insiders (pilots, crew members, air traffic controllers and engineers) and twenty 'strangers' (astronauts, psychologists, scientists and sociologists). Together they held four workshops (with four sessions in each) over the course of three days in June 1979, during which the insiders explained the nature of the problem to the strangers, who asked questions and shared their observations and insights.[17] They then broke the large group up into smaller subgroups to explore specific issues, ensuring as they did so that each subgroup also contained a mix of insiders and strangers. Each group explored a different aspect of the overall problem.[18]

The 200-page report that ultimately emerged made recommendations across a staggering range of issues and topics. It called, for example, for the redesign of cockpits to improve visibility, suggested ways in which flying technology could be enhanced, outlined new weather predictors, and drew on the insights of psychologists to suggest better training methods.[19] As the changes Nasa recommended were implemented, so the rate of accidents started to fall, from one in 200,000 flights at the time of the Tenerife disaster to one in 19 million three decades later.[20] It was an extraordinary achievement.

3.

Many breakthroughs in medical safety have occurred in similar ways. Take anaesthetics, for example. Back in the 1940s the American Society of Anesthesiologists (ASA) engaged two doctors from the Harvard Medical School to assess the risk factor involved in giving a patient a general anaesthetic. After analysing more than 6,000 cases, the doctors concluded that this relatively straightforward procedure led to significant problems in one in 10,000 cases and that 8 million people in the US died each year as a result.[21] 'Anaesthesia might be likened to a disease which afflicts 8,000,000 persons in the United States each year,' two medical doctors, Henry Beecher and Donald Todd, wrote in 1954. 'More than twice as many citizens out of the total population of the country die from anesthesia as die from poliomyelitis [or polio], which was considered to be one of the most dangerous diseases in the world at the time. Deaths from anesthesia are certainly a matter for "public health" concern.'[22] It was an important, if alarming finding. But while medics were able to pinpoint the extent of the problem, attempts to resolve it proved largely fruitless over the following two decades.[23]

Then in 1974 the ASA asked two engineers to study the problem. Applying a critical analysis technique that was second nature in their profession but unknown in medicine, they quickly established that the problem lay not with the drugs administered but with the humans who administered them.[24] Five million people in the US each year, they estimated, were needlessly dying because their breathing apparatus wasn't connected properly, or because the breathing tube had been inserted into the patient's stomach, or because dials had been incorrectly turned up or down, or because the wrong drug or the wrong dosage had been administered. 'Most of the preventable incidents involved human error (82%),' they wrote in their final report, 'with breathing-circuit disconnections, inadvertent changes in gas flow, and drug syringe errors being frequent problems. Overt equipment failures constituted only 14% of the total number of preventable incidents.'[25]

Once the engineers had delivered their findings, the ASA turned to another set of outside experts for further clarification. 'In 1984,' Frederick Cheney, an anaesthetist at the University of Washington School of Medicine in Seattle, explains, 'there was little comprehensive information on the scope and cause of anesthetic injury in the United States. Because significant anesthesia injury is a relatively rare occurrence, it is difficult to study prospectively or by retrospective medical record review, even from multiple institutions.'[26] However, the society suddenly realised that medical insurance companies had investigated all the claims made against anaesthetists in the last forty years – not just the fatal accidents, but the near accidents, and complications too. And since the insurance companies had a detailed record of every case – the hospital records, interview transcripts, expert witness reports, and jury decisions – it was possible to pinpoint what had gone wrong in each case where a claim had been made – and why.[27]

Thanks to the comprehensive data that medical insurance companies were able to share, patterns could be detected, common errors identified, and practical steps taken to reduce the risk of human error. Over the years that followed, breathing apparatus would be redesigned to make it more foolproof, monitors measuring blood oxygen levels would be improved, dials on equipment would be simplified, and a requirement that another medic should be present when an anaesthetic was administered would become standard. Changes that were all suggested by strangers – engineers, psychologists and scientists – who hadn't previously worked in medicine.[28] 'The history of anaesthesia is, in essence, a continuum of innovations and inventions,' the anaesthetist Bernie Liban explains.[29] Another anaesthetist, Alan Aitkenhead, points out that 'even simple and inexpensive changes in practice can have a major impact on safety'[30] – and, of course, it was just such 'simple and inexpensive changes' that outsiders were able to suggest. Thanks to their interventions, the number of medical accidents fell by a factor of twenty from one in 10,000 to one in 200,000. Millions of lives were thus saved each year.[31]

Medical researcher Ann Bonner, who has studied dozens of nurses both as an insider and an outsider, explains what is going on in such cases. '[As a stranger] I felt an instinctive ability to grasp the subtle differences with an open objectiveness . . . It also became apparent how an insider could simply lose intuition and sensitivity . . . As an outsider, however, I was able to observe and seek clarification of routine activities . . . [and] recognise patterns of nursing practice that could easily be missed by an observer familiar with the situation.'[32]

4.

A willingness to listen to outsiders may seem such an obviously sensible strategy that it scarcely needs to be stated. The fact is, though, that it is a vanishingly rare quality in most organisations. Taking account of an outside view requires a degree of humility that few are prepared to express. It's very hard to own up to the admission: 'We know we're not perfect'.

But there's more to it than that. Humans are by nature tribal; we have a deeply inbuilt sense of 'us' and 'them'. There is a natural, deep-rooted reason for this. As the neuroscientist Robert Sapolsky explains, treating outsiders with suspicion is a strategy 'to help keep us safe'.[33] Until we get to know someone a little, we can't be sure whether they might be a threat or a danger or how friendly they are. Brain scans of individuals who have been shown photos of someone who looks very different from them (by reason of race, nationality and so on) reveal there is an immediate flow of blood to that part of the brain that detects potential threat, the amygdala. Shown photos of people who live differently from them (for example, photos of drug addicts or homeless people), that part of the brain that registers disgust, the insula, is stimulated.[34] In other words, we are hardwired to treat outsiders with distrust and often with a lack of sympathy (hence the reason why we don't instinctively clench our hands if we see someone put a needle into a hand that doesn't resemble ours but do clench if it does).[35] 'Humans universally make us/them dichotomies,' Sapolsky explains, 'along lines of race, ethnicity, gender, language group, religion, age, socioeconomic status, and so on. And it's not a pretty picture. We do so with remarkable speed and neuro-biological efficiency.'[36] It's naturally hard for us to accept the wisdom of strangers.

But the fact that by nature we look on outsiders with suspicion is not an excuse to succumb to that tendency. And in any case, there are tried and trusted ways to reduce the friction that too often occurs when people who don't know each other are put in a position where one is invited to comment on the other's thoughts and ideas. It's always best, for example, if the process is eased in gently rather than imposed. Research has shown that when the benefits of using outsiders are properly explained to the insiders well before the outsiders are actually brought in, tensions are reduced. It also helps if those outsiders are used for only short periods at a time (so they don't become de facto insiders) but frequently enough that insiders start to become more relaxed around them. That way the insiders are likely to become more receptive to the ideas that are being offered to them.[37] Give people a 'task focus rather than a social focus', as the psychologist Laura Babbitt puts it.[38] 'Focus on shared goals. Practice perspective taking,' Sapolsky adds.[39]

Above all it is vitally important to bear in mind – and to reassure people – that while the stranger in one's midst may have valuable wisdom to impart, it's those inside the organisation – particularly the stable stewards – who have to be left to run with it. After all, they're the people who have the deepest understanding of what ultimately is in that organisation's interests.[40] The outsider should be valued for what they are able to contribute: dispassionate views, often involving the adoption of a new perspective. The insider should be valued as the expert who has the power of implementation. In other words, the relationship should be a symbiotic one. As the social researcher Harry Wolcott puts it: outsiders make the 'familiar strange', helping insiders find something new; the insiders make the 'strange familiar' and help execute it.[41]

5.

For the Centennials, involving strangers – performing in front of them – is an essential part of what they do and how they get better. The Royal Shakespeare Company regularly broadcasts rehearsals online. Nasa gets outside psychologists to sit in on team meetings. The Royal College of Art opens its artists' studios to the public. They're not alone. Among the non-Centennials, as I have witnessed for myself, Nordstrom utilises mystery shoppers. Jaguar Land Rover invites customers to watch their car being built. Harley-Davidson and Toyota let outsiders see how they work. Such activities are not just PR stunts. They are a way of gleaning useful information, of asking for and receiving feedback that can then be acted upon.[42]

Southwest Airlines actively invites its customers, staff and suppliers to share their experiences online so that everyone can see them, knowing that this will help improve the service this long-successful company offers in the future.[43] When I visited its headquarters in Dallas, Texas, the first thing I noticed as I entered the building was a big wall-mounted screen displaying live Facebook and Twitter feeds. 'We get over 4,000 tweets or posts each day,' Sarah Hicks, one of Southwest's social care specialists, told me.[44] Her colleague, Adam Scott, offered a concrete example of how the company reacts to such feedback. 'The other day, someone sent a tweet saying that the check-in queue at Midway airport was moving too slowly. So we contacted our manager there and found out there'd been a miscommunication about break times, and there weren't enough agents at the desk. So I sent a tweet back to the customer saying, "Hey, thanks for the catch. We're going to get some people out there right away." A couple of minutes later there were two more agents at the counter, and then the manager found the customer who'd sent the original tweet, who was standing in the queue, to thank them for letting us know there was a problem. All of that was done in less than eight minutes.' Brooks Thomas, a senior social business adviser at Southwest, said: 'Our goal is to essentially fully integrate social as a way of life throughout Southwest Airlines, whether you are on the front lines, or a communicator, or a marketer, or somebody hiring, or doing training.[45] Everyone at Southwest Airlines always performs in public.

So do the Centennials. 'Whether you're in an All Black environment,' Richie McCaw, their former captain, explains, 'or you're at home, or out and about, you're still an All Black and you're representing the team and so you should act as if you are. That's a tough one for a lot of the players to get their heads around. You've got downtime at home, you're not in the All Black environment, you're out with your mates, relaxing, switching off, winding down, chilling out . . . You're still an All Black, because that's what the headline will say if you stuff up.[46]

At the same time, that performative aspect of reaching out to strangers creates just the right adrenalin flow to stimulate people to do their best. 'By asking students to present their work,' Felicity Aylieff, the former head of ceramics and glass at the Royal College of Art, told me, 'we create a deadline that they have to hit, which forces them to take decisions and actions that might not otherwise happen. And by asking them to present their work to strangers we create a moment when they will have to do well.[47] For his part Peter Keen, the former British Cycling performance director, says: 'We've found that our best athletes always perform best under pressure, in the big moment or on the big stage, partly because we've planned it that way – we want them to peak at an Olympic Games – but also because the stage elevates their performance and encourages them to perform at their best.[48]

Obviously, no one can live at this elevated pitch all the time. The Centennials, therefore, balance the stress of performance with periods when there is no outside scrutiny, and open up different parts of their organisation at different times. Kieran Read, the former All Blacks captain, says: 'For me to perform well and play well, I need to get away at some point.[49]

All know, however, that those periodic injections of adrenalin are vital to the creative process.

6.

Even the greatest artists learn from strangers as they perform, and may well go through several iterations of a piece of work in response to the reactions they receive. The history of one of the most famous songs of all time – 'Hallelujah' – offers a case in point. Leonard Cohen came up

73

with it over a period of several years, writing more than eighty verses before he found the four he wanted. 'I filled two notebooks,' Cohen later recalled, 'and I remember being in the Royalton hotel [in New York], on the carpet in my underwear, banging my head on the floor and saying, "I can't finish this song."'[50] In terms of genre, his version was a slow gospel song – 'a cross between a hymn and a waltz', as Guy Garvey, the lead singer of Elbow, put it.[51] But it wasn't what Cohen's record label wanted. According to John Lissauer, the record's producer: 'It went to Walter Yetnikoff, who was the president of CBS Records, and he said, "What is this? This isn't pop music. We're not releasing it. This is a disaster."'[52]

'Hallelujah' was eventually released by the independent label PVC Records. It wasn't a commercial success. The journalist Alan Light later described how 'hardly anyone seemed to notice' the first track on the second side of the *Various Positions* LP. It didn't even merit a mention in Don Shewey's review in *Rolling Stone*, though he did note the album's 'surprising country and western flavour'.[53]

According to Light, when Cohen took the album on tour a year later, 'he soon started reconsidering the song's lyrics, experimenting with adding back and swapping out some of the verses that he had excised from the original sprawling manuscript' to create a version that was 'less theatrical and more human and personal'. He also added 'more melody' as 'two back-up singers replaced the choir'.[54]

It was this version that John Cale, co-founder of the Velvet Underground, heard in 1990 at the Beacon Theatre in New York. 'I was really an admirer of [Cohen's] poetry,' he later recalled. 'It never let you down. There's a timelessness to it.'[55] However, he didn't like the way in which the song was performed. So he stripped back the back-up singers and the instrumentation – to just a single voice and a piano – and made his own selection of the verses that Cohen sent him for a Cohen tribute album entitled *I'm Your Fan* that was released the following year. 'I called Leonard and asked him to send me the lyrics, and there were a lot of them, fifteen verses. It was a long roll of fax paper. And then I chose whichever ones were really me. Some of them were religious, and coming out of my mouth would have been a little difficult to believe. I chose the cheeky ones.'

Two years later Jeff Buckley heard the Cale version on a CD that was lying around in a friend's flat in New York. He liked the song so much he started performing it in bars across the city; a single voice accompanied by an electric guitar. Before long it had become the highlight of the show – and the last song performed each night. By the time Buckley recorded the song for his album *Grace* in 1994, he'd performed it in public more than 300 times, playing it in numerous versions and permutations, constantly amending and refining. Even the studio recording was made before a live audience.

'After dinner or whenever,' the album's producer, Andy Wallace, remembered, 'Jeff would just come in and run through his set. We tried to have some semblance of an audience, maybe six or twelve people around, so there was no temptation to stop, but just to play it all through. I wanted to record him as intimately as possible, so it felt like you were sitting two feet in front of him, which was the best place to see him in those tiny clubs.'[56]

'We didn't do "recording sessions",' Steve Berkowitz, the album's executive producer, explains. 'Jeff played the songs, and they got recorded. We tried hard not to have a barrier, just let him play, just be in it. To give him an atmosphere, an immediacy – like Dylan or Miles Davis – just to make music.'[57]

Buckley kept returning to the song in the studio, performing it over and over again in front of the studio audience, asking for their feedback, and making tiny adjustments, until he felt he'd got it just right. 'Even when we thought it was done,' Berkowitz recalled, 'and were doing the final mix, Jeff decided he needed to do one more overdub.'[58]

'The varieties and refinements weren't dramatic,' Light wrote later; 'they represented Buckley searching for the subtleties and nuances he wanted, for a precise shading in the ultimate delivery of this song . . . A pause here, a breath there, a guitar fill – he was teasing out the slight changes that would express the feelings he was striving to communicate.'[59]

It was these constant iterations that turned a song that had been largely ignored when it was first released into one that Buckley celebrated as a 'hymn to being alive. It's a hymn to love lost. To love. Even the pain of existence, which ties you to being human, should receive an amen – or a hallelujah.'[60]

'When you hear the Jeff Buckley version,' the musician Jake Shima-bukuro explains, 'it's so intimate it's almost like you're invading his personal space, or you're listening to something you weren't supposed to hear.'[61] For Daphne Brooks, an academic and author, 'it's that exhale at the beginning of "Hallelujah" that signals that he's going for broke, ready to let go and submit'.[62]

On 3 September 2007, Jeff Buckley's version of 'Hallelujah' – not Cohen's – was voted one of the ten most perfect songs of all time by fifty of the world's greatest songwriters.[63]

7.

In summary, Centennials perform in public to ensure that everyone performs at their best, by:

Understanding how strangers can improve decision-making, and the insights that they can bring

Creating specific moments that they want to 'perform' in front of strangers to ask them for advice, and show them what they can do

Asking strangers to watch both their most important activities and their most routine ones

Using the insights from these strangers to understand what's working and what's not, and so find new ways to improve

Having time away from strangers too, to rest, make improve-ments, and then get ready for their next 'performance'.

Habit 6

GIVE MORE, GET MORE

It's all about trust

1.

Elizabeth Holmes had always been competitive and ambitious. As a nine-year-old child, her short and simple answer to an aunt who had asked her what she wanted to be when she grew up was: 'A billionaire.'[1] She worked hard at school, got good grades and, in 2002, embarked on a chemical engineering degree at Stanford University.

It was a smart move at the right time. Silicon Valley had largely recovered from the dot-com meltdown that had taken place just a couple of years before, and there was renewed hunger for clever people with entrepreneurial minds.[2] Holmes helped out as a lab assistant, then spent some time in Singapore working at the country's genome institute. And it was while she was there, taking endless blood samples via syringes, that she hit on an ingenious concept: a wearable patch that could monitor a patient's blood, administer and adjust drug doses accordingly, and update doctors wirelessly with the data it recorded.

The following semester, she dropped out of college and devoted herself full-time to building a company – Theranos – that would manufacture and market her idea. At first, she focused on the patch technology. Then she embarked on an even more ambitious project: to produce a hand-held box that could run hundreds of tests in under a minute on just a pinprick of blood. She brought in Sunny Balwani – an MBA from University of California, Berkeley, who'd sold his previous enterprise for $40 million nine years earlier – to run the business on a day-to-day basis, and devoted her time to raising funds and achieving sales.[3]

On 10 September 2014 she stepped on to the stage at the TEDMED conference in San Francisco and delivered her pitch. 'I believe that the individual is the answer to the challenges of healthcare,' she said, 'but we can't engage the individual unless they have access to the information they need.[4] Her ambition, she said, was to 'create a world in which no one ever has to say "If only I'd known sooner", a world in which no one ever has to say "Goodbye" too soon.'

Money and support flooded in. Over the course of just two years, she raised more than $700 million, set up forty wellness centres in Walgreens stores across the US, established a lab that employed 500 scientists, and assembled what *Fortune* magazine described as 'one of the best management boards in history'.[5] It was a board that boasted two former US secretaries of state, a former defence secretary, two former senators and two former top military personnel. The company's investment board was no less impressive, comprising everyone from Larry Ellison, founder of Oracle, to the Walton family who owned Walmart, to Rupert Murdoch at News Corp. Interestingly, neither board contained any scientists or medics.[6]

Behind the scenes, though, things were not going so well. Holmes may have achieved her childhood ambition several times over – at one point she was worth $4.5 billion – but her scientists were struggling to make the technology work.[7] As Edmond Ku, an engineer who worked on the first prototype, later explained: 'The volume of blood that we had to work with was so small [because it was taken by using a pinprick rather than a syringe] that we had to thin it down with saline solution to create more volume. That made what would otherwise have been relatively routine chemistry work a lot more challenging.'[8] And because some of the blood cells were also ruptured by the pinprick, the tests became harder still.

Holmes, however, refused to listen to the doubters. As far as she was concerned, they were the non-believers – people who deserved to be marginalised or fired. She was interested in hearing only from those who thought it would all come right in the end. She set up two competing teams: Jurassic Park, which used the existing technology made by Siemens to run the blood tests that Theranos hoped to replace; and Normandy (named after the D-Day landings), which, she hoped, would storm ahead and make the necessary breakthroughs.

But those breakthroughs never happened. And before too long people outside the company were starting to ask awkward questions. Queries were raised as to why the company had not released any peer-reviewed research. Newspapers began to sniff around. Then, on 16 October 2015, the *Wall Street Journal*, which had interviewed various sceptical scientists and disgruntled former staff, ran a front-page story under the headline 'Hot Startup Theranos Has Struggled with Its Blood-Test Technology'.[9] The following week, the US Food and Drug Administration began an investigation.[10] On 14 June 2018 Holmes and Balwani were charged with nine counts of fraud.[11]

For many of those involved in the Theranos debacle, it must have seemed a black swan event – an unforeseeable business collapse brought about by behind-the-scenes dishonesty and greed. For the more objectively minded, though, all the danger signs were there. Here was a company that made grand claims but refused to allow outsiders to scrutinise them. A company that shut out contrary voices. A company whose culture was built on secrecy. 'Everything was so closed and secretive,' one former employee recalls, 'and we didn't trust each other so we all had to sign NDAs when we entered the building. Our emails were scanned to see what we were saying. Our security logs were checked to see when we entered and left the building. Some people were fired for putting USBs into computers, others were sued when they left, and we were told not to talk about our work to anyone in case they stole our ideas. Fingerprint scanners were put on doors so we couldn't walk around; partitions between desks so we couldn't talk to each other. And windows were tinted so we couldn't see each other. I mean, it was crazy. It was like a high-security prison!'[12]

Theranos was a company that operated in the shadows.

2.

The lesson of the Theranos story may seem an obvious one, but it's not one that many organisations take to heart. They may operate secretively but not because they have anything to hide. They worry about giving too much away. They fear that others will steal their ideas. They are convinced that if they share publicly what they're doing, they'll ultimately lose their competitive edge.

That's not how the Centennials operate. Indeed, they take the opposite approach. They go out of their way to share their stories with the rest of the world. In the 2018 Amazon Prime series *All or Nothing*, for example, we follow the All Blacks on and off the pitch as they discuss tactics, review matches and mull over individual performances. We witness Lima Sopoaga talk through his approach to a kick he made in a match against Argentina.[13] We listen to Steve Hansen, the head coach, as he discusses strategy with assistant head coach Ian Foster. Members of the All Blacks squad have also made other documentaries, written books and given interviews on television and in newspapers. Far from hiding what makes them unique, they share it with the world.[14]

It's the same with British Cycling. Various of its athletes, coaches, nutritionists, physiotherapists and psychologists have published articles, books and videos online. They're constantly offering tips and advice to others. Nasa, too, operates in broad daylight. One might assume that it would be keen to keep its multibillion-dollar technology under wraps, and be reluctant to share its ideas and strategies. After all, in its field it faces competition both from within the US and from outside. Far from it. Nasa is keen to share its research and air its ambitions in public. It even has a YouTube channel that to date has attracted 9 million subscribers. And it compiles and shares thousands of open datasets showing, for example, its management practices, equipment tests, weather predictions and planet orbital patterns, so outsiders can analyse them and help them spot new problems and develop new ideas.[15]

Why should the Centennials be so keen to operate in this way? There are two, closely interconnected reasons. First, they believe that openness creates trust. Second, they believe that trust attracts money and talent.

Trust – both from within and from without – is generally in short measure in the business world. According to an annual survey that has been conducted over the past couple of decades by Edelman – the world's largest public relations firm – only 51 per cent of the 34,000 people from twenty-eight countries around the world it asked in 2020 trust business leaders (for billionaires the figure is a mere 36 per cent). Eighty per cent, however, trust scientists.[16] The reason for this, according to the study, is that business people play their cards close to their chests. Scientists, by contrast, operate in a more open manner. Naomi Oreskes, professor of the history of science at Harvard University, says: 'Scientific progress is inextricably connected with the institutions of science, such as conferences and workshops, books and peer-reviewed journals, and scientific societies through which scientists share data, access evidence, grapple with criticism and adjust their views.'[17] In other words, by sharing their thought processes and publishing their findings, scientists show us what they're doing – and why they're doing it – and we therefore trust them. By hiding what they do, or being opaque about it, business people (and billionaires, in particular) invite distrust both within and outside the organisation they serve.

When trust is present, it oils the wheels of business. According to Paul Zak, the director of the Center for Neuroeconomics Studies, trust reduces transaction costs and thereby facilitates wealth creation, reducing job turnover, improving job satisfaction, and making people happier and healthier. Trust, he says, is 'associated with higher employee incomes, longer job tenure, greater job satisfaction, less chronic stress, improved satisfaction with life, and higher productivity.'[18] When people work in high-trust environments they are more energetic and collaborative. They work better together for longer, and as they do their performance slowly builds. People in low-trust environments, by contrast, are more closed and more secretive. They waste time playing politics and worrying about things that don't matter. They are therefore less productive. Over time their stress levels increase; they then either take leaves of absence or simply leave.[19]

There's a powerful physiological reason why trust should affect people in these ways. When humans interact positively with one another the brain releases the hormone oxytocin.[20] It is a process that occurs when mothers breastfeed their babies, and when people hug and kiss each other.[21] It also accompanies non-physical acts of social bonding, such as communal eating, drinking, dancing, singing and storytelling.[22] And when oxytocin is released, it makes us more relaxed and empathetic. In one experiment, those administered oxytocin by nasal spray were found to be more trusting of others in a control group than those who hadn't been, to the point where they were twice as likely to lend money to a stranger as those who hadn't received an oxytocin hit. In fact, the administration of oxytocin triggered a virtuous circle: the more volunteers in the experiment trusted a stranger, the more the oxytocin levels within that stranger were in turn boosted. Granting trust, in other words, wins trust.[23] And trust is created by openness and frankness, not by secrecy and evasion.

3.

Once trust is there, money and talent follow. Take British Cycling. 'Being secretive might help you in the short term,' Peter Keen, their former performance director, told me, 'as it might help you get more from what you've already got, so you can win at this Olympics or even the next one. But it won't help you attract the next generation of money and talent that you'll need for the one after that, or the one after that.'[24]

The organisation's general willingness to open up to outsiders has brought huge benefits over the years. Lotus Cars, for example, has helped with bike design. The McLaren Formula 1 team have offered technological advice. Rampton Hospital has become involved in mental health programmes. The Royal Ballet has offered touring tips.[25] (By the same token, British Cycling's darker side – accusations of doping cover-ups – has served to weaken bonds of trust, proving corrosively damaging to the organisation's image in the process.)[26]

If trust brings in outside help and expertise, it also attracts new recruits and enlarges the internal talent pool. The story of Disney's CalArts and of those of its alumni who went on to work at the Pixar Animation Studios offers a case in point. CalArts is a private arts university in Santa Clarita, California, that was set up by Walt Disney in 1961, shortly before his death.[27] 'I don't want a lot of theorists,' Disney had told people. 'I want people who know how to make films.'[28] He had therefore bought an old house in Valencia, just north of Los Angeles, and turned it into a school where there were none of the fraternities or sports teams one would expect to find at a traditional college, but a more bohemian set-up where pets and graffiti were encouraged. 'It was like an open floor plan,' one former student, Craig McCracken, recalls. 'Everybody just went out and found cardboard or whatever they could. It seemed like this shanty town. We found couches or whatever we could in Valencia and just started creating this hive.'[29] Students at CalArts learnt how to do everything from cutting film and recording sound, to creating the effect of light and shadows. They were also endlessly encouraged to look at things in different ways, to bend rules and break routines. According to Joe Ranft, another former student: '[The professors] would say stuff like: "Don't drive home the same way every day! Drive home a different way just to go different! Look at things backward and upside-down!"'[30]

Disney was keen to share all his secrets. He therefore involved his fabled 'nine old men', who'd made such classics as *Snow White and the Seven Dwarfs*, *Bambi* and *101 Dalmatians*, and got them to tell the assembled students how they had achieved their success, and what challenges they had overcome. In particular, they divulged Disney's twelve basic principles of animated film – from 'give your story a sense of weight and purpose' (squash and stretch) to 'highlight certain elements, to make them more exciting' (exaggeration) to 'look at your characters, from lots of angles, to make them real' (solid drawing).[31] 'Now I recognise exactly what they were doing,' John Lasseter later realised. 'They were handing the torch to us.'[32]

One student at CalArts, who studied character animation there for four years, was *Toy Story* director-to-be John Lasseter. After graduating, he went on to secure a job at Disney. Ironically, though, it didn't last that long. He was surrounded by talent, including former classmates such as Brad Bird (who would go on to make *The Incredibles*), Chris Buck (*Frozen*), John Musker (*The Little Mermaid*), Michael Giaimo (*Pocahontas*) and Tim Burton (*Edward Scissorhands*). But times had changed. Disney was no longer the outward-looking company it had once been. It had become more inward looking and insular. The crunch came when

Lasseter proposed a project of his own, a computer-graphic animation he named *The Brave Little Toaster*. 'They basically heard his pitch,' Brad Bird remembers, 'and said, "OK, that's it. You're out of here." He was just kind of dumbfounded because, like me, he had been prepped by the old masters, and suddenly no one was interested in all the stuff we were inspired to do.'[33]

Now out of a job, Lasseter went to a computer graphics conference in Long Beach a few weeks later to search for someone who might be interested in his idea. Here he bumped into Alvy Ray Smith and Ed Catmull, who had set up Pixar four years before.

Pixar had an openness to it that Disney once had and had now lost. 'Most [of our competitors] embraced a culture of strictly enforced, even CIA-like secrecy,' Catmull later recalled. 'We were in a race, after all, to be the first to make a computer-animated feature film. So many who were pursuing this technology held their discoveries close to their vests. After talking about it, however, Alvy and I decided to do the opposite – to share our work with the outside world. My view was that we were all so far from achieving our goal that to hoard ideas only impeded our ability to get to the finishing line. Instead, [we] engaged with the computer graphics community, publishing everything we discovered, participating in committees to review papers written by all manner of researchers, and taking active roles at the major academic conferences. The benefit of this transparency was not immediately felt. But the relationships and connections we formed, over time, proved far more valuable than we could have imagined.'[34]

Pixar soon reaped the benefits this openness brought, as various people stepped in to help solve the many technical challenges it faced, not least how to make an object walk or talk. In Lasseter they found a master storyteller. 'John's genius was creating an emotional tension, even in the briefest of formats,' Catmull said. When Pixar showed its first short film – *The Adventures of André and Wally B.* – at the same computer graphics conference the following year, so strong was the narrative line that nobody cared that, owing to a technical problem, some parts of the film were shown in black and white. 'This was my first encounter with a phenomenon that I would notice again and again, throughout my career,' Catmull continued. 'For all the care you put into artistry, visual polish frequently doesn't matter if you are getting the story right.'[35]

In a further twist of fate, Disney now reappeared. Impressed by the work that Pixar was doing and the software it had developed – software that Disney itself was now using in such films as *The Little Mermaid* and *The Rescuers Down Under* – it commissioned Pixar to make three feature films over the next eight years. The first of these was *Toy Story*, Lasseter's story of the relationship between a boy and his toys, told from the vantage point of the toys. Signed off in 1993 and attracting a team of talent that included such CalArts alumni as Andrew Stanton, Joe Ranft and Pete Docter, it was to be the world's first fully computer-animated feature film. On its first weekend in November 1995, it took nearly $30 million and would go on to take over $300 million in its first year. It also transformed how animated films were made.[36]

The Pixar success story, then, is quite literally about a willingness to share its stories. Those who created its first major success were beneficiaries of an open culture created by Walt Disney. For its part Pixar's mastery of computer graphics technology was achieved by sharing its secrets and its ambitions with others. And the more it opened itself up, the more money and talent flowed. The hits over the next ten years speak for themselves: *A Bug's Life* (1998), *Toy Story 2* (1999), *Monsters, Inc.* (2001), *Finding Nemo* (2003), *The Incredibles* (2004) and *Cars* (2006). In January 2006 the animation story came full circle when Disney came to Pixar with a proposal to buy it for $7 billion.[37]

As Catherine Mallyon, the executive director of the Royal Shakespeare Company, put it to me: 'We believe we're all in this together. And the more we do to help others, the better we all get, and the more money and talent will come into the arts, which helps everyone.'[38]

4.

Sharing stories involves a willingness not just to share successes, but failures too. Only in that way can trust truly be created. After all, if trust demands openness, openness demands a willingness to show vulnerability.[39]

Nasa learnt this lesson the hard way. In the 1960s, the space agency developed an open and collaborative culture – a culture that ensured that President John F. Kennedy's ambition to put a man on the Moon before the end of the decade was realised. However, by the 1980s, it had become more self-enclosed and secretive, creating an inward-looking culture whose shortcomings were fatally exposed by the *Challenger* disaster of 1986, when a design fault caused the Space Shuttle to explode shortly after take-off, killing all seven of the astronauts on board. The fact that an accurate analysis of that disaster had to be left to an outsider – the physicist Richard Feynman – shows both how cut off Nasa had become from what was actually happening, and how essential it was for the space agency's future to share its story with others.

Improvements were made and things seemed to get better, but then disaster struck again in 2003 when the *Columbia* shuttle exploded, killing its seven astronauts. Nasa now fully embraced the lessons it had learnt. Technical experts were invited in to shed light on what had gone wrong. Psychologists were brought in to advise on how to communicate better. Simultaneously, changes were made inside Nasa to build trust and create a more collaborative culture, notably making engineers (not managers) responsible for their own work. The results were transformational.[40]

5.

Not all the stories that an organisation shares have to be big, ambitious ones. Anecdotes about the small details, the rituals and routines that are part of that organisation's DNA are crucial too. Indeed, by virtue of the fact they don't involve seismic research and major breakthroughs, they can often be easier to understand and to connect with. British Cycling, for example, talks about its big successes, but shares everyday stories too: how its athletes eat, sleep and train each day, how they develop the mental strength to perform under pressure, and how they measure and adjust their performance when they're cycling.[41] Such practical insights can readily be exploited by competitors, of course. But, as British Cycling has calculated, the long-term gains far outweigh any short-term disadvantages. The fact that it doubled its income and quadrupled its membership between 2010 and 2020 suggests its strategy was a wise one.[42]

Proof of such long-term gains also comes from a study undertaken in a very different sphere. Cystic fibrosis is a genetic disorder that can be passed from one generation to the next if both parents possess the same recessive gene. It's relatively rare – affecting around 3,000 babies in the US each year, for example – but its effects can be devastating. The cells of those who suffer from the condition produce too much chloride, which leads to a build-up of mucus in the liver and lungs and eventually stops them from working.

Back in the 1960s most children with cystic fibrosis did not survive to celebrate their third birthday.[43] Experts noticed, however, that life expectancy for those treated in certain medical centres was much better, with children on average living an additional decade. The Cystic Fibrosis Foundation therefore asked Warren Warwick, a paediatrician from Minnesota University, to undertake research to explain the disparity. Over the next four years, he set out to compare the different methods adopted by thirty care centres across the country.

When he reported back he noted several ways in which the approaches of high-performing centres differed from the norm. They tested babies for cystic fibrosis symptoms much earlier, he said. They started treatment earlier too, getting sufferers to sleep in mist tents, and clapping on their chest twice a day to stop the mucus from building up. They even got sufferers to cough in a different way from the norm to help dislodge the mucus.[44] After his report was published in 1968, and his recommendations were adopted, life expectancy for those with the condition tripled over the next two years, and doubled in the six years after that. By 1976, they were living for eighteen years on average.[45]

When progress started to stall – by 1980, the life expectancy of those with cystic fibrosis was still only nineteen years – the foundation published a league table, the first of its kind, showing each centre how it was performing and how it could improve. The foundation also set up training and research facilities to help individual centres.[46] As it shared its findings more funds and talent flooded in and there was a further spate of breakthroughs. First, geneticists identified the cystic fibrosis gene. Then surgeons developed techniques for lung, liver and kidney transplants. In the early 2000s researchers announced that they could now edit the CF gene, and so significantly reduce a patient's symptoms. By 2020 life expectancy had risen to more than forty-five years – a fifteenfold increase on the state of affairs sixty years earlier.[47]

What is interesting is that even though the foundation was careful to share its research and breakthroughs with everyone, the best-performing centres always stayed ahead of the pack – ten years ahead, in fact – and there was a remarkable consistency to their overperformance. In the 1960s, they helped sufferers survive until they were thirteen, when other centres expected to see their patients die before they were three. In 2020, when the average cystic fibrosis sufferer was living until they were forty-five, those treated at the best-performing centres could expect to see their fifty-fifth birthdays. That decade gap remained unchanged even though the lower-performing centres were improving. 'Most people think that if you share your ideas then others will catch you up,' Bruce Marshall, a senior vice-president at the Cystic Fibrosis Foundation, explained. 'But that's not what we found. We found that when the high-performing centres did this, more money and talent went to them, so more breakthroughs happened. And although the other centres were improving, they stayed ahead of the pack.[48] The essential rule – that openness leads to improvement – always applies. Excellence and openness are a powerful team.

6.

If there's one area of the commercial world that demonstrates this truth it's Silicon Valley. These days, we tend to think of it as a collection of independent companies. But its ecosystem is rather more complex than that. Ultimately, it's a community of experts and entrepreneurs who often share funds and ideas, and frequently move from one company to a direct competitor. A study in 2006 found that more than a quarter of the 200,000 people who worked there had changed company in the last year, a proportion 40 per cent higher than that to be found in other tech clusters they studied.[49] Thanks to such fluidity and co-dependence, this community has thrived and grown exponentially. In 1959 there were

18,000 high-tech jobs in the region. By 1971 there were 117,000, climbing to 498,000 in 1999. In 2020 there were more than 1.7 million.[50]

Arguably, Silicon Valley has its origins in a decision made by Frederick Terman at Stanford University at the end of the Second World War to open the engineering school, of which he was dean, up to business. At the time it was regarded as a revolutionary and somewhat controversial move. According to Jamis MacNiven, who worked for Apple in the 1970s: 'Stanford was the first major university that reached out, in a big way, into the business community and said, "Hey, we have this open-door policy. Come on in, do business: go out and do business!"'[51]

'Contrast that with the Ivy League,' says Jim Clark, the founder of Silicon Graphics in 1981 and Netscape in 1994. 'They had their nose in the cloud: "We are beyond business. Business is dirty. We are not talking about applications. We are about advancing knowledge and research."'[52] Terman sensibly ignored the naysayers. He leased half a square mile of university land, invited high-tech businesses to set up shop there, and also encouraged them to discuss their ideas with the university: to create business courses, clubs and societies from which they all could benefit. And he also reached out to investors.[53]

Over the next few years, money and talent started to arrive – from venture capitalists such as Draper, Gaither & Anderson, and Venrock,[54] and businesses such as General Electric, Hewlett-Packard and Lockheed Martin.[55] And with them came the breakthroughs: semiconductors (Bell Labs) and the internet (Stanford) in the 1960s; microprocessors (Intel), computer games (Atari) and PCs (Apple) in the 1970s.

Then in 1971, William Shockley, who'd invented semiconductors at Bell Labs and was now at Fairchild, asked a journalist from *Electronic News* – a newspaper set up by Fairchild fourteen years earlier – to share the Stanford story with a wider public. The journalist obliged and in the course of a three-part series described how what he termed 'Silicon Valley' – a fifty-square-mile region, from Redwood City down to San Jose – had been created and nurtured, and what achievements they had made. The story was duly picked up by the national press. It started to spread.[56]

As it did so, more money and talent arrived, more businesses were established, and more breakthroughs started to happen: from graphics

(Silicon Graphics), networks (Cisco) and workstations (Sun) in the 1980s; to e-commerce (eBay), search engines (Google) and servers (Oracle) in the 1990s; to smartphones (Apple), social media (Facebook) and taxis (Uber) in the 2000s; to electric cars (Tesla), tablets (Apple) and smartwatches (Apple) in the 2010s.[57] All the while more magazines and newspapers were set up to share the new stories that were constantly breaking – publications such as *Macworld*, *PC Magazine* and *PC World* in the 1980s, and *Wired* in the 1990s. Amid all this, Silicon Valley boomed. In 2020 it was home to four of the six most valuable companies in the world: Apple, Google, Facebook and Tesla, who, between them, had a combined value of more than $4 trillion.[58] The two other companies that make up the six of this exclusive club – Amazon and Microsoft – may not be headquartered in Silicon Valley, but they still have offices and research centres there.

Within Silicon Valley, people frequently move around, learning from one company and then applying the skills they learnt at another. Gordon Moore and Robert Noyce worked for Fairchild before they started Intel. Steve Jobs worked for Atari and Steve Wozniak for Hewlett-Packard (HP) before they started Apple. Elon Musk helped set up PayPal, and Martin Eberhard worked for Wyse before they started Tesla. Biz Stone worked for Google and Evan Williams for HP before they started Twitter. The list is endless.[59] For those who believe in an inward-facing company culture, such fluidity – which they would no doubt describe as disloyalty – is anathema. But it's actually what makes Silicon Valley tick and is why it is so immensely powerful as a competing entity against the rest of the world. Aaron Sittig, who worked for both Napster and Facebook in the 2000s, puts it like this: 'The best way to think about Silicon Valley is as one large company, and what we think of as companies are actually just divisions. Sometimes divisions get shut down, but everyone who is capable gets put elsewhere in the company: maybe at a new start-up, maybe at an existing division that's successful, like Google, but everyone always just circulates.'[60] Openness is everything.

It's a mindset constantly to be found among the Centennials. Even when they're dealing with potential competitors, they share their stories, their achievements and their disappointments so everyone can learn and improve. And as they do – just like the high-performing cystic fibrosis centres – more money and talent comes to them, and more breakthroughs happen. Which is why Eton has outreach programmes for other schools, Nasa helps other space agencies, and the Royal Shakespeare Company supports other theatres. Some would argue that such an approach is too generous – foolish, even – and is not in the interests of the organisation reaching out. In fact, the very opposite is the case.

7.

In summary, Centennials gain trust, and the advantages trust brings with it, by:

Sharing their stories of success and failure to help them understand what happened and what they can learn

Sharing these stories not just by talking about them but by giving interviews and talks, making documentaries and films, and writing articles and books

Creating and sharing open datasets that reveal what has worked and what has failed in order to encourage people to step in to help

Working with insiders, outsiders and competitors to find ways to bring money and talent into their sector.

Part 2: Disruptive edge

Experts

Habit 7

BE POROUS

Use brilliant people part-time

1.

Over the course of just three years in the early 1970s, British pop legend David Bowie did what few British artists ever managed to achieve: he made it big in the US. The Thin White Duke, as he characterised himself during his stay in Los Angeles, stormed his way to a top-five US single ('Fame') and a top-five album (*Station to Station*). He was on a roll. And then in 1976, he threw this all up, killing off the Thin White Duke and moving to Berlin, where he embarked on a new phase of his life, recording five albums in just three years, two with Iggy Pop (*The Idiot* and *Lust for Life*), and three with Brian Eno and Tony Visconti (*Low*, '*Heroes*' and *Lodger*).

It wasn't the first time he'd radically changed direction. In the late 1960s, having achieved his first top-five UK single ('Space Oddity'), he adopted the hugely successful persona of Ziggy Stardust. And Berlin wasn't his final move either. Throughout the rest of his career he would continually shift gears every few years and find something new to do – in France, London and then New York. Many were disconcerted by the transformations he underwent. Visconti, who produced twelve of the twenty-six studio albums Bowie made over his forty-seven year career, said: 'Every time Bowie put out a new album, there were a lot of people who hated it . . . People would say, why didn't he record "Rebel Rebel" again or why couldn't he write another "Space Oddity"?' Visconti also explained why Bowie constantly changed, saying, quite simply: 'Because he'd done it.'[1]

Bowie was always on the search for something new. He was restlessly creative. And such was his creative genius that while many were resistant at first, they ultimately came round to Bowie's self-reinventions. 'With *Young Americans*,' said Visconti, 'you heard people saying that white people weren't meant to make soul, and with *Low* the record company almost rejected it because there weren't enough vocals on it. But everybody loves *Low* – that album gave birth to Gary Numan and a lot of other styles of British electronic music.' By the time he died in 2016, Bowie was widely acknowledged to have been one of the most influential musicians of all time, his songs covered by everyone from R&B stars to punks and hip-hop fanatics. He had achieved nineteen top-five albums in the UK, and a further five in the US. His last album, *Blackstar*, a fusion of art rock and jazz, went to number one in both countries.[2]

Much of Bowie's continuing success was down to his willingness to constantly explore the new and the different. As he said of his move to Berlin: 'It's a strange singular place, Berlin. After the war, when it became sucked into the middle of East Germany – and it was just an island in the middle of East Germany – all the industry, all big business moved out of Berlin. It just left big factories and warehouses that were empty. So what happened is students and artists moved in. So the whole place became like a workshop. And it was just a wonderful place to be in, for that.'[3]

He was artistically inspired, too, by the presence of the Berlin Wall that then snaked its way between East and West Berlin. So inspired, in fact, that he decided to record his new albums right up against it. 'You'd see the soldiers on the towers,' Eno explained, 'but I mean I don't think anyone for one moment thought they were going to start taking pot shots at us or anything. But it certainly added a thread to the sort of geography of the record in that we were in a place with a very strong personality. And I suppose the way that translates is in making you think you're going to do something strong as well. It's no use releasing something mediocre, or pallid, in an atmosphere like that. You tend to make strong statements then.[4]

But another key factor was involved. Bowie might have been a global superstar, but he was never afraid to turn to others for help and inspiration. Recalling his work on *Low*, Visconti described how Bowie worked: 'He always had a core to the band, which [in this case] was Dennis Davis on drums – one of the best drummers I have ever worked with – Carlos Alomar on guitar, and George Murray on bass. They had been with him, more or less, since *Young Americans* – and David took them on the road, so they were the core of the band.'[5] And then they would bring in seven or eight new musicians for each album – guitarists, keyboard players and vocalists – to give a different edge to each song. Over the course of his career Bowie would work with nearly 200 musicians – an average of twelve per album. Around a quarter would be people he'd played with in the past on a previous album; they were the stable stewards who knew how he worked. The others – the majority – were people he admired who were new to him, who he hoped would help challenge and change him.

The way in which *Low* was made exemplifies how Bowie worked. At the core of the recording were three musicians – on bass, lead guitar and drums – he had played with over the previous three years. Then there was the fresh talent: six artists Bowie would never work with again and, most notably, Brian Eno, who had made his name with Roxy Music five years earlier. Eno had developed a set of 127 cards – Oblique Strategies, as he called them – that he used to help break familiar patterns and shake things up. Each card proposed an action that forced you to look at something differently or behave in a different way:[6] 'Ask people to work against their better judgement'; 'Change instrument roles'; 'Do something boring'; 'Emphasise the flaws'.

'We would each take a card but keep it secret,' Eno explained. 'Each Oblique Strategy tells you a way of operating – it's a technique on each card – and then we'd each start working on the same piece of music, but with entirely separate and secret agendas. For example, one of them said "Make something as quiet and discreet as possible" when the other would say "Make a horrible mess" or something like that. So there were the two of us trying to pull this thing in completely different directions. And of course this can make for a great composition when there's that kind of tension.'

'We would devise systems where I would put down a piano, say,' Bowie recalled, 'and then take the faders down, so that you could only hear the drums, and [Brian] knew only what key it was in. And then he would come in and put an alternative piece in – not hearing my part but knowing what the key was. And then we'd leapfrog with each other – not hearing each other's parts – and then at the end of the day put all the parts up and see what happened. See what it was like. "Oh, parts three, seven and five sound great." So we took all the rest down – and just had fader three, five and seven – and that would become the basis for that song.'[7] The pair weren't afraid to put others outside their comfort zone either. Robert Fripp, the lead guitar on the third track of the *Heroes* album, was asked, for example, to launch into songs at full speed without having heard them before. Then, once all the other parts had been recorded, Bowie would go into a booth and record the vocal, responding directly to what the others had produced. The creative tension this approach engendered was, according to Visconti, the cause of the soaring and distinctive guitar melody that we hear at the beginning of the album's title track '"Heroes"'.

Carlos Alomar, the guitarist who played on eleven of Bowie's albums, summed up his philosophy: 'He was such a restless person. He didn't like being comfortable. Comfortable is genre-driven, and be careful because it will outlive you and it will surpass you. David had a lovely saying: "Let go, or be dragged." He was David 2.0, 3.0. If I wanted five amplifiers, he'd get them for me; if I wanted to mike something differently, we'd do it. It was change, change, change. [Other artists] would introduce something and stay there. David would introduce something and leave it.'[8]

2.

Changing geographical location to inspire creativity and fresh perspectives, as Bowie periodically did, may be too radical and impractical for most. Bringing in outsiders, though, is neither of these things. All too often, though, people resent the very notion that it's worthwhile considering things from a different angle or that an external expert might have something useful to teach them. It takes a degree of humility – as Bowie demonstrated – to open yourself up to external scrutiny and ideas.

And yet the dangers of a closed mindset are constantly demonstrated. Organisations that close in on themselves perpetuate their mistakes and bad or inefficient ways of working. They fail to spot opportunities and threats. Ultimately, their bunker approach may well destroy them.

The fate of BlackBerry, the mobile phone company, clearly illustrates this. It had, for a long time, been an extraordinarily successful and cutting-edge company. Founder Mike Lazaridis, who had trained as an electrical engineer during the day and acquired computing science skills at night, had set it up in the mid-1980s (when it was called Research in Motion) when he was just twenty-three.[9] He'd then spent eight years working on various ideas before he teamed up with Harvard MBA Jim Balsillie, who encouraged him to focus on developing a two-way pager. This then became a mobile phone, before morphing into the BlackBerry – the first smartphone with easy-to-use email and a full-size keyboard. The new phone was an instant hit with business people. By 2006, the company, which now employed 6,000-plus people, was selling more than 50,000 phones a day, and constantly coming up with new and improved versions each year.[10] At its height – in 2009 – it controlled nearly half of the world's smartphone market.[11]

By the time Apple launched the iPhone in 2007, however, Black-Berry had become complacent. It thought its core market was safe and the company was dismissive of rivals. 'It isn't secure,' BlackBerry COO Larry Conlee told a journalist when the iPhone came out, 'it has rapid battery drain and a lousy keyboard.' BlackBerry's CEO Balsillie added: 'It's kind of one more entrant into an already very busy space, with lots of choice for consumers. But in terms of a sort of sea-change for Black-Berry, I would think that's overstating it.'[12] BlackBerry was reassured by a report prepared by the Monitor Group – a management consultancy set up by Harvard professor Michael Porter – that suggested the iPhone would never become a major threat and that all BlackBerry needed to do to protect its current market dominance was to 'step up advertising and product promotions'.[13]

The problem was that BlackBerry didn't appreciate what the iPhone actually represented. It saw it as just another phone, albeit a well-designed one. BlackBerry didn't realise that it was in fact a computer that happened to have the capabilities of a phone.[14] Compared with the iPhone's software, BlackBerry's was antiquated. Moreover, it followed a traditional proprietary route at a time when companies such as Apple and Google were each developing an operating system and then getting thousands of independent developers to create apps for them. Consequently, while Apple and Android phones could constantly claim 'There's an app for that!', app developers were complaining via their blogs how impossible it was to work with BlackBerry.[15]

By the time BlackBerry saw the light, it was too late. In 2013, there were 80,000 apps on the BlackBerry store. Apple and Android customers, by contrast, could choose from more than 1 million. BlackBerry was able to keep going for a few years by expanding into markets where price was crucial and innovatory products tended to make their way more slowly: Asia, Latin America and the Middle East. But when cheaper Samsung phones with Google software came out, and network speeds started to increase, sales fell dramatically – from $20 billion in 2011 to $2 billion five years later. On 28 September 2016, the company announced that it was selling its hardware business to TCL, a Chinese electronics company, after losing 97 per cent of its market share. Four years later, it stopped making phones altogether.[16]

The closed BlackBerry mindset is scarcely unique. Nor are the circumstances that led to its downfall. In each of the past sixty years, Standard & Poor's – the US credit-rating firm – has published a list of the 500 most valuable companies on the US stock exchange (the S&P 500).[17] When in 2017 three US researchers studied the index, they discovered that the reason why individual companies slipped out of the index was invariably that they had been blindsided by a company operating in a different sector.[18] In BlackBerry's case, the existential threat had come from a computer company. Elsewhere, the car industry was being transformed by an energy company (Tesla), media was undergoing a fundamental change because of a software company (Facebook), and the retail sector had been altered beyond all recognition by a technology company (Amazon). The researchers also found that the rate of change (i.e., the rate at which companies moved in and out of the index) was increasing.

What disruptive companies such as Tesla were doing was not in itself necessarily revolutionary. The ideas and technologies they were using were already there. They were just applying them in a market that had not previously used them. After all, touchscreens had existed for a number of years before Apple put them on phones, just as battery technology had been around for decades before Tesla put it in a car. It took a fresh mind from a different discipline to make the connection and spot the potential.

Yet although such disruption is now very well documented and the casualties continue to mount – whether BlackBerry, General Motors, Blockbuster (videos), Borders (book retailers) or a whole host of others – most companies continue to be woefully blind to the challenges and threats that may be coming down the road. And the reason for this is that almost without exception they are looking in the wrong direction. According to the study done of the S&P 500, while four-fifths of the CEOs surveyed believed that their company would face a threat in the next fifteen years, three-quarters of them believed it would come from existing players in their sector, not from outside.[19] They were so focused on the job in hand that they could only see what was right in front of them. They never looked from side to side or checked what was coming up behind.[20]

These CEOs tended to suffer from another mental block too – one that is common to most humans. Essentially, as a species, we tend to overvalue the ideas with which we agree, and we undervalue those with which we disagree.[21] Consequently, when faced with a truth or possibility that contradicts our world view, we take refuge in what psychologists call confirmation bias. Two-thirds of us will reject the new idea outright. Half of us won't look for it in the first place if we think it might undermine our existing opinion or prejudice.[22] Instead, our default position is to consider only evidence that supports our ideas, and listen to people with whom we know we will agree.[23]

There are sound practical reasons for behaving in this way. Confirmation bias can lead to poor decision-making, but it also makes it easier to get things done, and to convince others to follow our lead and believe that our ideas are good ones. As one psychologist put it to me: 'If we all agree on the same ideas then we don't waste time discussing things, and can just crack on.'[24] Confirmation bias, in other words, can work well when things are simple, stable and predictable.

The problem is that it can be a disaster when things are not.

3.

The Centennials not only understand this basic truth, but they know how to avoid its pitfalls. To steer away from confirmation bias, to keep new ideas flowing, to pinpoint best practice and approaches, they turn not to people with MBAs or management consultants focused simply on such short-term goals as making more money, but to disruptive outsiders and experts who question and challenge everything.

As Peter Keen, the former British Cycling performance director, explained to me: 'Our biggest breakthroughs always came when we worked with a brilliant expert from outside who looked at our problem in a completely different way.'[25] It was thanks to outsiders, he said, that British Cycling completely changed the designs of their helmets and bikes, how their cyclists sit on their bikes, and how they mentally prepare for each race. Chris Boardman, one of the Olympic gold medallists who worked with Keen, describes this approach as 'the perfect mix of expertise and ignorance that can bring about giant leaps of innovation'.[26] Taking a leaf out of the British Cycling book, Nasa turns to nutritionists and psychologists to problem-solve and the Royal College of Art brings in engineers and scientists to inspire students to think of new and better ways to change the world.

There are two ways in which such experts are utilised. Either they work for the organisation in question part-time so that they can continue to work on other cutting-edge projects elsewhere and bring the benefits of those projects to bear as they come to fruition. Or they are employed full-time but are spread across at least three different projects at once.

The former are the people the Royal Academy of Music turns to. 'We learnt early on', Timothy Jones, the academy's deputy principal, explained to me, 'that people go out of date if they spend too much time with us, as they only work on our problems with our ideas. So we ask them to work with us part-time. We've found it's easier to recruit the best people when we do this as we're only asking for part of their time.'[27] British Cycling's nutritionists, psychologists and scientists similarly work with two other Olympic teams at the same time. The latter type of staff are to be found among Nasa's biologists, engineers and meteorologists. They are employed by the space agency on a full-time basis but usually work on several programmes at once.

The benefits of this approach can manifest themselves in often unpredictable and surprising ways, as the All Blacks have learnt from hard experience. Back in 2004, they faced a real problem. They found that they had been going into tournaments as the firm favourites but then time and time again were losing their grip. They pondered what might be causing this. Perhaps the leadership of the team was at fault. They decided to broaden the leadership base beyond the captain and allow the players to pick who led them. Perhaps it was the culture. Rugby union had turned professional nine years earlier, and there was a concern that players had become more preoccupied with what would serve them rather than what would help the team. A 'no dickheads' policy and a 'better people make better All Blacks' philosophy were therefore instituted. Perhaps it was a problem with talent. Over the next four years thirty new players were rotated in and out of different positions to see who worked best and where.[28]

But, although the team continued to be world-class, the next World Cup in 2007 showed all the signs of history repeating itself. The All Blacks dominated their first four games, scoring eight times as many points as their opponents. Then they got to the quarter-finals, faltered – and ended up losing to France in what was their worst World Cup performance ever. 'After the final whistle blew,' Dan Carter, their fly-half that day, recalls, 'we assembled in one of the bleakest dressing-rooms of my career. We'd lost in the quarter-final of a tournament we were heavily favoured to win.'[29]

'We hadn't played to our best,' Richie McCaw, their captain, said, 'and that was the tough part to take. On top of that, what was it going to be like when we got home? Obviously the whole country was disappointed, all the emotion, and you just thought, "This shouldn't be happening," but it was.'[30]

Now the team turned to an unlikely source for help. Ceri Evans was a former football player who had become a forensic psychiatrist. He now worked as an expert witness in criminal court cases, as a mental health expert on national health programmes, and as a performance psychologist who helped business leaders, lawyers, doctors and special forces alike to perform well under pressure. Sure enough, it was Evans – coming at things from a completely different angle – who pinpointed the problem.

'When a large dog suddenly appears in front of us,' he explained, 'all we need to see and sense is that it's angry and growling, not its name, species or favourite park. The defining feature of this system is speed. Because it's linked to emotions such as fear, it has been called "the hot system". I call this system Red.

'Once we're safe from the dog,' Evans continued, 'we can think about how to avoid crossing its path in the future . . . This system allows us to solve problems, set goals, learn and adapt. Because it's linked more to thinking and rational analysis, it has been described as "the cool system". I call this system Blue.'

In technical terms, Evans was distinguishing between the amygdala region of the brain, which responds to a sudden crisis with a fight, flight or freeze response, and the cerebral cortex, where considered thought takes place. His point was that, under pressure, the All Blacks were seeing Red. They needed, he said, to learn to see Blue.

'Ceri gave us exercises,' McCaw remembers, 'to help us make that transition from Red to Blue. Breathe slowly and deliberately, nose or mouth, with a two-second pause. While breathing, hold your wrist on the out breath. Then shift your attention to something external – the ground or your feet, or the ball in the hand, or even alternating big toes, or the grandstand.' 'The other thing you've got to do . . .' he says of Evans' approach, 'is plan for the unpredictable, so that when it happens, it's expected and you don't feel helpless.'[31]

The crunch came in the final of the 2011 World Cup against France in Auckland. As so often before, the All Blacks had taken an early lead, only to see it slowly slip away. Now McCaw stood in the middle of the pitch, pondering what to do. He wasn't panicking or losing control, though. He was breathing slowly – with a two-second pause between each breath – to calm himself down. And he was holding his wrist and stamping his feet to bring himself back into the moment.

'Instead of feeling shocked,' he recalls, 'I feel it's playing out exactly the way I always knew it would. The guys are all around me. I'm talking, they're listening . . . There are no glazed eyes, no one in the Red Zone.' 'Don't panic,' he told them. 'We knew it was going to be like this. We're ready for it.'[32]

Half an hour later, the All Blacks won the World Cup for the first time in twenty-four years.

It didn't stop there. As soon as the World Cup was over the team went looking for more ideas from outside their world. They worked with Brazilian cage fighters to learn how to grapple better. They asked British ballet dancers to show them how to lift better. They turned to British motor racing teams to understand how to use technology better. They called on US basketball teams to gain insights into how to attack better. And they talked to US Marines to find out how to debrief better.[33] Four years later, they secured their second World Cup in a row.

4.

These days, Centennials don't just bring in disruptive experts on an occasional basis. They use them all the time, and they make sure that such people make up a significant proportion of their total workforce: typically between a third and two-thirds. They are, as it were, the grit in the oyster that produces the pearl, while the stable stewards (typically a quarter) guide and the effective executors (typically a tenth to a half of the workforce) see things through.

To involve so many disruptive experts overall may seem either extravagant or potentially risky. The total number involved, however, needs to be that high if all the potential talent out there is to be tapped. In any case, the Centennials use their disruptive experts sparingly

– at particular moments, on particular projects – so that they avoid the disruption overload that might otherwise knock them off track. Three-quarters of the 1,200 All Blacks who've played for the team over the past 120 years could be termed disruptive experts in that they each played in fewer than ten Tests, but then only a third of this cohort has ever been on the pitch at any given time.[34] British Cycling, the Royal Academy of Music and the Royal College of Art all use large numbers of outside experts, but they use them on a part-time basis and balance them carefully with full-time staff.

The fact that the Centennials tend to utilise such people on a part-time basis or get them to work on several projects at the same time is also highly significant. They're not simply thinking about practical expediency or economic necessity. They know that if experts are to stay at their creative best, they themselves require a degree of disruption in their daily lives. Working on a single project can lead to mental staleness. Working on several keeps the creative juices flowing, and allows cross-fertilisation of ideas.

It's no coincidence in this respect that the possessors of so many of the great creative minds of history have had more than one passion. Studies of the 700-plus scientists who have won Nobel prizes over the past 100 years, for example, have shown that most have not only been expert in their fields but have had other interests too.[35] Indeed pursuing other enthusiasms has been shown to be a better predictor of Nobel success than a high IQ. 'A high IQ is like height in a basketball player,' David Perkins, a professor at Harvard University, explains. 'It's very important, but there's a lot more to being a good basketball player than being tall.'[36] In any case, as several studies have shown – most notably the Terman study that tracked the lives of 1,521 children with an IQ above 135 from 1921 to 1996 – a high IQ doesn't in itself mean that you'll achieve anything significant.[37] The physiologist Robert Root-Bernstein and his team, who set out to compare Nobel Prize winners with 7,000 scientists who did not win this prestigious award, found that the laureates were seven times more likely also to be a visual artist, sculptor or printmaker; eight times more likely also to be a craftsperson engaged in woodwork, mechanics, electronics or glass-blowing; twelve times more likely also to write poetry, short stories, plays, essays, novels or popular books; and twenty-two times more likely also to be an amateur actor, dancer, magician or other performer.[38] Names and hobbies speak for themselves. Max Planck, who won the Nobel Prize in Physics in 1918, played the piano and composed music. Albert Einstein (the 1921 winner) enjoyed bird-watching, sailing and playing the violin. Emmanuelle Charpentier, whose work on DNA editing secured her a laureateship in 2020, is also a keen dancer and pianist.

What is true of Nobel scientists is also true of Nobel writers, who are on average also at least twice as likely to pursue a hobby as the average US citizen.[39] Ernest Hemingway (1954 winner) enjoyed boxing, fishing and hunting; Nelly Sachs (1966) music, dancing; William Golding (1983) archaeology, chess, music, sailing; Nadine Gordimer (1991) sculpture; Louise Glück (2020) painting.

Laureates who have been asked about this phenomenon have explained how these other interests have helped clarify challenges and ideas. Wilhelm Ostwald (1909), Albert Einstein (1921), Barbara McClintock (1983) and Christiane Nüsslein-Volhard (1995) all said that playing music helped their mind wander (by giving it a different focus) and so ultimately gave it the space to bring clarity to the problem they were trying to solve.[40] Einstein, who always took up his violin when he was stuck, said: 'The theory of relativity occurred to me by intuition, and music is the driving force behind this intuition.'[41] Those whose hobby has been painting or drawing have said how this interest has helped them to visualise what it was that they have been trying to comprehend. 'Still I had a lurking question,' Dorothy Hodgkin (1964) recalled of her attempts to unravel the secrets of the insulin molecule: 'Would it not be better if one could really "see" [the] molecule?'[42] She then proceeded to use an X-ray machine to photograph it. In the words of one laureate, Santiago Ramón y Cajal (1906): to achieve breakthroughs you must employ scientists 'with an abundance of restless imagination, [who] spend their energy in the pursuit of literature, art, philosophy, and all the recreations of mind and body. To an observer from afar, it appears as though they are scattering and dissipating their energies, while in reality, they are channelling and strengthening them.'[43]

Disruptive experts frequently change the topics they study, too. As Root-Bernstein explained: 'Lifelong producers of breakthroughs constantly explore other research problems even as they focus on one or two major ones . . . [and often] report that they must abandon a problem before a solution occurs to them, or find that the solution only arrives as a result of addressing another, related problem. [And they often] kept problems "simmering on a back burner" until adequate data, a new technique, or some insight finally [came to] them.[44] It's an approach that has been described by some as slow-motion multitasking.[45] Charles Darwin studied barnacles, earthworms and orchids while he was writing *On the Origin of Species*. Leonardo da Vinci famously moved between painting and drawing, and the study of biology, chemistry and physics.[46] Such slow-motion multitasking kept the creative juices flowing.

When it comes to how best to deploy disruptive experts within an organisation, it's crucial to play to their undoubted strengths, not their potential weaknesses. They're not there to process paperwork. And they're not there to manage. A common mistake many organisations make is to reward an expert by promoting them to a role where they assume responsibility for others or to ask them continually to fill out forms or sit in meetings to explain what they are doing. It's possible, of course, that they may fulfil such roles well. But it's far more likely that they'll end up either struggling, underperforming or wasting their talents on something that they're not very good at. As a rule, management is best left to stable stewards, and administration to effective executers. Experts are there for the new ideas and breakthroughs. The Root-Bernstein study found that only two of the Nobel scientists it considered 'became engaged in administrative work and then only for very short periods of time', concluding that 'lifelong producers of breakthroughs are not content simply to rework old fields or to refine prior insights or to become administrators of other people's research'.[47] The study also suggested that handing administration to research scientists all too often proves a self-defeating exercise: it takes them away from their research, so reducing the chances of their making a breakthrough.

If it's essential to keep disruptive experts away from tasks for which they are either not suited or that could be equally well or better done by others, it's also vitally important to give them space and time. Historically, Nobel Prize-winning scientists worked in their field for at least ten years (usually twenty) before they won their prize. And, although they were all affiliated with a university, only a quarter of them worked there full-time.[48] Such luxuries might not be feasible for the average organisation, but the principles behind them nevertheless still hold.

5.

In summary, Centennials bring in the best ideas from everywhere by:

Employing disruptive experts who are at the top of their game and have at least one, normally two, other serious projects or hobbies on the go

Making sure that a third to two-thirds of their total workforce are disruptive experts, who can be deployed to help on specific projects at specific moments

Asking these experts to work with them either part-time for around a third of their time, or full-time but on at least two (usually three) different projects at once

Asking them to choose the projects they want to work on and where they think they can create most impact

Encouraging them to move between projects whenever they need to

Ensuring that they do as little administration and management as possible, so they can focus on finding new breakthroughs.

Habit 8

SHAKE ALL TREES

Hire talent, not CVs

1.

In 2020 Nasa announced that it would be recruiting ten new astronauts. Twelve thousand people applied for the vacancies, all of whom then completed a two-hour online test.[1] Four years earlier, during their previous recruiting drive, Nasa received 16,000 applications. On both occasions, they assessed all of them.

Why would the space agency put itself to such trouble to invite and then sift through so many applications?

The simple fact is they know that everything comes down to the quality of the people they recruit, and that these people should be drawn from the widest possible skills pool. 'The missions we're recruiting for now are longer and more complex than ever before,' Doug McCuistion, director of the Mars Exploration Program, explains. 'We're no longer looking for people who can fly to the Moon and come home safely in a couple of days. We're looking for people who can spend one to three years in space – on the Space Station or on a Mars mission.'[2]

'One of the first questions we've asked ourselves', Professor Noshir Contractor, a Nasa psychologist, says, 'is: is "the right stuff" – that Tom Wolfe wrote about when referring to the Mercury astronauts John Glenn and Alan Shepard among others – still "the right stuff" for a team that would go to Mars? And I think we're pretty confident that it's not.'[3] One of the astronauts involved in recent projects clarifies: 'Some of the things we're looking for haven't changed. We still want good team players who are calm under pressure and can lead a team if they need to. But we're looking for a range of backgrounds and skills too: not just military-trained test pilots but university-trained biologists, engineers, geologists, medics and physicists, who can help us solve the complex, ever-changing problems that we know we'll face in space.'[4]

The initiatives that Nasa undertakes to reach out to the staff of the future when they're still at school has already been described (see Habit 2). This painstaking, strategic approach also extends to the moment when those people apply for a job. No filters are there to reduce the number of applications. No one is ruled out until they can be properly assessed. 'We try to reach all segments of society,' Duane Ross, manager of the astronaut selection office at Johnson Space Center, explains. 'Not just the space cadets and folks like that, but anybody who might be interested and has the background and wants to come down here and help us.'[5]

The end result is that Nasa personnel are drawn from an astonishingly diverse range of people. Over the past ten years, half the twenty astronauts they have recruited have been women, a fifth have come from a mixed heritage background and, in terms of their academic and professional backgrounds, half were previously pilots, a third scientists and a sixth each were either medics, or from the air force or the army.[6]

Given the number of people who apply, such diversity should perhaps not come as a surprise. What may astonish many is just how long the process is from initial application to appointment. It takes eighteen months.

'It's hard to pick people!' Ross continues. 'It's not one thing. We want a good, diverse group of people because that's where you get the best result. There are some basic academic requirements. We'll typically find folks with good preparation in math, engineering or science. The biggest thing is how applicable and relatable the comparison is we can draw to jobs the applicants have done with what the astronauts have to do when they get here. We also look at outside activities the applicants do to get some idea if they are adaptable to new situations and environments. Everything we do at JSC [Johnson Space Center] and the other centres is a team effort, whether a big team or as small as a flight crew. You have to be able to pass a Nasa flight physical too.[7] After rigorous assessment, the initial list of thousands is whittled down to 500. From those, 100 are selected to come in for a six-week assessment. Fifty are then invited back for another five-week assessment. Finally ten are offered a job at the space agency.[8]

'Some people think we're crazy assessing 12,000 people and taking eighteen months to find the ten we want,' admits Janet Kavandi, director of flight crew operations at the Johnson Space Center, 'but it's one of the most important decisions we make so we need to get it right.'[9]

2.

Many would argue that such a long and extensive recruitment process makes sense for a future astronaut but is either a luxury or unnecessary – or both – for more everyday organisations. It's true, of course, that few enterprises have the time or the resources to undertake a Nasa-type employment operation. But all too many go to the opposite extreme. They advertise, select a handful of candidates for interview, and then make their choice at a second (or, more unusually, a third) interview.

It may be a truism that if you want your organisation to be successful, you need to find and keep great talent. It's certainly a truism that appears at the top of the list in every CEO survey.[10] But it's also one that invariably gets ignored at the moment when it matters the most. In the majority of cases so little work goes into recruiting the right people for the right roles that, according to a recent study of US companies, a third then quit their job within a year, and half leave within five years.[11] Such constant dislocation of the workforce has a whole range of adverse effects. Recruitment costs money – money that is wasted if the person recruited does not stay around for long. It can take several months for a new employee to settle in and start doing their best work – again time and money that is wasted if they choose to leave. It's been suggested that, because of the disruption caused, it costs between half and twice someone's salary to replace them. Put another way, given that a quarter of the working population of the US change jobs each year, US businesses waste $1 trillion annually on staff changes.[12] The costs are not just financial, either. Morale can also be hit if there's a constant flow of people leaving and new staff arriving.[13]

Experts believe that traditional approaches to recruitment invariably yield poor results. And even though managers continue to use them, they generally concur with this gloomy verdict. In a typical US company, according to various recent studies, four-fifths of managers reckon they have not always recruited the right people, and two-thirds of their staff think they're in the wrong job.[14] Quite simply, the whole CV-interview-reference approach doesn't work.[15] Most managers rely only on CVs to assess applicants. They rely on CVs and interviews to assess a few. And they then rely on CVs, interviews and references to assess a couple. By this point they've probably already decided who they're hiring, so the references are actually largely redundant.[16] Essentially, then, it's a crude two-step process. Some psychologists have suggested that plucking a name out of a hat at random would probably yield better results. It would avoid the bias and prejudice that so often slips into the recruitment process. And, of course, it would save a lot of time and money.[17]

There's a common assumption that dissatisfaction at work is directly correlated with dissatisfaction with levels of remuneration. That's not strictly true. The evidence suggests that most people are content with a sum sufficient to cover their basic costs and provide a few luxuries; and the sum that has been shown to be 'sufficient' is 'a surprisingly small amount', according to Andrew Jebb, a psychologist at Purdue University who has analysed the findings of the World Happiness Survey of some 2 million people over the past twenty years. His estimate for a 'sufficient' salary is 'somewhere between $30,000 and $90,000 per year, depending on where you live, and how many children you've got'.[18] Above that level, as other studies have shown, there always seems to be a point when a higher salary doesn't make you any happier and may indeed start to render you less so. You start to obsess whether you're really being paid enough and how your pay compares with what others receive. You stop asking yourself whether you're actually happy in your job, whether your work is important, whether you feel you're learning, and whether you feel supported.[19] Interestingly, that ballpark upper limit that Andrew Jebb has arrived at is very close to what an All Blacks coach, an Eton tutor and a Nasa astronaut are paid (just over $100,000 a year, on average). That may be twice the US average, but it's still a hundredth of what the average US CEO receives.[20]

In other words, while remuneration is an important aspect of recruitment, it's not the only factor. People are looking for work that will pay the bills and cover the small luxuries of life. But they're also seeking roles that they will find fulfilling, that will make them feel they're doing something worthwhile, and that will allow them to learn and to develop. A recruitment process that fails to take account of these complex and subtle variables will inevitably fall short. Focusing on someone's CV, for example, may reveal what they've done in the past, but it won't tell you what they might be capable of or wish to do in the future. Interview questions are all too often skewed to reflect the biases and prejudices of the interviewer rather than to elicit useful information about a candidate's suitability for a particular role. And if those questions are plucked at random out of the air, then it becomes impossible to make properly informed comparisons between different applicants. The statistics speak for themselves. An exhaustive analysis, led by Frank Schmidt from Iowa University, of thousands of studies conducted in the past eighty-five years has found that the standard approach to recruitment – CVs, interviews and references – helps predict, at best, a quarter of someone's potential if all three component parts are properly applied, and a tenth or less if only one component is fully considered.[21]

3.

So how do the Centennials and other great organisations approach recruitment?

As we've already seen, enterprises such as Nasa start by doing a huge amount of preparatory work, both in terms of helping to encourage and create future generations of space experts and in ensuring that as many applicants as possible from as many different walks of life apply and are considered. The All Blacks reach out to the whole community, holding hundreds of workshops for thousands of children to encourage them to seek to be an All Black or a Black Fern (the women's team, which has achieved one of the best winning percentages in international rugby).[22] The Royal Shakespeare Company similarly seeks to make contact with the widest possible pool of talent through workshops and outreach programmes.[23] They also take their time to make their final selections. The Royal Academy of Music spends three weeks choosing the following year's cohort. As one of their tutors says in justification of this lengthy process: 'If we get it right, then everything works. If we don't, then it can all go wrong.' Often, too, they'll look beyond the line manager who is seeking a new recruit and the human resources department that might be on hand to help to utilise the skills of outside experts and former members of staff. The Royal College of Art turns to recruitment consultants. 'The best people are usually in a job and don't plan to leave,' an insider explains, 'so you need to find them first and then persuade them to come. That's why we use a recruitment consultant for every appointment we make: to shake the trees and see what happens, rather than sitting back and waiting for people to apply.' The All Blacks ask coaches and players who left at least five years before to come back to help select and support the new ones. Former Nasa astronauts are called on in the same way.[24]

As the exhaustive Nasa approach suggests, such organisations also go well beyond the standard CV-interview approach. They'll employ personality tests. Some give promising candidates trial periods. For example, global café Pret a Manger, UK hi-fi chain Richer Sounds, and Southwest Airlines in the US often ask people to work with them for several weeks – or even longer – before they decide whether to recruit them and they also ask the people they've worked with during their trial to help assess them. They all believe that such an approach ensures a happier workplace, not just because there's an opportunity to see whether applicants and their prospective future colleagues will gel but because they can see how well the applicants respond to customers.[25] As Frank Schmidt puts it: 'The best way to judge someone's potential is to see them in action, to see how well they absorb information, work with others and make decisions in a particular moment or situation.'

It's been suggested that while the CV, interview and reference approach yields at best a one in four chance of correctly judging someone's potential, seeing them in action raises the odds to one in three. When those two approaches are combined with properly designed ability and personality tests, the odds increase further to four in five. And if the trouble is taken to calibrate and refine those tests over time by cross-checking previous test results and outcomes, then it's possible to predict potential in nine out of ten cases.[26] It should come as no surprise that all the Centennials ask people to work with them part-time, and do ability and personality tests, before they recruit them.[27]

4.

If one enterprise offers a casebook study in the dividends that such a painstaking approach to recruitment can reap, it's the British codebreaking centre at Bletchley Park during the Second World War. The challenges it faced were immense. The German Enigma code that the Bletchley Park experts were seeking to crack used a machine that deployed three rotors that could be put in any one of six settings, each with twenty-six possible positions, that fed into a plugboard with ten places and 600 positions. In all there were more than 150 trillion permutations available to the codemakers. And the code was changed every day.[28] It seemed uncrackable.

When war broke out in 1939 there were just over 100 people working at Bletchley. Soon the pressure was on to find thousands of additional staff. But they had to be the right staff. Joan Joslin, who was recruited in 1942, later recalled the hoops through which she had to jump when she turned up for her interview at the Foreign Office in London on Christmas Eve. 'I met a very off-putting woman named Miss Moore, sitting behind a huge desk in a very grand office, who then proceeded to ask me a number of questions about my favourite subjects, hobbies and general topics,' she said. 'I remember telling her that I'd loved mathematics and English.'[29] Joslin then had to undertake a series of puzzles and tests, followed by further interviews conducted by other people. 'First they were stern,' she remembered, 'then they were nice, and then they were stern again – to keep me on my toes I think.' At the end of it all she was given a travel warrant, told to go home and pack a case, and take a train to Bletchley the following morning.

People were brought in from all walks of life. According to Gordon Welchman, who was one of the first four recruits Bletchley Park took on: 'At first we recruited receptionists, linguists and typists to intercept, decode and translate the messages we received, but this only got us so far. So we then started recruiting mathematicians and scientists, too, to see if they could spot any patterns in the data, and engineers and mechanics as well to see if they could design machines to speed things up.'[30] Many early approaches were to individuals that people at Bletchley Park already knew, but it didn't take long for this network to be exhausted. The recruiters therefore started to look further afield and in particular to take on more women. The historian Sinclair McKay has described how 'thousands of bright young female recruits . . . hailing from all sorts of different educational backgrounds and from all over the country, were selected by means of an innocuous-looking question on their application forms. The question asked if the candidates enjoyed mental recreations in the form of cryptic crosswords, or similar. If the answer to this was yes, there followed several discreet intelligence tests.'[31] Between 1942 and 1944 the number of women recruited tripled to the point where they accounted for nearly three-quarters of all the personnel at Bletchley Park. Over the same period, the number of codebreakers who did not have a university degree quadrupled to two-thirds of all staff.[32]

As the numbers recruited rose, so did the sophistication of the recruitment methods deployed. By the end of the war Bletchley Park had developed a battery of standardised tests.[33] McKay identifies crossword puzzles as being 'the most famous of the butterfly nets', but also points to the use of other 'conundrums . . . ranging from lateral thinking tests to problems involving invented mythical languages . . . from Egyptian symbolism to surreal Lewis Carroll-style logic problems that would involve looking at the world upside down'.[34]

As the pool of talent widened, so the culture changed and diversified. 'The place was unusual in every way,' wrote Alan Stripp, a linguist who worked at Bletchley for three years. 'Civilians and personnel of all three services, British and Allied, rubbed shoulders almost regardless of age, rank, and background. Such discipline as was needed sprang naturally from the job rather than from being imposed from above. If the eight-hour shift was too short to complete an urgent task, it was too engrossing to leave.'[35]

'Those of us who were commissioned officers wore uniform only when we felt like it, or when some top brass was expected on visit,' said Peter Calvocoressi, a lawyer who worked at Bletchley Park for six years. '[It] was not a place where people went around saluting one another.' In their leisure time the codebreakers would join one of Bletchley's many clubs. Mimi Gallilee, a typist there, recalled 'country dancing, Morris dancing, different kinds of music'; mathematician Oliver Lawn remembered 'play readings and play acting. Quite a bit of amateur dramatics and concerts of all kinds.' The sheer variety of gifted people gathered in one place ensured that it 'fizzed with youthful intellectual and artistic energy'. 'For every socially awkward mathematician, there was a hilariously confident debutante; for every owlish classicist, conversing in ancient Greek, there was a swing-music-loving Wren who would pass the time with the most ferociously fiendish crosswords.'[36] 'Despite the high tension of the work,' Edward Thomas, another veteran, explained, 'a spirit of relaxation prevailed. Anyone of any rank or degree could approach anyone else, however venerable, with any idea or suggestion, however crazy.'[37]

This unique mix of skills and backgrounds paid dividends. First, the linguists and typists noticed that enemy messages often started with a standard word or phrase – such as 'To', 'One', 'Heil Hitler' or 'All clear' – which came to be known as a 'Crib' and which helped with the cracking of elements of the code. Then the mathematicians and engineers designed a machine – called a bombe – that could sift through millions of potential letter combinations in under a minute. Ultimately the codebreakers were able to decipher more than 4,000 messages a day, shortening the war by at least two years, according to some estimates, and saving more than 14 million lives in the process.[38]

5.

As the Bletchley Park experience demonstrates, good recruitment practice is about more than finding people to fill prescribed roles. It's about looking into the future to see how those roles might develop, and what new skills and mindsets might be required. This is something the Centennials are invariably very good at. They constantly challenge their own status quo to ensure that the people they recruit will equip them to keep abreast of the latest developments in their field, and, ideally, place them one step ahead. The Royal College of Art, for example, has introduced at least one new programme each year (in such fields as healthcare, information experience and service design) to keep itself on its toes, just as Eton constantly seeks to set up new societies, disciplines and approaches.[39] 'We noticed that we hadn't produced a science Nobel Prize winner in the last fifty years,' William Waldegrave, Eton's provost, says, 'so we built a new science block, hoping that something different might happen.'[40] In much the same way, the All Blacks, British Cycling and Nasa brought in nutritionists and psychologists years before their peers did in the expectation that useful breakthroughs would ultimately occur.[41]

Good recruitment also involves thinking not just in terms of the individual but the team that that individual will join. Nasa, for instance, seeks to ensure both that it has the right mix of medics, pilots and scientists for each mission – and that there's a clown there too. 'Groups work best when they have somebody who takes on the role of class clown,' Jeffrey Johnson, an anthropologist who works with Nasa, explains. 'These are people that have the ability to pull everyone together, bridge gaps and boost morale.'[42] Nasa cites the earlier example of Norwegian Adolf Lindstrøm, who was the cook on Amundsen's successful race to the South Pole in 1912 and also the team's clown – the man who listened to their problems, defused the tensions between them, and kept them together as they chatted and relaxed over the meals he served them around the campfire each night. In much the same way, Ringo Starr was the Beatles' funny man, and Ronnie Wood fulfilled a similar role for the Rolling Stones.[43] Neither man may have been the driving creative force of their group, but they helped keep it together, relieving pressure and tension through laughter and so helping the others perform at their best.[44] 'It can get you down, not being the creative one,' Ringo Starr has said. 'But out of four people, you wouldn't expect them to all be creative, would you? Fifty per cent is enough.'[45] It's worth noting that he was the only one of the four to perform on all the other Beatles' solo albums after they split up, and that his two solo albums, *Ringo* in 1973 and *Ringo's Rotogravure* in 1976, were the only albums on which the others returned the favour, albeit on different songs.[46]

It's also worth bearing in mind that complementary teams can often achieve more than an individual team can do. This was certainly the experience of Netflix when it sought to improve its individualised recommendations algorithm back in 2009. The company's co-founder and CEO, Reed Hastings, was concerned that greater viewing choice without some form of custodianship could prove off-puttingly daunting ('I think that once you get beyond 1,000 choices a recommendation system becomes critical,' he said. 'People have limited cognitive time they want to spend on picking a movie.')[47] The company therefore launched the Netflix Prize – $1 million that would be given to anyone who could improve the Netflix algorithm by 10 per cent, and make it 85 per cent accurate.[48] Fifty thousand people from 186 countries took up the challenge, crunching data supplied by Netflix that showed 480,000 customer ratings of 17,000 films over the previous seven years (the figure may seem high, but it represented just 1 per cent of the number of actual ratings made over that period – and the contestants had to work out what the other ratings were, to show their model was better than the current Netflix algorithm).[49] What's interesting, though, is that while individual teams performed quite well, progress ultimately stalled. It was only when it was realised that although the various teams were using much the same programming tools, they were using them in different ways, and that they would do better if they pooled their efforts, that the 10 per cent improvement barrier was broken. As Neil Hunt, Netflix's chief product officer, later said: 'It [the combined approach] was fairly unintuitive to many people – because you generally take the smartest two people and say "come up with a solution" – [but] when you get this combining of these algorithms in certain ways, it started this "second frenzy". In combination, the teams could get better and better and better.'[50]

The huge benefits that accrue from having team members who embody different strengths and attributes is part of the reason why organisations that go out of their way to attract diverse talent tend to be better at solving problems and coming up with fresh ideas.[51] It also explains why the best organisations take their time over recruitment and cast their net as wide as possible. 'It's pretty simple really,' Steve Tew, the former All Blacks CEO, explains. 'If you want to get the best people you can then you need to take your time, and look in as many different places as possible. That's why having a diverse range of talent is so important. Not only does it help you play better on the pitch – as you can see and respond to things in different ways – but it helps you attract future talent too as more people look at you and think, "They look like me. I can do that!"'

'Most people find it easier to work with people who are similar to them, who come from similar backgrounds with similar expertise,' Paul Thompson, the vice-chancellor of the Royal College of Art, said to me. 'But if you do this, then you won't find anything new – as everything's too easy and too safe. Instead, you need to work with people who are different to you and keep a constant flow of new talent, with fresh ideas.'[52]

And, to return to Nasa's recruitment strategy that opened this chapter, it's precisely because talent is needed from everywhere and can come from anywhere that it's so essential to accommodate a very wide and deep pool of candidates. British Cycling therefore assesses 12,000 athletes for just fifty places. The Royal College of Art considers the relative merits of 6,000 students each year before selecting just 1,000 of them. The Royal Shakespeare Company looks at 6,000 actors and takes on 600 of them.

In many cases, recruitment of the best doesn't just involve placing an ad and waiting for applications. It's essential to reach out too. As Laszlo Bock, the former senior vice-president of people operations at Google, explains: 'You need to build a recruitment machine and ask everyone you know to help you find the talent you need by asking them very specific questions, such as: Who's the best finance person you've worked with? Who's the best Japanese salesperson you've heard of? Or who's the best Ruby programmer you know? So you can start to build a database of great people, and then work out how to get them to work with you.'

'And sometimes,' he adds, 'you need to hire a whole team rather than an individual.'[53] Randy Knaflic, Google's former director of recruiting and outreach programmes, elaborates on this latter point with a specific example. 'We knew of this small team of brilliant engineers working from Aarhus [in Denmark]. They sold off their previous company and were trying to figure out what to do next. Microsoft got wind of them and was all over them. Microsoft wanted to hire all of them, but they would have to move to Redmond [in the US]. The engineers said, "No way." We swooped in, ran some aggressive hiring efforts, and said, "Work from Aarhus, start a new office of Google, build great things." We hired the entire team and it's this group that built the JavaScript engine in Chrome.'[54]

Knaflic's approach deserves serious consideration. After all, if any organisation understands how to find talent, it's Google. In 2021 its recruitment machine brought in 20,000 new people.[55]

6.

In summary, the Centennials retain their cutting edge by:

> Using competitions, puzzles and tests to help them find the talent they need
>
> Working with people part-time for at least six months, and normally a year, before they work with them full-time
>
> Recruiting from the largest and most diverse pool of talent that they can
>
> Recruiting teams rather than individuals when they need to
>
> Putting a 'class clown' in every team, to help draw it together
>
> Working out what skills and talent they might need in the future, and then finding ways to start working with them today.

Nervousness

Habit 9

GET BETTER, NOT BIGGER

Think neighbourhoods, not cities

1.

The story of British cycling success is not one of an overnight break-through but of painstaking, incremental improvement. Arguably it begins back in 1986 when future Olympic hopeful Chris Boardman first met Peter Keen, the team's physiologist and later its performance director. Keen proceeded to put Boardman on an exercise bike with a pulley on one side, a cradle on the other, and a rubber tube in his mouth. 'The whole set-up was an odd assortment of high-tech and low budget,' Boardman recalls. 'It looked like something Doctor Who might have knocked up!'[1]

Keen asked Boardman to ride at a steady pace for as long as he could, while he dropped weights into the cradle every minute – to increase his workload and test his endurance to the point where he either gave up or threw up. Then he stabbed him in the thumb with a needle, took a blood sample, and ran some tests. After that he asked Boardman to ride as fast as he could for ten minutes while he pricked him in the neck every minute, taking more samples and doing more tests. This went on for five hours. Then Keen left the room and ran the numbers through a computer.

The report he shared with Boardman – along with a thin smile to let him know that he wasn't impressed – showed the aspiring cyclist for the first time exactly where he was in terms of endurance, power and speed. It also pointed the way to a precise future training plan. 'It was like nothing I'd ever seen before,' Boardman remembers. 'Up until then I'd only heard coaches describe effort in vague terms such as "flat out" or "dead easy". Here was something very different. Each level was expressed as a ten or twenty heartbeat range and accompanied by a brief description of what it should feel like to ride in that zone. Pete had created what amounted to a training language for cyclists: a method for people to discuss effort without ambiguity or misinterpretation. To my knowledge, he was the first person in British sport to use evidence-based reasoning rather than history or reputation to make his case. I was impressed – and inspired.'[2]

Over the next two years, Boardman followed Keen's plans and his body changed. He lost weight, gained power, and his performance improved. Even so he and his team pursuit squad came only thirteenth at the 1988 Seoul Olympics. His fellow team members were similarly unsuccessful, even though they had all followed Keen's schedule.

So Keen turned his attention to the bikes the team were riding. Graeme Obree, another British cyclist, had been testing different bike designs over the last few years, using straight handles to rest his arms on, putting them closer to his seat to make him more aerodynamic, removing the top bar so he could pedal harder, putting one fork at the front to reduce drag, and using washing machine bearings in the wheels to make them spin faster. Keen now went a step further, bringing in Richard Hill, an aerodynamicist from Lotus Cars, to help question and challenge everything.

Hill put Boardman on a bike in a wind tunnel, and made him sit in lots of different positions – with his arms together, then out wide; elbows out, then at his side; hands in the air, then on his thighs; his body bent over, then straight up. And, as he did this, Hill taped bits of cardboard to Boardman's bike, helmet and shoes to see what combination would make him most aerodynamic. 'His sole focus was reducing drag,' Boardman says, 'bending me into a shape to make the air flow as smoothly over me as possible. He neither knew nor really cared about what might be comfortable or biomechanically efficient.' 'He won't be able to ride in that position!' Rudy Thomann, a Lotus test driver, kept saying. 'Why not?' Hill asked.[3]

After two months Hill had got Boardman to adopt a new seating position and an innovative helmet design. He had also introduced him to a new type of bike, with a curved frame, a one-piece fork and flat handlebars for him to lean against. 'It was a thing of beauty,' Boardman remembers, 'but it no longer looked like a bike!' Worried that the new design might stir up controversy, Keen first tried it out in public with another cyclist a month before the Barcelona Olympics. It went largely unnoticed. So he reckoned it would be fine to unveil it to a wider public at the Olympic Games.

In the lead-up to the event, John Syer, a psychologist from the English football club Tottenham Hotspur, was brought in to work with the team. He sat with Boardman as he geared himself up for the big day, listening to his anxieties, talking him through the challenges. 'Well, I guess I can only do my best,' Boardman finally said. Syer smiled and nodded.

Boardman went on to become the first British cyclist in seventy years to win an Olympic gold medal. He also became the first individual pursuit cyclist ever to lap his opponent – it was only a two-person race – in the final.

It was a turning point, but there was no single eureka moment here. Boardman's success was the result of thousands of tiny step-by-step advances arrived at through constant analysis, experimentation and enquiry. It was a combination of individual striving, improved engineering and carefully honed training over several years. British Cycling had embarked on a programme of what has now become known as 'marginal gains', and had ultimately reaped the benefits. Over the next seven Olympic Games – from 1996 to 2020 – the team went on to win thirty-one gold medals, sixteen silver medals and eleven bronze medals – twice as many as any other country.

Most organisations that achieve such success immediately look to grow, to capitalise on what they've done and look for new opportunities to do it elsewhere. British Cycling didn't. For its leadership team, getting better was infinitely more important than getting bigger. Throughout this extraordinary medal-winning period they remained intensely focused on making tiny improvements. They examined how their athletes ate, slept and drank. They studied how their bodies, brains and bikes worked. They assessed how they trained by themselves and how they trained with each other. Their team as a whole did indeed slowly expand over time, but even today it remains relatively small and very tight-knit, with fewer than 300 athletes and 300 staff in total, and fewer than fifty athletes and twenty coaches on both the Olympic and Paralympic teams. Their focus is on constant, incremental improvement, not expansion.[4] 'It's hard to explain what makes the team so special,' Chris Hoy, the six-time Olympic gold medallist, says. 'It's all of it – the science, the training, the coaches – but most of all we point the mirror at ourselves and ask "How can we get better?"'[5]

2.

Growth for most enterprises is the reason they exist. Growth for Centennials is something to be cautious – even nervous – about. They worry that expansion all too often occurs at the expense of standards, that the pursuit of growth at all costs can all too easily be a distraction from core goals and values. Excellence can change the world. Growth on its own won't.

And it's not just that growth won't transform long-term fortunes. Growth for its own sake can also be dangerous – even lethal.

The growth and then implosion of phone giant Nokia offers a cautionary tale here. The company entered the mobile phone market in 1979 when it launched Mobira, a joint venture with Finnish TV maker Salora, but it really took off after 1992 when Jorma Ollila became CEO. An economist by training, and previously a banker and then Nokia's CFO, Ollila's raison d'être was growth. As far as he was concerned, Nokia was no different to any of the economies he'd studied or the finances he'd managed. Expansion was everything. When he took over, Nokia controlled only a tenth of the world's mobile phone market. He pushed his engineers to develop cheaper, smaller versions of their existing models and to move into new markets. He also set ambitious new sales targets and linked them to generous bonus plans. 'Many people at Nokia became millionaires because of the way our incentives were structured,' he said.[6]

In the short term, this proved a successful strategy. By pushing for growth and by selling off such non-core businesses as cable, which had proved very successful but whose sale (along with the sale of half the company's equity) released much-needed funds, Nokia expanded exponentially. Between 1992 and 2007, as the workforce increased fifteenfold to more than 50,000 people, sales multiplied sixtyfold to more than $50 billion. The company's share price tripled. It became the largest mobile phone company in the world.

And then the iPhone appeared.

When a groundbreaking new technology appears the narrative is often that existing players didn't see it coming and were therefore blindsided. That was certainly not the case with Nokia. Its engineers had known that the iPhone was on the horizon for at least a year before it was released, and had been aware of the technology that would power and shape it for even longer. 'We had pretty good specifications for it,' one middle manager said. ' . . . The first thing [a marketing manager] flagged up [in a market review] was that we didn't have touchscreens or touchscreen development . . . That message went right up to the top of the organisation, and was well received too.'

The manager went on to explain how Olli-Pekka Kallasvuo, who took over as CEO when Ollila stepped down in 2005, forwarded the email to his subordinates. 'Our market analysis showed that our biggest competitive weakness was the lack of touchscreen products; he agreed, and wrote, 'Please take action on this.'[7]

'One of the first things [the CEO] brought up was the touchscreen,' a technical director said. 'He felt it was the next big thing . . . He brought it up with the executive group every way he could. And he spoke directly with technical middle management . . . In every single executive group meeting, they went over our outlook with the touchscreen. And this was right after he was made CEO [eighteen months before the iPhone launch] . . . I recall many such cases vividly, where he brought up the right concern, he discussed it directly with the technical middle and upper management, he went straight to the topic, put pressure on people, put it up in all possible goals, followed up on it in every single meeting.'[8]

But nothing changed.

The problem was that for fifteen years Nokia had focused on growth and beating its great rival Motorola to the exclusion of just about every other consideration. In the process it had become too large and too bureaucratic to enact change swiftly. Yves Doz, a professor at the French business school INSEAD, has shown how staff were 'spending more and more time in committee meetings and less time actually working'.[9] Alberto Torres, Nokia's head of strategy, has described how the company's matrix structure – ironically, intended to ensure open and swift communication between teams – served to slow the corporation down.[10] 'A matrix is not good for speed,' he said. 'In high-speed, high-complexity contexts like the mobile phone industry, you need very fast decisions and in Nokia's matrix, decisions were negotiated very slowly.'[11] Nokia knew that the iPhone was a serious threat. But so baked into its DNA was its growth philosophy that it found it impossible to alter course. It simply carried on doing what it had always done – just on an even greater scale. Previously, it had launched two new smaller, cheaper phones a month. Now it launched three. Previously, it had recruited an average of twelve people a day. Now it was bringing twenty-four on board. Instead of seeking to regain ground through innovation, it desperately tried to grow its way out of trouble.[12]

Over the next five years – as the company launched more and more of the wrong products, and none that could compete with the iPhone – its sales halved and its workforce had to be cut by a third. On 3 September 2013, Nokia sold its mobile phone business to Microsoft, for a twentieth of what it had been worth five years earlier. Five years later, Microsoft sold the business for a twentieth of what it paid for it.[13]

3.

Getting better not bigger is a constant Centennial mantra. 'We could easily grow,' Timothy Jones, the deputy principal at the Royal Academy of Music, told me, 'as we get at least four applicants for every student place each year. But we don't want to. We'd rather stay small and try to produce the best conductors, composers and musicians we can – who will, hopefully, transform what music is played, and how it is played, in the future.'[14]

It's even possible to put a maximum number on a Centennial organisation: 300. According to a study undertaken by the Bank of Korea more than a decade ago, 90 per cent of all the Centennials in the world employ fewer than 300 people (interestingly, most of them are in Japan, a country with a very long-term philosophy).[15] That number holds for the All Blacks, British Cycling, Eton College and the Royal Academy of Music too. And, if they feel the need to grow – to increase their impact or become more financially stable – then organisations ranging from the Royal College of Art to the Royal Shakespeare Company make sure the number of staff on any one site does not exceed that magical 300 figure. Even Nasa, which, with 16,000 on the payroll, is a giant in comparison to the other Centennials, keeps the number of people on most of its sites to 300 or fewer.[16] In the case of many other Centennials, staff numbers have barely changed over the past fifty years, even though the organisations in question have flourished and consistently outperformed their peers during that period.

It's not difficult to see why such tight control of team size and the demand for excellence and constant improvement go so closely hand in hand. If not very carefully handled, expansion can cause the nature and structure of the organisation to become more significant in people's minds than what that organisation is seeking to achieve. Looking back at Nokia's fall from grace, one engineer explained how, when he arrived, 'we were just a small team, trying to do something special – "connecting people" – by trying to give everyone a phone. It was really exciting!' But then the company grew, some sites expanded to accommodate more than 1,000 staff, and extra layers of management were added (up to eight by the time the iPhone came out). '[By] the time the iPhone arrived,' the engineer went on, 'the business was so big and complex. You didn't know who anyone was and you couldn't get anything done – especially something new.'[17] 'We created huge additional complexity,' former CEO Olli-Pekka Kallasvuo admitted, 'with many more interface and articulation points.'[18] 'The close relationships that enabled us to utilise cross-company synergies, link operational strategy and get things done had gone,' chief technology officer Pertti Korhonen said.[19]

Nokia is far from being the only company in history to fall into this trap. A study undertaken at California Polytechnic State University back in 2002 that analysed the performance of more than 2,000 US businesses over the previous eleven years showed – in the words of Cyrus Ramezani, one of the lead researchers – that 'although the corporate profitability measures generally rise with earnings and sales growth, an optimal point exists beyond which further growth destroys shareholder value and adversely affects profitability'. At a certain size, he concluded, so vast, sprawling and complex does an organisation become that economies of scale cease to function.[20] In a similar vein the Ewing Marion Kauffman Foundation demonstrated that two-thirds of the 1,300 fastest-growing US companies on the Inc. 500 index between 2000 and 2006 died within four years of their dash for growth.[21] Unrestrained growth caused their costs to spiral. Their management structures came under strain. They lost control.

If this is a phenomenon that occurs in well-established companies, it's also one that is all too common among start-ups. Back in 2011 a group of six researchers from UC Berkeley and Stanford University analysed more than 3,000 fast-growing start-ups that had been set up in Silicon Valley over the previous decade. Ninety per cent, they found, had failed in the five years after they grew.[22] And they had generally failed for much the same reason: they had focused on getting bigger, not better. In their dash to build revenues and profits they had settled for the wrong type of investors. They had rushed to launch a project before it was ready and before they understood their target market. They had taken on the wrong kind of staff with ideas that were incompatible with their vision. They had recruited too many salespeople and had taken them on before they knew precisely what product it was they were trying to sell.

'Having been both an entrepreneur and investor,' Michael Jackson, a serial entrepreneur and investor, said, 'I've seen many entrepreneurs (myself included) try to scale blindly. No one takes venture money to stay a small business, and scaling successfully is what separates eventual industry leaders from long-forgotten start-ups in the deadpool. Far too often, though, entrepreneurs start scaling before they know what is going to work.'[23] He likened venture capital to 'putting a rocket engine on the back of a car': 'Scaling comes down to making sure the machine is ready to handle the speed before hitting the accelerator.'[24] Bernard Moon, co-founder and partner at SparkLabs Group, sounded a similar note of caution. 'If you raise too much capital,' he said, 'you can become undisciplined and anxious from the pressure to succeed and grow big. You might hire too many people, hire too quickly without adequate checks, you might rush to launch when it might be better to launch late, or you might let inertia takeover.'[25] Dashes for growth rarely end well.

4.

There's another reason why an obsession with growth so often mis-fires, and it goes to the heart of what makes people tick. Humans are, by nature, social animals, but the size of the neocortex in our brain limits the number of relationships we can manage at any point in time. The anthropologist and psychologist Robin Dunbar, who has dedicated thirty years to studying this phenomenon, has discovered that, regard-less of where we live or the nature of our society, there are very strict natural rules that govern our relations with others, whether we're part of a company of soldiers, a church congregation, a farming commu-nity or a hunting tribe in any part of the world.[26] Essentially, he argues, all our relationships fit into four concentric circles. The central circle is the 'family' – the small group of four or five people we see every day. Then comes the 'extended family' of around fifteen, who we have contact with most days. After that is the 'community' of fifty, whom we see most weeks. And finally there is the 'site' of 150 whom we bump into most months. That 150 is the maximum number of contacts that we can manage in our brains at any point in time: we simply cannot cope mentally with a larger number. 'There is a cognitive limit,' Dunbar explains, 'to the number of individuals with whom any one person can maintain stable relationships that is a direct function of their relative neocortex size.'[27]

Armies show these relationship circles at work in an institutional setting. Every soldier will belong to a small group with whom they work and relax every day (a squad or section), and in the course of a week they will also often work closely with two or three other small groups (other squads or sections). Collectively there are around ten small groups in a wider group of fifty (the platoon or troop), and two or three of these 'communities' in a 'site' of 100 to 150 (an army company or squadron). As Dunbar has shown, when communities exceed 150 their natural tendency is to subdivide or – if they are forced to stay together – to fracture. The Hutterites, a fundamentalist Anabaptist Christian community based principally in Pennsylvania, have more than 50,000 members, but whenever an individual community reaches its natural 150 limit, it will subdivide and give birth to a new community of around fifty people.[28] In the same way, the 5,000 or so Mormons who moved from Illinois to Salt Lake City in the 1800s did so in groups of 150. 'Once a community exceeds 150 people,' one Hutterite leader explained, 'it becomes increasingly difficult to control its members with peer pressure alone. With smaller groups, a quiet word in the corner of the field is enough to persuade an offender not to behave badly in future. But with larger groups, that quiet word is more likely to elicit a brusque and dismissive response.'[29]

This maximum group size, incidentally, is not just a human phenomenon. Among baboons, whose brains are on average a third the size of humans, the maximum group number is fifty. Among lemurs (a tenth the brain capacity of humans) the maximum is fifteen. If the group exceeds that number then their stress levels – which can be measured by the level of corticoid in their faeces – double or treble.[30] For all such groups there is a Goldilocks size. If they're too small in number, they will struggle to compete against other groups for food and mates and will be left very vulnerable if one of their members dies. If they're too large, they will spend too much time trying to find their position in the hierarchy and maintain the stable relationships that keep it together (via mutual grooming) and will struggle to find sufficient food to keep all their members healthy or find a new place to live.

Such careful management of group size is rare among most modern human organisations. The Centennials, however, are acutely aware of its importance. True, the 150 maximum for any given site is not always practicable (at the Royal Shakespeare Company, for example, executive director Catherine Mallyon told me that where resources are expensive or difficult to share it can prove necessary to accept a total group size of 200 or 250). But even then, efforts are made to preserve the 150 grouping within the larger setting (the US materials manufacturer Gore, see below, follows a similar approach). When it comes to the inner circles of the Dunbar thesis, British Cycling is careful to have no more than around fifty athletes in any of its podium, pro road, senior academy or junior academy teams. Eton normally has fifty students in a house. The Royal Academy of Music has fifty students in a department. Nasa has fifty astronauts on its space programme. And when it comes to the key inner teams where people have to work very closely together, where trust and support is so important, and where innovation and problem-solving mark the difference between success and failure, you will find that there are normally five athletes in a British Cycling squad, five students in an Eton or Royal Academy of Music seminar, and five astronauts on a Nasa space mission. Those teams are all at the forefront of what they do, breaking new ground and finding new edges, and then they pass their discoveries on to wider circles – the extended families, communities and sites – of which they are all part.

Because tight organisation, according to Dunbar's principles, suits the way humans tick, it's also more economical. As the California Polytechnic State University study mentioned earlier showed, very large companies tend to be inefficient. To handle armies of staff, additional layers of management are deemed necessary. Miscommunication abounds. Agility is lost. According to recent estimates, a third of the workforce in the US is now employed by organisations of 5,000 personnel or more. That's a tenth more than it was twenty years ago. Far from achieving economies of scale, such organisations have seen their overheads rocket, increasing by twice their direct costs. It's been suggested that simply to keep their bureaucracies functioning, more than $3 trillion has to be pumped into them each year – money that could be more productively spent on incremental improvement.[31] Dunbar-sized enterprises avoid such pitfalls.

5.

One organisation that understands these dynamics and has made them an integral part of its structure is Gore, founded in 1958 by a chemical engineer who had seen for himself what happens when you ignore the natural rules that govern human groups. Before he started his own company, Bill Gore had worked for DuPont for sixteen years. During that time he had become increasingly dissatisfied. The company he had joined was a creative family business. The company he was working for a decade and a half later was on its way to becoming a corporate giant. The transition had been accompanied by a huge growth in sales and an accompanying mushrooming of the workforce from 30,000 when Gore started to 90,000 fifteen years later.[32] Gore worried that in the process the company had lost its creative edge, that it had become distracted by the challenges of managing what it had rather than revelling in the possibilities of what it might do in the future, and that it was in danger of losing control. The products it had pioneered and that had made it great – neoprene, dynamite, paint and cellophane – were no longer cutting-edge. It hadn't launched anything new in over a decade. And it was resisting Gore's proposal to find new uses for PTFE, the polymer the business had developed twenty years earlier. It just wanted to make money from what it had.

So Gore left.

Over the next three years, working with his wife and son in the basement of their home, he developed all sorts of products that might profitably make use of PTFE – from communication cords, to computer cables, to electric wires. In 1960, the family team secured their first big order, from Denver Water, for seven miles of computer cabling. They built their first factory later that year, and were awarded their first patent in 1963.[33]

Gore knew they had to grow if they were to survive. But he also knew he didn't want to create another DuPont behemoth. And it was then that he came across a book that transformed his life. Douglas McGregor's *The Human Side of Enterprise* posits two approaches to management. Theory X is based on the assumption that people are lazy, unengaged and motivated only by money and so argues that they need to be commanded, controlled and incentivised. Theory Y holds that people are motivated, curious and keen to do meaningful work and therefore believes that, to do their best work, they simply need to be nurtured, encouraged and recognised.[34]

Gore rejected Theory X. He decided that he would expand his business along the principles of Theory Y. Such an approach, he came to believe, offered the best chance of avoiding the problems he had noted at DuPont. It would also create an environment in which people would work on problems they wanted to solve with like-minded colleagues, and would come up with fresh and innovative ideas accordingly. 'He created a place with hardly any hierarchy and few ranks and titles,' journalist Alan Deutschman wrote. 'He insisted on direct, one-on-one communication; anyone in the company could speak to anyone else. In essence, he organised the company as though it were a bunch of small task forces.'[35] Terri Kelly, who worked at Gore for thirty-seven years (fifteen of which were spent as the company's CEO), described the ethos of the company in these terms: 'We're a lattice or a network, not a hierarchy, and associates can go directly to anyone in the organisation to get what they need to be successful. We try to resist titles. We have a lot of people in responsible positions in the organisation, but the whole notion of a title puts you in a box, and worse, it puts you in a position where you can assume you have authority to command others in the organisation. So we resist this.'[36]

Even today, Gore continues to be driven by the insights that inspired its founder back in the 1960s. Everyone is referred to as an 'associate', whose roles and responsibilities are negotiated with the other associates in their team – usually a team of five. These colleagues also judge their performance, and help set their bonus, at the end of each year.[37] In addition, each associate is allocated to a 'sponsor', who, in Kelly's words, 'makes a personal commitment to an associate's success and development'.[38] Enormous care is taken not to add too many new people to the company (rarely more than one a month to each business) and to control the number of personnel per site so that the maximum of 300 is not exceeded. 'If a plant gets too big or a business gets too large – more than 250 or 300 people – you start to see a very different dynamic,' Kelly says. 'The sense of ownership, the involvement in decision-making, the feeling that I can make an impact starts to get diluted.'[39]

Each site operates as its own hub, complete with all the departments necessary: research, development, engineering, manufacturing and sales. And when a site threatens to become too big, new offshoots are created, each with its own full complement of departments (Bill Gore pithily described this approach as 'Divide so we can multiply').[40] 'We like to have the functions co-located,' Kelly explains, 'because innovation depends on having research, manufacturing and sales all in the same place, where they can build off each other. This also helps us develop leaders. [And] we co-locate different businesses together. If a particular industry has a downturn, you want to be able to move the associates to another opportunity. If our plants were all in isolated locations, this would be much more difficult. So we like the idea of campuses where a number of small factories are co-located within a twenty-mile radius. This way, people don't fear moving on to something else, and are less hesitant to take on a new opportunity. This lessens the risk the associates will try to preserve a business or product area that may no longer be so promising to the company.'[41] Gore has also found that by putting different businesses together – aerospace, chemical, medical and military, for example – it becomes easier to attract fresh talent, since prospective employees like the prospect of being able to switch roles if they want to.

Gore may now be one of the largest privately owned businesses in the US, with more than $3 billion annual sales and more than 10,000 people on the payroll.[42] But it continues to grow slowly and carefully, valuing excellence and incremental improvement far higher than expansion. There are still fewer than 300 people per site and there are generally at least two sites within twenty miles of each other in the various territories in which it operates – from Delaware (where the company was founded) and Arizona in the US, to Germany, China and Japan.

The company's record speaks for itself. It has appeared on *Fortune*'s list of the 100 best places to work every year for the last twenty years. It has never made a loss. And it continues to develop hundreds of new products each year that have secured the company dozens of innovation awards. It remains at its sector's cutting edge, producing high-tech fabrics for astronauts, explorers and soldiers, heart patches and blood vessels for hospital patients, and Gore-Tex products for everyone. Which is why, in 2021, *Fast Company* said it still had the second most innovative culture in America – second only to Moderna, which had developed the Covid vaccine earlier that year.[43]

6.

Once organisations focus on how they can get better rather than bigger, various advantages start to flow. Hierarchies are simplified (the Centennials have fewer than five layers of management). Costs are therefore reduced (management within the Centennials normally accounts for around a tenth of their financial outlay). Money saved on bureaucracy is spent more productively on building the financial reserves that are so necessary for long-term survival (the Centennials have all built up endowments and investments that, in some cases, are responsible for a third of their income). And because no site exceeds 300 employees, it's possible to create a degree of flexibility that monolithic concerns find hard to create: new departments and programmes can be introduced as and when required.[44]

Above all, the smaller, modular forms such organisations adopt help them become more creative. Instead of focusing on how much more they can make from what they've already got, they ask themselves how they can do new things and make what they've got even better. And if it happens that an opportunity presents itself and they have to grow quickly, then they normally do this by setting up a spin-off – such as Nasa's spin-offs division or the Royal Shakespeare Company's Matilda programme – to preserve the size of the core and ensure continuing agility. The spin-off, which can learn from the core while generating its own revenue, can then thrive (or, perhaps, ultimately decline) without having any collateral impact.[45]

The use of the different Dunbar numbers is also crucial. Centennial structures are not monolithic. As already mentioned, they break up naturally into families of five, extended families of fifteen, communities of fifty and sites of 150. And because they do so, they operate in a completely different way from most organisations. Most companies have a top-down structure, but the Centennials don't. They look to their smallest groups – their families – to be the powerhouses that break new ground, and push things forward. It's the families, not the senior team, who make the initial running. They then share their breakthroughs and findings with the larger groups. The role of the those at the top is not to regulate their work, but to enable it.

It's something the US National Transportation Safety Board discovered the hard way when, in 1979, it asked Nasa to explain why the airline industry had suffered so many fatal accidents in the previous decade.[46] Nasa came to the conclusion that these failures arose from a command and control approach to management that simply didn't work in such a complex, cutting-edge environment.[47] It was far better, Nasa concluded, to leave such matters to the tightly knit team in the cockpit – and not just the captain or air traffic control. After all, if something goes wrong – such as a landing gear failure or a warning light coming on – the whole of the cockpit team needs to respond immediately, to try different ideas as quickly as possible, and to try to find a way to fix things. In such situations, a top-down approach is far too cumbersome and slow – and the chances are that those at the top won't have the answers anyway.[48]

This is the reason why Nasa leaves its core team of astronauts to make the key decisions in space, even if a larger group is involved in planning the mission. In another arena it's why the All Blacks coaches leave most of the decisions on the pitch to their players, even though they're obviously very closely involved in their training beforehand. Indeed, instead of giving the traditional motivational speech before each match (the All Blacks players said it didn't help), the coaches now ask four senior players (a quarter of the team on the pitch, referred to as 'the back of the bus'), to talk through necessary preparations in the dressing room and to take the lead on the pitch.[49] The coaches' role is to plan match strategies and tactics beforehand, to review the match afterwards, and to develop a training plan for the next one.

The coaches also look to the players to guide the larger community (the thirty or so players who make up the squad). These three senior players will work with the four 'back of the bus' players to bring new talent into the squad, to help maintain the team's morale over the course of a season, and to manage the team's diary each week.

Constant interaction between the four groups – family, extended family, community and site – is absolutely crucial to the coherence of the whole. And not just within a company. The rule also applies more generally. When the US Department of Health and Human Services reviewed studies of thousands of families over the previous forty years it discovered that families and communities flourish only when they share similar beliefs and values, know how to support – and challenge – each other so that they keep moving forward, and understand the importance of changing roles and responsibilities over time so that there is constant evolution.[50] The street on which I live in London houses around 300 people, but we tend to split into two sites – the top and the bottom of the street – as a recent street party demonstrated. My own family relies heavily on two or three other families (around ten people in total) to help us when we need assistance, and we know around ten other families on the street to say hello to. There's nothing unique about this. It's a pattern you will find in most other thriving communities – whether it's a village in Italy, a tower block in Singapore, or a city block in New York.[51] Each community needs a mix of communities and families that are all different from each other, but are willing to work together – to help buffer the storms and find new ways to improve – so that they can collectively sustain their survival and success over time.

In the same way, Eton College may be based on the community principle of the house, but it makes sure that all its houses have a similar mix of arts and science students and that there is constant interaction between houses.[52] The Royal College of Art similarly makes art, design and technology programmes available on each of its sites, and makes sure that the students work on projects with people from other programmes each month.[53] If incremental improvement comes from the 'family', it will only spread and be of value to the overall organisation if it permeates through the various circles of the Dunbar number.

7.

In summary, Centennials focus on getting better not bigger, so that they don't get distracted or lose control, by:

Dividing themselves into families of five, extended families of fifteen, communities of fifty and sites of 150

Putting two or more sites close together so they can help and support each other

Building up financial reserves to help them weather the storms

Using spin-offs if they need to grow quickly, so their core can stay small

Having fewer than five levels of management in all parts of their organisation

Asking their families to drive their innovation, and then share their learning with their other families, communities and sites, so they all get better.

Habit 10

X-RAY EVERYTHING

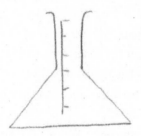

Everything has a formula

1.

It's 16 December 2015 and Meekyoung Shin, a first-year student on the ceramics and glass master's programme at the Royal College of Art, is presenting her latest work to a couple of tutors and the programme director. It consists of three statues. All have collapsed. 'As you can see, the project didn't go quite as planned,' she says.

A flurry of questions follows. Some are the obvious ones. 'Why, where, when and how did it all go wrong?' 'What would you do differently next time?' But soon they become far more wide-ranging. 'What surprised you most about the project?' 'What was the happy accident that you'd like to repeat in the future?' 'What do you think went wrong with the things that worked?' One of the tutors, Alison Britton, who also runs a successful ceramics business, asks: 'Who is your work for and why would they buy it?' 'What would they do with it, and how would it make them think and feel?' The to and fro of questions and answers goes on for almost an hour, digging ever deeper, seeking to help Meekyoung understand not just why things have gone wrong but what she could do better next time and what her broader goals are.

'Every student completes five main projects in the two years they're here,' Felicity Aylieff, the programme director, explains. 'The first year is designed to break them down – to make them work on topics and in mediums they've never encountered before, to make things go wrong and to create as much learning as possible. Then, at the end of the year, we sit down with them and ask them what they want to do when they graduate. Then we design the second year around each student – bringing in the appropriate visiting tutors and creating the right amount of challenge and support for each one – so they're ready to do what they want to do when they leave.'

It's a pretty intense approach and it's not surprising that some students should feel in their first few months that they are merely stumbling from one failure to the next. One student, who now runs her own ceramics business, ruefully recalls how she went from being top of her class at school to becoming convinced that she didn't know what she was doing when she started at the college. But the teaching staff are on hand on an almost daily basis to review and discuss each project as it develops. They then undertake a more formal critique – in front of the student's peers and with a visiting tutor – once the project has been completed. 'We tell the students they should expect 90 per cent failure and 50 per cent surprise, if they want to work at the cutting edge,' Martin Smith, the former head and now a tutor on the programme, says. 'If this isn't happening, we tell them to be more adventurous and more unusual, so that they're always pushing the boundaries, and never stay still.'

2.

Many organisations claim to embrace failure. Tolerate is probably a more accurate word. But the Royal College of Art, along with other Centennials, seeks it out. It recognises the simple fact that failure is an inevitable part of any process and that it's around us all the time (after all, 80 per cent of the world's largest companies a century ago aren't here today, nor are 95 per cent of the 4 billion species that have ever lived on the Earth).[1] If accepted as such, failure becomes not something to be shunned but something from which people genuinely learn. It becomes a form of deep practice.

Not just that, but a healthy attitude to failure guards against complacency. Talk to any leader of any Centennial and you get the sense that success makes them a little nervous. 'What have we missed? I know we've missed something,' Peter Keen, the former performance director at British Cycling, said to me after he'd just described how the team had won nearly half the Olympic gold medals on offer – five times as many as any other country – over the previous twenty years. 'We haven't always played that well,' Steve Hansen, the former All Blacks head coach, admitted after explaining how the team had won 85 per cent of their matches in the previous two decades. 'I don't think we're as good as we once were,' a design tutor at the Royal College of Art confided to me, despite the fact that their graduates had gone on to constitute half of Apple's product designers and a large proportion of the world's leading car designers in the previous twenty years. Because an understanding of the inevitability and value of failure runs through them all, they all embody what is perhaps best described as a disruptive nervousness. They're restless. They're always trying to do things better. Failure for them is what spurs breakthrough and achievement.

The explosion of the *Challenger* Space Shuttle on 28 January 1986, in which all seven astronauts aboard were killed, offers a classic warning story here of what can happen when this disruptive nervousness disappears.

Since Nasa's Moon landing triumph in 1969, the space agency had undergone significant internal change. When it had first entered the space race – just over a decade earlier – it had drawn on the knowledge of in-house experts who were, as one engineer later recalled, 'expected to take risks and make mistakes, but not make the same mistake twice'.[2] 'There wasn't somebody keeping score in the way that you might think of it now,' said another engineer. 'The philosophy was different. We knew we were learning.'[3]

After the Moon landing, however, the agency became more bureaucratic and fragmented. The number of managers tripled. The number of contractors increased fivefold. And the authority to make decisions moved to Washington.[4] In the process, discussions became less open and Nasa's engineers lost their power. 'Our meetings are not as open as I think they used to be,' one engineer complained, 'in the sense of having good technical arguments and penetrating questions asked. I've been at too many meetings where somebody will start out on that track and the recipient gets extremely defensive.'[5] 'On the one hand,' another engineer said, 'the upper levels of management have been diverted by the Washington bureaucracy into having to spend a lot more time on nontechnical subjects – administrative and political affairs. At the other end of the organisation our whole attitude on demanding technical and cost accountability has slackened.'[6] As a result, the more interesting conversations stopped – or started happening behind closed doors – creating 'underground decision-making', as Hans Mark, an administrator at the Marshall Space Flight Center, put it.[7]

That was bad enough. But what the events that immediately preceded the *Challenger* disaster show is that amid all this change Nasa and those who worked closely with it forgot how a culture that embodied disruptive nervousness actually functions. The night before *Challenger* was due to launch, engineers at the Morton Thiokol plant in Utah who had worked on the O-rings that sealed the two solid rocket boosters expressed concerns that the rings had not been tested at the low temperatures they would have to endure during the launch the following morning. They shared their concerns with Nasa. But in an organisation where disruptive nervousness had first been discouraged and then dispensed with, the message was mishandled and the warning it contained went unheeded. The engineers at Morton Thiokol failed to unpick the potential problem fully and didn't present their conclusions clearly.[8] The thirteen slides they shared with Nasa contained lots of confusing and conflicting information. 'In their haste to get ready for the call,' Joseph Hall, a professor at UC Berkeley later argued, 'the engineering team mistakenly included slides that had been used in previous Flight Readiness Reviews to argue that the O-rings would not be a problem despite damage and blow-by incidents.'[9] Those at Nasa who spoke to the Morton Thiokol engineers failed to interrogate the data with which they were presented, and fell back on the dangerous assumption that since there hadn't been problems with the O-rings in the past, it was unlikely that any would arise in the future. 'My God, Thiokol,' Lawrence Mulloy, the shuttle programme manager, exclaimed, 'when do you want me to launch, next April?' George Hardy, the Marshall Center's deputy director of science and engineering, also said he was 'appalled' at the Thiokol recommendation. So the launch went ahead.[10]

The *Challenger* disaster was followed by the inevitable inquiry that uncovered the reason why the O-rings in the space craft's right booster had failed so catastrophically: they simply didn't work below 65 degrees Fahrenheit.[11] But only half a lesson was learnt. Nasa realised that it would need to re-engineer that part of its shuttles. What it didn't appreciate was that if it didn't change its approach to failure and the constant potential for failure, all the *Challenger* inquiry could guard against was a recurrence of that particular mistake. The space agency continued to add management layers, outsourced more work, and looked to achieve more cost-cutting measures.[12] 'In hindsight,' Julianne Mahler, a professor of government and politics at George Mason University, argued, 'it was only a matter of time before another accident happened.'[13]

Seventeen years later, it did. At 8.59 a.m. Eastern Standard Time on 1 February 2003, the *Columbia* Space Shuttle disintegrated as it re-entered the Earth's atmosphere. All seven astronauts aboard perished. The particular cause of the disaster was a piece of foam that had broken off from the shuttle's tank and damaged its wing during take-off. Arguably, the deeper cause was the same as it had been in 1986.

And now Nasa woke up to its more fundamental problems. According to Stephen Johnson, a safety engineer at the Marshall Space Flight Center: 'What caught the attention of the Columbia Accident Investigation Board and others was the resemblance of the decisions and factors leading up to the accident to those behind the *Challenger* accident seventeen years earlier.' Julianne Mahler, who studied the *Challenger* and *Columbia* disasters closely, wrote how, in more general terms, 'investigators found that decision makers were isolated and failed to listen'.[14] People came to realise that seeking to legislate against individual problems was not sufficient – there were simply too many variables in play at any given time. What needed to change was the culture.[15]

Over the next months and years, psychologists were brought in to help the space agency understand how to explain and listen better.

Responsibility for work done was taken from managers and returned to engineers. Everyone was given a 'stop work' card, which they could play if they thought something might go wrong.[16] 'These simple changes completely changed how Nasa worked,' Robert Zimmerman, an author of several books on space exploration, wrote as the cultural shift took hold. 'Before the *Columbia* accident, the managers were in charge. But over the past two years, those tables have turned. The managers have backed off and are letting the engineers do their thing.'[17] Gerald Smith, who worked at Nasa for twenty years, said: 'We made it very clear at meetings that if anyone had a concern or issue, let's raise it. Do not, do not hold back. If you've got a problem, let's say it. If you don't like a decision, let's hear it, let's talk about it.'[18]

Nasa's approach today is perhaps best summed up by astronaut Charles Camarda. 'Our motto is: Where there is failure, there is knowledge and understanding that doesn't come with success.'[19]

It's worth bearing in mind in this context that when a group of four researchers from the US research company the Standish Group analysed 50,000 projects that should have delivered over the previous thirty years they came to the conclusion that two-thirds had failed to meet their targets. They also noted that the proportion of failure to success hadn't shifted over that time period. Failure is inevitable. It's how you approach it that matters.[20]

3.

It would be a mistake, though, to assume that we learn only from things that have gone wrong. We need to learn from successes too, particularly if we want to sustain it. As one All Blacks mantra has it: 'You don't have to lose to learn.'[21] Someone building a new bridge, say, will learn not only what to do from the handful that have collapsed, but from the vast majority that are still standing. Some psychologists today talk about the power of positive psychology (also known as appreciative inquiry or strengths-based learning), focusing on doing more of the things you're already doing that work, rather than trying to fix the things that don't.[22] That approach arguably downplays the value of learning from mistakes.

But it does remind us that we don't just learn from negatives. We learn from positives, too.

The experience of Jerry Sternin, Save the Children's country director in Vietnam in the 1990s, nicely exemplifies this. When he arrived in the country in December 1991 Vietnam was still recovering from a war that had ended fifteen years previously.[23] Literacy rates were low, sanitation was poor and food provision was inadequate. The communist government that now held sway had allowed people to own their own farms in a bid to encourage them to grow more crops, but despite their best efforts half the nation's children were still malnourished. The Vietnamese health minister told Sternin bluntly: 'You have six months to make an impact, or you're out!'[24]

The temptation when faced with such an enormous challenge is generally to look at what has gone wrong and seek to fix it. But Sternin adopted a different approach. He had recently come across a review of thirty development projects by Marian Zeitlin, a nutritionist at Tufts University, who concluded that when faced with a difficult problem, it can make more sense to try to scale success than to fix failure.[25] Seeing the wisdom of this in his particular sphere, Sternin decided to look for what Zeitlin termed the 'positive deviants' – children who should be malnourished but weren't – and see what could be learnt from their experience. 'Redirect attention from "what's wrong" to "what's right",' he later put it as he described his quest to pinpoint 'observable exceptions that succeed against all odds'.[26]

It took him a while to persuade the government that this was the way to go. But eventually they agreed to let him study four villages in the Thanh Hóa province, 100 miles south of Hanoi. Each had a population of around 20,000 people. Each depended on rice farmers who grew rice for themselves, as well as sold it to others, and who normally had two or three of their own children to feed. 'We asked for five volunteers from each village,' Sternin said, 'which meant we had twenty volunteers across the region, to help us improve the level of child nutrition in the area. We brought them together and asked them: "Is it possible for a child to be poor, but well nourished?" "Co co, co co!" they shouted. "It is, it is!" That's when we knew we were on to something.'[27]

Over the next two months, Sternin worked with the volunteers to select 2,000 children under the age of three from across the region and from a range of family backgrounds. They weighed each child and recorded the amount of rice produced by their family every month for the next three months. They plotted their weight against family income on a graph. What they found was that – surprisingly – a third of the children were both poor and well nourished. That immediately suggested to the researchers that weight and wealth were not correlated (further confirmation of this insight came from a study of two children who came from relatively affluent families but were nevertheless malnourished).[28] Sternin's team therefore now zeroed in on a smaller group of four poor but well-nourished children, and spent two weeks with them to see exactly how they lived.

Three months later, they were ready to report their findings. According to World Health Organization guidelines, children should be given easily digestible vegetables, such as corn, rice and sweet potato, in medium portions twice a day. That's not, however, what the poor, well-nourished children were doing. They were supplementing their vegetables with small quantities of high-protein food, such as crab, shrimp and snails, three to five times a day. In the process they both consumed twice as many nutrients as other children and found them easier to absorb. 'The parents of the healthy children were doing all the things we were telling them not to do!' one volunteer explained. 'Not because they didn't understand what we were saying, but because they knew it didn't work.'[29] For his part Sternin noted that crabs, shrimps and snails were all readily found on all rice farms. They were, he realised, essentially free – and easy to share.

Inferring new strategies from current successes is something that others have done too. Back in 2005 Merck changed its sales approach in Mexico when it realised that its most effective salespeople there were cold-calling fewer customers than the company mandated but were spending longer with each one to build up a sense of rapport.[30] Sales rose by a third when the practices of this small group of salespeople (10 per cent of the total) were rolled out more widely. Goldman Sachs has followed a similar route in its bid to improve client management, as has Hewlett-Packard, which gleaned valuable lessons about products and services by getting groups of staff to study how the company's high performers operate (these high performers constitute less than 10 per cent of the total workforce).[31] The positive deviant approach has also been successfully adopted to reduce gang violence in New Jersey, increase entrepreneurism in South Africa, reduce the spread of HIV/Aids in Jakarta, and reduce the infant mortality rate in Pakistan.[32] Focusing on the small number of people – generally less than 10 per cent of a given population – who have already worked out an answer to the problem in hand pays dividends.

Sternin's success in Vietnam was also contingent on another key factor. When he and his volunteers started to roll out the new programme, they were careful not simply to prescribe it to people. 'Most development programmes fail when people tell everyone what to do,' he said.[33] Instead they recruited more volunteers and set up a nutrition centre in each of Vietnam's fifty provinces, where the parents could come to get their children measured each month and learn from other parents, who were trying to raise their own offspring in similar circumstances. People swapped ideas. They uncovered the solutions in their own time. And they then stuck with them. By the end of the six-month period Sternin had been allocated, more than half of the 2,000 children they'd worked with were well nourished. By the end of the first year, nearly all were. Five years later, when the model had been rolled out across the country – by the Vietnamese government and the National Institute of Nutrition – nearly all the children in the country were benefiting from improved nutrition.[34]

'People learn best when they discover things for themselves,' Sternin explained. 'Knowledge is usually insufficient to change behaviour. It is our own discoveries that change behaviour. A basic belief of the "positive deviant approach" is that when someone from the outside provides the solution, those to whom it is directed may not believe it and do not have an investment in it.'[35] Finding the solution, then, is only half the challenge. The other half is getting people to accept it and adopt it. In an ideal world, this should involve giving them the tools to solve the problem for themselves, so that they can see first-hand that it works. That's not always practicable. But the fact remains that time and patience should be factored into getting people to go along with new ideas.

Interestingly, experts have found that take-up is hugely improved if new ideas are framed in terms of what would be lost if they weren't adopted rather than what would be gained if they were.[36] Double-glazing salespeople, for example, win more customers by telling them what they will lose out on if they don't install new windows than what they will gain if they do. It's a valuable lesson to bear in mind.

4.

The ancient Greeks made a distinction between knowledge (which they called *techne* or *episteme*) and wisdom (*metis* or *phronesis*). The former is the technical knowledge that can be gathered from doing the same thing over and over again, and can often be passed on through theories and rules. The latter is an adaptive process where mastery comes from doing different things over time, and learning through experience, examination and experimentation. Knowledge tends to come first, as it generally relates to particular tasks (the what and how). Wisdom develops as we start to understand the context (the where and when).[37] Both are crucial. Both require an ability to learn from failure and success.

It's only by obsessively picking over every action, moment and decision that the Centennials are able to develop the knowledge and wisdom they need to stay ahead, as they seek to find the success in failure, and the failure in success that keeps them moving forward. British Cycling, for example, soon acquired the knowledge necessary to determine which tyres it should use and how they should grip the track during a race, but only after time did it gain the wisdom that came from gradually realising that tyres need to grip the track in one way at the start of a race and in a different way as the race proceeds. That wisdom gave the organisation the idea of spraying the tyres with alcohol before the start of each race so as to provide extra grip over those crucial first metres.[38] For its part the Royal Academy of Music first worked out what experiences its students needed to have to develop their skills (knowledge), and then realised where and when those skills would best be developed (wisdom). Now it makes sure skills are acquired in an optimal sequence over a three-year programme; small, but vital, refinements and improvements that rely on both knowledge and wisdom, techne and metis.

Achieving such a mindset takes time and effort. But there are ways to facilitate it. One is to develop the habit of systematically and scientifically analysing everything that you reckon might affect your performance in a particular task or context by writing down a list of everything that you can think of, for at least ten minutes. Ideally, you want to come up with forty or so separate items, covering such topics as the mental and physical health of your people, the equipment they use, the environment they work in, or the people they work with, and so on. Remember, the crazier the idea the better, as it is more likely to stimulate you to find something new. Then take a break. Go for a walk or do some exercise (getting more oxygen to your brain can increase your creative impulses by more than 60 per cent).[39] Sit back down again and spend another ten minutes coming up with forty more ideas. Repeat the process of writing and exercising until you are convinced you have nothing left to add. Take a break. Try again. Then ask other members of your team to try the exercise on an individual basis. Once everyone has come up with their own set of ideas and perspectives, draw them all together and see what connections and cross-fertilisations can be made.[40]

The next step is to pick one of the most promising ideas. Try to think of eight ways in which you might be able to improve it, and see if you can draw them in eight minutes (the Royal College of Art calls this the 'Crazy 8'). Giving an idea visual form can help. So too can flicking through a magazine or a book as you search for inspiration. It's a good notion, as well – once you've thought through your best ideas – to try some terrible ones as well. Clive Grinyer, the head of the service design programme at the Royal College of Art, assured me that bad ideas can help you 'reframe your thinking'.[41]

Turning to outsiders is the final stage of brainstorming: asking for ideas from people within the organisation you don't normally work with and people from outside who have different perspectives and areas of expertise. The Royal Academy of Music turned to surgeons when it was seeking to work out how to perform better under pressure. British Cycling approached the Royal Ballet for ideas on touring. Nasa asked Norwegian explorers to help it improve the way it planned. It can also be worth trying what intelligence, military and security services call 'red teaming'. This involves getting a 'blue team' to come up with a new and innovative idea, and then asking a 'red team' to pull it apart. As the debate unfolds you can tell pretty quickly whether the idea has legs – though, of course, it will take creating a model or simulation to know for sure whether it actually works in practice.[42]

For British Cycling it was only when it went through these exhaustive processes that it started addressing fundamental issues about aspects of performance that would really shift the dial. How should our bike tyres grip the track at the beginning, and during each race? Where, when and how can our athletes stay warm and focused between races? Why, when and how do our athletes get distracted before a race?

For the Royal Academy of Music the questions that started to arise included: How should our students hang out together when they're not practising? Where, when and how should they fail if they want to learn? Why, when and how can we help them adapt when things go wrong?

It obviously takes self-discipline to reach the point where this kind of open mindset feels natural. And it takes time too. Which is why, as a rule of thumb, all the Centennials normally spend at least one day a week reviewing all the current projects they are working on to see how they can be improved and if any patterns are forming that they need to be aware of. Are new technologies or types of competition emerging? Are there new economic or social factors that need to be taken into account? And they spend at least one day a month reviewing their previous projects, to see if they reveal any useful patterns or trends. Such critical self-examination helps them not only maximise their current performance, but prepare for the future.

Former US secretary of state Colin Powell evoked what he called the '40/70 rule' to explain best practice here. Essentially, you need to be confident that you have a good understanding of the problem you're seeking to solve before you think about turning theory into practice (the 40 per cent element), but you should not wait so long (to the point, in other words, where you think you have a 70 per cent understanding) before you act.[43] In other words, you need to start moving forward when you think you have a fair grasp of what is involved. But if you wait until you think you have all the answers you'll probably end up being too late.

5.

Preserving the proper degree of objectivity throughout such processes is the other great challenge (hence the reason why constantly involving outside – corrective – voices is so important). One of our great human weaknesses, according to the Israeli psychologists Danny Kahneman and Amos Tversky, is that our individual judgement is prone to be wrong-footed by the smallest of – often unrelated – influences.[44] In one experiment the two researchers invited volunteers to spin a wheel of fortune that was rigged to land on ten or sixty-five and then to guess the percentage of African countries that are in the United Nations. Those who scored the lower number tended to go on to assume a lower level of United Nations membership among African countries (20 per cent lower on average), even though there was, of course, absolutely no connection between fortune wheel outcomes and the question they were then posed. In other experiments, people asked to write down the last three digits of their phone number were shown to be unconsciously influenced by that number when they were then asked to estimate how many marbles there were in a jar; dice-rolling outcomes affected views of sentencing for shoplifting; the number on a player's shirt affected people's judgement of how many goals that player would go on to score.[45] The only way to guard against being influenced by irrelevant factors is constantly to seek reality checks from those who are not involved on a day-to-day basis on the project or decision-making in hand.[46]

Even seemingly unimpeachable data and statistics can prove slippery entities to interpret. In one experiment students were asked to take a map of the US and colour in the counties with the highest levels of kidney cancer deaths over the previous decade. The data clearly showed that most deaths occurred in the most rural areas.[47] Asked to explain why this should be, the students said it was because people living there were, on average, older, had worse diets, limited access to good healthcare, and were more exposed to agricultural chemicals. They established their data, in other words, and drew plausible conclusions from it. It was only when they were asked to measure the lowest level of kidney cancer deaths and found that they, too, occurred in these very rural areas that they realised how misled they had allowed themselves to be by the original data, and how quickly they had been prepared to jump to conclusions. In fact, what they were witnessing was the wild fluctuation in results that invariably occur when the statistical base is low. Rural America is relatively sparsely populated. It doesn't take much, therefore, to tip a statistical survey one way or the other.

It's also worryingly easy to measure the wrong data. Robert McNamara, who was secretary of defence during the early part of the Vietnam War, had previously been a brilliant leader at Ford Motor Company. While there, he had used his experience as a mathematician and statistician to cut costs, achieve economies of scale, and ensure not just that Ford made the cheapest cars on the market but that revenue grew consistently in the fifteen years he was with the company (it actually rose fortyfold between his arrival in 1946 and his departure in 1961).[48] His analytical approach worked brilliantly in an industry that at that time was very stable. But when he applied the same mindset to conducting a war, the result was a complete disaster.[49] The questions he asked were precisely what one would expect someone from his background to ask. How many bombs are we dropping? How many targets have we destroyed? How many of the enemy have we killed?[50] By answering these, he thought, he would be able to 'create the highest national security for the lowest possible cost', as he put it.[51] But it didn't work. McNamara's data-gathering told the US what it had done, not what it should do next. Because it measured effort and not the success of military tactics, it gave the impression that the war was going well, when at best it was a stalemate. And by failing to articulate larger questions – such as: How does a conventional military force 'win' against a largely guerrilla one? – it skewed the US's strategy and tactics. The US viewed the war as a proxy fight with communist superpowers, involving day fighting, above ground, in the jungle. In fact, it was a civil war involving forces who were fighting at night via a network of tunnels. At the same time, vitally important factors, such as the morale of the South Vietnamese troops or the relative sympathy of Vietnamese peasants towards the communist Vietcong, went largely ignored.

Colin Powell, who was a soldier in Vietnam at the time, later recalled a visit by McNamara to the camp where Powell was stationed. At the end of his forty-eight hours there McNamara announced that 'every quantitative measurement shows that we are winning the war'. 'Measure it and it has meaning,' Powell wrote. 'Measure it and it is real. Yet, nothing I had witnessed in the A Shau Valley indicated we were beating the Viet Cong. Beating them? Most of the time we could not even find them.'[52]

After collecting the wrong data for seven years, McNamara finally resigned in 1968. The US quit Vietnam five years later, having fought the wrong war, for the wrong reasons, in the wrong places, at the wrong time. In the process, nearly 2 million Vietnamese and 60,000 US lives were lost.[53]

Two important lessons flow from the experiences of McNamara and of those students who were looking at patterns of kidney disease. First, it is essential to understand what you're looking at – the task (what, how) and the context (where, when) – by opening your mind to self-reflection and analysis, and seeking the questions and advice of others. Second, you need to make any datasets you gather as large, clean and free from bias as possible by looking at the total population and as many people and instances as possible.[54] If you want to know how deadly a disease is, for example, you should not just look at the people in one region; you need to look at the rest of the population too. If you want to be 80 per cent confident in your findings, then – as a rule of thumb, and assuming your data is clean and unbiased – you need to study the impact of the disease on 100 people to achieve a confidence level of 90 per cent (how likely it is that your findings will be accurate) and a margin error of 10 per cent (how likely it is that your sample will reflect the total population); which gives you an overall confidence level of 81 per cent (90 per cent, multiplied by 100 minus 10 per cent). If you want to be 90 per cent confident in your findings then you need a sample of 200. To achieve 95 per cent confidence, you need a sample of 1,000. The 'sample size calculators' available on the internet are useful here.[55]

It was such careful use of reliable statistical evidence that ultimately saw an end to smallpox – once one of the world's great killers, responsible for millions of deaths each year. The World Health Organization, which in 1967 set itself the goal of eradicating the disease through a comprehensive programme of immunisation, evolved a multi-pronged approach that involved constant surveillance and, where necessary, containment. But throughout the process the WHO made sure that it focused on key, relevant data: not the number of vaccinations given or the funds spent (factors that someone like McNamara would no doubt have considered) but on actual recorded cases.[56] As it did so it made a series of vital discoveries: that adult females rarely contracted the disease (and so didn't require vaccination), that more than 95 per cent of sufferers had never previously been vaccinated (so it made most sense to administer as many first doses as possible before second doses were rolled out),[57] and that patterns of outbreaks had a regional and cultural aspect to them (for example, it proved harder to eradicate smallpox in India because afflicted families tended to travel between remote villages).[58] As such findings were made, the WHO constantly refined and adapted its approach.

The last recorded case of smallpox was in Somalia in October 1977.[59]

6.

Self-examination for most organisations is something they undertake on only an occasional basis – when they have experienced a major problem or need to make a big decision. At other times, the time and mental discipline required invariably mean that self-examination is put on the back burner. The Centennials, by contrast, build it into their DNA. The All Blacks players, for example, taking their lead from the military, talk of the 'OODA loop' that lies at the heart of everything they do: observe (what's happening), orientate (by synthesising all the available information), decide (if and how they want to move forward), act (quickly and decisively), observe again. In a similar way, Royal College of Art students use a 'design thinking loop' whereby they discover (what's already out there and is working or not working), define (what might work better), design (something new that 'wows' and could change people's lives), deliver (that idea), discover again.[60]

Such deep, reflective practice is embedded in everything they do. It's the way they channel their disruptive nervousness into genuine achievement.

7.

In summary, Centennials unpick success and failure to avoid complacency and ensure that they continue to move forward by:

Spending at least one day a week reviewing their current projects, to see how they can be improved

Spending at least one day a month reviewing previous projects, to see if any patterns are emerging that they can learn from

Asking both insiders and outsiders to question and challenge them, and help them review what they do

Looking for the success in the failure, and the failure in the success, as they try to find new ways to improve

Scientifically analysing anything that they think might affect their performance, and constantly tweaking everything to see what works.

Accidents

Habit 11

MAKE TIME FOR RANDOM

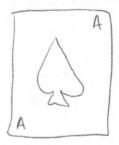

Increase the chance of chance

1.

Six Sigma was the brainchild of naval engineer turned business executive Bill Smith. And it seemed the answer to a vexed problem. Motorola, where Smith worked from the mid-1980s until his death in 1993, had started out in the 1920s making 'battery eliminators' for portable radios that allowed them to be plugged into the mains when they weren't being carried around. For half a century it had been at the forefront of mobile technology, working with the military during the Second World War and with Nasa in the 1960s. It had also produced the first commercial mobile phone in the 1970s, and the first mass-market version in the 1980s. But quality control had become a problem. At the time Smith joined the company, Motorola estimated that it was spending £800 million a year checking and fixing its mobile products. A tenth of its output, it estimated, required subsequent adjustment. When Motorola's president and CEO, Bob Galvin, asked at a specially convened meeting what the problem was, he received a blunt assessment from Art Sundry, one of his sales managers: 'I'll tell you what's wrong with this company: our quality stinks!'[1]

Bill Smith convinced Galvin that the only way to turn things around was to employ a ruthlessly empirical and statistical approach to quality control. His Six Sigma doctrine, honed over several years, involved the application of precise methods and models to define, measure, analyse, improve and control ('DMAIC') everything. Consistency was the goal. Error and variability were anathema. Smith's goal – and that of his 'black belt' Six Sigma engineers – was to create an environment where, if you did something a million times, you would make fewer than three mistakes. 'A product is built in the shortest time and at the lowest cost,' Smith explained, 'if no mistake is made in the process.'[2]

The doctrine proved astonishingly successful when applied to Motorola's manufacturing process – so successful, in fact, that in the first four years that Smith worked there, its production costs dropped by over $2 billion.[3] The company therefore took the principles embodied in Six Sigma and rolled them out to other areas of its operation, notably research and development. It wasn't long before other companies started to get in on the act. Polaroid, Chrysler, General Motors, Nortel and General Electric all became Six Sigma devotees. By the mid-2000s, according to *Fortune* magazine, a third of America's 200 largest companies were using Six Sigma methodologies. All, like Motorola, experienced immediate benefits in terms of accuracy, cost and quality.[4]

And then, one by one, they all faltered. Polaroid went bankrupt twice – in 2001 and 2008. Chrysler, General Motors and Nortel collapsed in 2009. General Electric eventually tumbled in 2017. Motorola itself saw its profits halve in the late 2000s. In the last quarter of 2008 it posted a $3.6 billion loss.[5]

Why? There's no doubt that Six Sigma had its merits when applied to repetitive manufacturing processes. But when adopted as an overall business approach, it proved deeply flawed. An obsession with measurement, with guaranteed outputs, with the elimination of error, and the possibility of error, certainly achieved an important short-term goal: increased profitability through reduced costs, from less wastage and greater efficiency. But that's all it did. When it came to long-term survival, it was a disaster.

A 2013 study by two Deloitte management consultants, Michael Raynor and Mumtaz Ahmed, shed valuable light on the problem of focusing too narrowly on the here and now.[6] Their analysis of 25,000 companies whose shares had been traded on the US stock market over the previous forty-five years showed that those enterprises whose strategy simply involved reducing costs and competing on price invariably failed to survive in the long term. Doing the things you already do, or selling things you've already got, as cheaply and efficiently as possible might yield immediate results, but they don't prepare you for future unforeseen challenges or new competition. (As Raynor pointed out: 'When you try to compete on price, a faster gun always seems to come to town.')[7] 'Companies don't become truly great by reducing costs or assets,' Raynor concluded. 'They earn their way to greatness. Exceptional companies often – even typically – accept higher costs as the price of excellence.'[8]

As the fates of the leading Six Sigma adherents show, the stability their strategy depended on never lasts for long. Nor does the competition they face stand still. Motorola died faster than the others because its rivals – first Nokia, then Apple and Samsung – brought out new and innovative products every two years. General Motors lasted longer because its competitors moved quite slowly and because its customers changed their cars only every five to ten years. General Electric proved to be the last person standing because there was little innovation in its sector and customers tended to renew the products they bought only every ten to fifteen years.[9] Sooner or later, though, the Six Sigma organisations' lack of innovation caught up with all of them – and they collapsed or died.

The Deloitte researchers argued – not surprisingly – that to be successful in the long term you need to take a very different approach. Don't focus on reducing costs, they said; focus on finding ways to increase price. Don't compete on price; focus on finding ways to be different and better than your competitors. 'A revenue advantage', Raynor stated, 'can be [either] driven by higher unit price or higher unit volume, and exceptional companies tend to rely more on price.'[10] Their findings were very much in line with those of the Organisation for Economic Co-operation and Development (OECD), which found in a 2007 report that what drives a country's long-term economic performance and standard of living is its ability to innovate.[11] 'Levels of research and development spend, investment in new technology, and new patent and trademark applications,' the OECD report showed, 'are all good indicators of the future economic and social health of a country, and are crucial for the long-term success of the whole world too.'[12]

2.

The impact of these two very different philosophies – a focus on cost versus a focus on innovation – is well illustrated by the varying fortunes of 3M in the early 2000s. Under the leadership of Jim McNerney from 2001 to 2005, it followed a strictly Six Sigma path. McNerney had previously served at General Electric for twenty years, where he had absorbed the doctrine of Six Sigma via its then CEO Jack Welch.[13] He was also a former McKinsey stalwart and had an MBA from Harvard. Over the course of his time at 3M he ruthlessly applied Six Sigma, trimming and tightening, cutting expenditure and extracting more profit. A tenth of the workforce went, as did a quarter of 3M's research budget and two-thirds of its capital investment.[14]

In the short term, his approach paid dividends. Profits doubled. Dividends soared. But when McNerney announced in 2005 that he was leaving 3M to join Boeing, and George Buckley was brought in as an interim and then a full-time CEO, the long-term price of McNerney's approach became clear. Buckley asked to see what proportion of the previous year's sales had come from products developed in the last five years (the 'vitality index', as 3M calls it). Since he knew that 3M's customers generally bought a new product from them every fifteen years, he assumed the answer would be 'a third'. The answer that came back a couple of weeks later was 'a twelfth'. According to Dennis Carey, who worked alongside Buckley: 'Some important divisions were even zero, where new product development and innovation had been completely eliminated.'[15] 'No one in the company knew these numbers any more,'

Buckley later said. 'They should have been front and central to them, but they had fallen into disuse . . . Once I showed my team the numbers I'd derived, there was a "holy shit" reaction. So I said, "Look guys, we've got to get back to innovating."'[16]

Buckley told his scientists and developers to stop trying to meet short-term financial targets. Instead, he said, they should dream and experiment again. He also increased their budget by a fifth. Over the next five years 3M developed thousands of new products. Its vitality index quadrupled. By 2010 more than a third of its sales came from products developed in those previous five years. It was back where it needed to be.[17] '3M is a technology company,' Buckley explained, 'so it's essential that we keep investing in and creating new technology.'[18] 'What's remarkable is how fast a culture can be torn apart. [McNerney] didn't kill it, because he wasn't here long enough,' said Art Fry, the scientist who invented the Post-it Note. 'But if he had been here much longer, I think he could have.'[19]

McNerney, meanwhile, was applying at Boeing the principles he had applied at 3M. Budgets were slashed, costs cut and profits maximised. In the short term it worked. But it also wrong-footed the corporation. Suddenly faced with competition from Airbus's new A320neo, which had a superior cabin, engine and wing design, and used a fifth less fuel than the Boeing 737 Next Generation, the company had to go into overdrive to develop a rival, the 737 Max, and to do so in half the time normally required to develop a new aircraft: four years rather than eight. 'The company was trying to avoid costs, and trying to contain the level of change,' said Rick Ludtke, an engineer who worked at Boeing. 'They wanted the minimum change to simplify the training differences, minimum change to reduce costs, and to get it done quickly.'[20] 'The timeline was extremely compressed,' said another engineer. 'It was go, go, go.'[21]

The combination of a tight schedule and a work culture that had sought to remove the possibility of wrinkles, errors and miscalculations proved fatal. Boeing failed to notice that the lift created by the new position of its engines (higher than normal), and the automated software used to correct this (to tilt its nose down), didn't work in certain conditions.[22] The new planes weren't tested properly. Three years later, after two fatal crashes in which more than 300 people perished, the whole fleet had to be grounded. The financial consequences for Boeing were dire as its share price fell and sales stalled. The human consequences were incalculable.[23]

3.

That innovation is essential for long-term success may seem an obvious statement. But it's extraordinary how few organisations embrace it (just 1 per cent of Raynor and Ahmed's 2013 survey).[24] They may talk about creating space and time for innovation, and giving people permission to experiment, but they don't do it. They claim they want their staff to come together in cross-functional teams so that they will come up with great new ideas, but they place them in siloed departments to increase their 'efficiency'. The fate of Boeing, Chrysler, General Electric, General Motors, Motorola, Polaroid and others shows that such approaches are simply not compatible with creativity and new thinking. There is often a year – often the year before things take a sudden turn for the worse – when such companies enjoy great financial success because they've cut costs as far as they can, but then the lack of innovation starts to bite.[25]

The Centennials, by contrast, know that these approaches don't ultimately work. So they set up environments that are the very opposite of slick production lines. People with different perspectives and from different departments sit alongside one another. They move around on a regular basis and make the best possible use of random encounters. They are expected to make mistakes, not go out of their way to avoid them.

Nasa, for example, far from creating fixed teams, creates fluid ones that work with lots of different people. British Cycling swaps around training sessions so that different athletes train with different coaches, in different facilities, each week. Eton moves its students between different classes, classrooms and teachers several times each day. Toyota famously tried to eliminate seven 'wastes' in its manufacturing processes – waiting, transporting, processing, inventory, motion, defects/rework and overproduction – a core principle of any Six Sigma or Lean initiative.[26] The Centennials make a point of keeping two of them: motion and defects. And they are pretty happy if there's some waiting time too.

Given that the point of Six Sigma is to stop waste and to save money, it would seem fair to assume that building in a degree of 'creative inefficiency' is bound to involve additional expense. And, to a degree, it does. The creative process is, by its nature, very time-consuming, and may demand numerous detours and iterations. But the removal of many of the checks, controls and layers of management that a Six Sigma process requires – to give people the freedom to manage themselves and experiment – offers compensatory advantages. As Timothy Jones, deputy principal at the Royal Academy of Music, told me: 'We recruit the best people we can, and then let them get on with it. We don't ask them to fill out loads of paperwork to prove they've done something, or employ loads of managers to check it's been done.'[27] In practical terms, this means less bureaucracy, less management and leaner operations. Most organisations would expect overheads to account for at least a fifth of turnover – and, in some cases, even a half.[28] Among Centennials, it's typically a tenth.[29]

The Royal College of Art exemplifies how a creative organisation looks in practice. People from different departments sit next to each other – for example, the fashion students sit next to the architecture students in an open-plan studio, and the ceramics and glass students are next to the information experience design ones. Building entrances, cafés and toilets are placed in strategic, central places so people have to walk around the building each day – 'four or five times each day, I'd say,' according to one of a group of architecture, ceramics, fashion and service design students. At least one new programme is created annually – to stimulate some fresh ideas. And each year students have to work on at least one 'AcrossRCA' project that involves collaborating with students from other programmes. The 'London Ambulance Project' involved information experience design, fashion, healthcare and vehicle design students who came together with ambulance crews to propose improvements to the layout and equipment design of an emergency vehicle, and develop a full-scale model to show how these improvements would work in practice.[30] The 'Dementia Project' saw architecture, information experience design, healthcare and visual communication students working with carers and patients in residential care homes to redesign the bedrooms and eating areas so that those with mobility issues or poor memory or eyesight would find them easier to negotiate. Other cross-programme teams have grappled with the challenges of creating more sustainable clothes, repurposing food waste and improving city travel.[31]

Such projects help solve important societal problems. They are also hugely beneficial to students. 'Some of them loathe it,' vice-chancellor Paul Thompson admitted to me, 'because they are there with a very single purpose: they want to be a car designer [for example] and they don't want to waste their time dealing with a project that is a global challenge and that involves a bunch of other people. They go into it sometimes a bit resistant. They come out of it saying: "This is the most fantastic thing ever."' It's always the thing that comes out as being the highest ranked in our student satisfaction survey, and it's also, ironically, one of the cheapest things we do at the RCA. It doesn't cost us a lot to run that programme, but it's unbelievably successful.'[32]

Fresh ideas also arise from wholly random, unplanned encounters in the RCA's communal spaces. Thompson described how a student might hear about a technical approach or a particular piece of equipment from someone working in a wholly unrelated field and immediately see the possibilities these present in their own. Or they might come across someone on their own or another course with whom they ended up collaborating. It should come as no surprise that over the past fifteen years the InnovationRCA centre has helped more than 100 graduates launch more than fifty spin-offs that have generated more than £100 million of sales and created more than a thousand jobs. Concrete Canvas, for example, was set up by two innovation design students who came up with a concrete fabric that helps people quickly build emergency fire- and water-resistant structures. Quirk Money was the brainchild of two service design students who wanted to help people better manage their finances. Olombria brought together the very different skills of architecture, information experience design and fashion students who have sought to tackle declining pollination levels in regions where bee populations have declined by using hormones to increase pollination by flies. Revive Innovations combined the skills of a critical writing and a design products student who developed a wearable adrenaline auto-injector for people suffering from severe allergies.[33]

4.

Perhaps the best non-Centennial exemplar of this approach is not an organisation but a country: Israel. Home to a population (9.3 million) that ranks only ninetieth in the world in terms of size, it nevertheless stands at thirtieth in global output rankings, and enjoys the twentieth highest standard of living.[34] According to the OECD it is also, per head of population, the most innovative country in the world, with both more start-ups per person (one for every 1,400 people) and more venture capital funding too ($170 per person).[35] It attracts investment from all over the world, and is home to some of the world's most innovative companies: 3M and Amazon, Apple and eBay, Facebook and Google, Intel and IBM, Microsoft and Nokia, PayPal and Samsung, Starbucks and Tesla, all have operations there. 'If you're a multinational company today,' says Yair Snir, managing director at Dell Technologies Capital, 'one of your assets must be an R&D centre in Israel.'[36] In 2022 more than 100 of the companies set up in Israel over the previous twenty years were considered 'unicorns', valued at more than $1 billion.[37] Not for nothing is the country known as the start-up nation.[38]

It might be tempting to assume that the country has achieved this status because of its low-tax laws and high capital funding that brings in both internal and external investment. Or because it encourages highly qualified and talented outsiders to settle there. Its record in both areas, however, is not that different from other OECD countries.[39] What is different is its culture. Essentially, Israelis operate in a far less siloed, more fluid way than the citizens of most other countries. They co-operate more readily and are more prepared to work with people from different sectors.

The main reason for this – as most Israelis will tell you – is that before people join the world of work, all who are not exempt for religious reasons have to serve in the military for at least two years. As Dan Senor, who has written extensively about Israel's success, puts it: 'While students in other countries are preoccupied with deciding which college to attend, Israel's are weighing the merits of different military units.'[40] Here they're thrown together with others of a similar age but – often – from very different backgrounds. They have to learn to get on with each other, to co-operate, to achieve particular demanding tasks, and work together as an effective team. 'Nobody tells you exactly what to do,' explained Dor Skuler, who went on to set up Intuition Robotics after he left the army. 'They tell you: "This is the problem, go figure it out." With a crazy deadline. So you're inventing, being entrepreneurial and only understanding what you were doing after the fact. But you have to do it, because you don't have any other choice to meet the mission you were given.[41]

Not just that. During their years of military service, Israelis build up a network of contacts that they can then draw on long after they move back into civilian life. 'The whole country is one degree of separation,' explained Yossi Vardi, an entrepreneur and investor who has helped set up more than eighty companies over the past forty years. 'The social graph is very simple here. Everybody knows everybody; everybody was serving in the army with the brother of everybody; the mother of everybody was the teacher in their school; the uncle was the commander of somebody else's unit. Nobody can hide.[42] Such connections that are made are then rekindled and strengthened via periodic service in the 'reserve forces' after the main period of conscription has come to an end.

This networked route to success is very much how Waze – one of Israel's most successful start-ups – got going.[43] It originated as a community project set up in 2006 by a computer science and philosophy student who wanted to create the first Hebrew road map of Israel. Two years later, at a social event in Tel Aviv, they happened to meet an Israeli entrepreneur – through a friend of a friend – who pointed out that, as the software they had developed gathers real-time information about traffic flow and accidents from its users, it could be used to serve the road-using public more generally, by guiding people around the whole of Israel. Two years later – after another chance encounter, this time with a US investor – the company decided to open an office in America and start making maps that covered US states. And then – after another chance encounter seven years after its initial set-up – Waze was bought by Google for a billion dollars. It is now used by governments and motorists all over the world to analyse traffic flows, plan routes and deploy emergency services.[44]

This journey to global success was not a linear one. It consisted of a series of movements and bumps, over a number of years, involving a number of sectors, communities and disciplines. In essence, it was an idea dreamt up by an Israeli scientist and philosopher, that was brought to life by a community of Hebrew speakers, that was then made into a company by an Israeli entrepreneur, and that was then scaled by a US investor before being bought by a global technology giant. Its success was not preset; it was networked. Interestingly, even after the Google buyout, Waze opted to keep its R&D team in Israel. Its rationale was that Israel was where its network was, and so was where future networked innovation was 'more likely to happen'.[45]

It's a very similar picture to one of the inventions that made 3M such a global power in the last decades of the twentieth century, before the arrival of Jim McNerney: the Post-it Note. Essentially, that came about by accident. Back in 1968, Dr Spencer Silver, a chemist at 3M researching powerful glues, accidentally came up with a very weak one. He knew at once that it was something different and something new. He just wasn't sure what application it could possibly have in the wider world. Nevertheless, he became obsessed with it, endlessly talking about it to friends and co-workers. 'I became known as Mr Persistent,' he later recalled, 'because I wouldn't give up.[46]

Six years later, a colleague, Art Fry, faced with the problem of a bookmark that fell out of his hymn book when he was singing in church, tried Silver's invention after hearing about it in one of his seminars. Not only did the glue stop the bookmark slipping, but it was weak enough that the bookmark could be moved around the book without damaging the pages. Hymn book markers, however, were scarcely a market, nor was the Press 'n Peel product that 3M launched in 1977. It was only after another three years of development, and countless conversations with a whole array of people, that Silver finally came up with the Post-it Note.

A decade later it was a billion-dollar business.

As George Buckley said: 'Invention is by its very nature a disorderly process. You can't put a Six Sigma process into that area and say, well, I'm getting behind on invention, so I'm going to schedule myself for three good ideas on Wednesday and two on Friday. That's not how creativity works.[47]

'The more you hardwire a company on total quality management, [the more] it is going to hurt breakthrough innovation,' said Vijay Govindarajan, a professor of innovation at Dartmouth's Tuck School of Business. 'The mindset that is needed, the capabilities that are needed, the metrics that are needed, the whole culture that is needed for disruptive innovation, are fundamentally different.[48]

Innovation, in other words, cannot be precisely engineered. But the environment in which it takes root can certainly be nurtured.

5.

It cannot, however, be an overnight process. Creating the right culture takes time, and also requires a mindset that people obsessed with process often find difficult to adopt.

The best starting point, arguably, is to seek to identify the different natures of the people who serve the organisation. Who are the disruptive experts who move things forward? Who are the stable stewards who keep things on track? What precisely do individual members of staff do? Do they develop new customers or suppliers, processes or products, talents or technologies, practices or policies? Are they by nature doers or thinkers, practical or theoretical, logical or empathetic, planned or spontaneous? Do they buy or sell, serve or shape, make or measure, learn or teach?

Once individuals have been characterised in this way, then the next step is to find people they might be paired with who embody their opposite in some way. They might have a similar purpose, but a different personality or perspective. They might have a similar personality, but a different purpose or perspective. Or they might have a similar perspective, but a different purpose or personality.

British Cycling, for example, put its engineers together with its psychologists. What they had in common was their personalities (both groups tend to be logical and planned). Where they differed was in their purpose (engineers develop new technologies and policies, while psychologists develop new talent and practices) and in their perspectives (engineers make, psychologists measure). In much the same way,

Nasa put its engineers and meteorologists together, as both have similar personalities (logical and planned), but different purposes (engineers develop new products and practices, meteorologists develop new processes and policies) and different perspectives (engineers make, meteorologists measure). Meanwhile, the Royal College of Art put its fashion and architecture students together, as they have a similar purpose (both develop new products for new customers) and similar perspective (both make things), but different personalities (people in fashion tend to be more empathetic and spontaneous, architects more logical and planned).

It goes without saying that this cannot be an exact science. No individual can be wholly compartmentalised; no two members of any group are entirely alike. The trick, therefore, is to look for generalities, not specifics; to find people who have some commonalities, but some differences too, and bring them together. Nor will the process happen overnight. It's taken years for the Centennials to develop these approaches and embed them into their organisations – and even they sometimes take a wrong path too. So, if something isn't working, try a different approach. Alter pairings. Mix things up. Expect trial, error and random events. This is all part of the culture that you're creating, and you need to lead by example.

6.

Identifying contrasting people and placing them together is just the start. After all, there's no guarantee that simply putting different groups together will encourage them to work together. You need to encourage them to collaborate by tapping into their daily rituals and routines. Moving meeting rooms – or just the coffee machine – so that they sit at the centre of the workplace may do the trick. It's also worth considering replacing smaller tables in the café with larger, more communal ones, or offering free food and drink in communal spaces at set times on set days, or having a 'no eating at your desk' policy to encourage people to spend downtime together, or clearing corridors so it's easier for people to stop and chat, or ensuring that there's just one entrance to each building so that staff are more likely to bump into each other.[49]

If there's one place that fully embodies this approach it's Pixar's head office in California, which Steve Jobs redesigned in 1999 and which became known as 'Steve's movie'. Jobs worked closely with Pixar over a number of years, both before and after his reappointment at Apple in late 1996; and while Pixar was careful to keep him at arm's length when it came to the daily running of its business, it was keen to tap into his imagination and insights for the redesign of the company's offices. Jobs played around with different ideas. He considered putting Pixar's creatives, engineers and executives in three separate buildings. He wondered whether it might be an idea to give each film in development a dedicated building. Eventually, though, inspired by a visit to Lockheed Martin's top-secret Skunk Works division that designs jet fighters and spy planes, he decided that everyone should work together, all the time, in one building. 'There's a temptation in our networked age to think that ideas can be developed by email and iChat,' Jobs said. 'That's crazy. Creativity comes from spontaneous meetings, from random discussions. You run into someone, you ask them what they're doing, you say "Wow", and soon you're cooking up all sorts of ideas.'[50]

Today, as in Jobs' day, Pixar creatives sit on one side, engineers on another, executives occupy the second floor and – in the middle of the building, drawing everyone together – is a vast atrium that can accommodate all 1,000 staff. The dynamic hub of the building, it's complete with a reception area, bathrooms, cafés, cinemas, gym, post room, games, sofas, tables and chairs. 'The atrium initially might seem like a waste of space,' said Brad Bird, who directed *The Incredibles* and *Ratatouille*. 'But Steve realised that when people run into each other, when they make eye contact, things happen.'[51] Ed Catmull, Pixar's former president, described how the 'cross-traffic' the atrium created 'meant a better flow of communication and increased the possibility of chance encounters'. 'You felt the energy in the building,' he said.[52] The Pixar approach may not be practicable for everyone. But the principles that lie behind it certainly are.

Bringing people together is not a process with a clearly defined end-point. It has to be dynamic and ongoing. Individuals need to be continually encouraged to work on different ideas and different projects – hence the reason why British Cycling swaps round its scientists for each new Olympic cycle, the Royal Shakespeare Company changes its line-up of creatives for each new production, Nasa asks its engineers to review programmes that they are not directly involved with, and the Royal Academy of Music gets its tutors to assess programmes they don't teach. According to Timothy Jones, deputy principal at the Royal Academy of Music: 'We try to create a culture of questions – catalytic questions that knock down doors, find new paths, and create something new. We see the answers to these questions as stepping stones to the next set of questions. You're always examining and questioning what you do, and how you do it, so you're continually improving, and constantly evolving.'[53]

Again, Pixar offers a useful model here. Four years after it finished its first film, *Toy Story*, and while its head office was being redesigned, Pixar set up the 'Braintrust' – comprising a team of twelve directors and writers – to help anyone who gets stuck with some aspect of the film that they are working on. Crucially, the Braintrust doesn't seek to come up with or impose any answers: it's not a managerial tool or a quick-fix operation. It's there to open up a director's perspective and consider solutions they might not previously have thought of, by asking them a series of questions that tease out different ideas and angles. It opens their minds, allowing them the space to think of solutions.

In his book *Creativity, Inc.*, Catmull explained the Braintrust's philosophy. 'You may be thinking: How is the Braintrust different from any other feedback mechanism? There are two key differences, as I see it. First, it is that the Braintrust is made up of people with a deep understanding of storytelling and, usually, people who have been through the process themselves. While the directors welcome critiques from many sources along the way (and in fact, when our films are screened in-house, all Pixar employees are asked to send notes), they particularly prize feedback from fellow directors and storytellers.'[54]

'The second difference', he continued, 'is that the Braintrust has no authority. This is crucial. The director does not have to follow any of the specific suggestions given. After a Braintrust meeting, it is up to him or her to figure out how to address the feedback. Braintrust meetings are not top-down, do-this-or-else affairs. By removing from the Braintrust the power to mandate solutions, we affect the dynamics of the group in ways I believe are essential.'[55]

The Braintrust was there to help when films such as *Finding Nemo*, *The Incredibles* and *Inside Out* got stuck. When Catmull took over Disney Animation in 2006, the Storytrust he instituted was there to help with films such as *Tangled*, *Frozen* and *The Lion King*. The success of all those films is testament to the power of truly innovative thinking.

The Braintrust is a clever 'organised' solution to the challenge of getting disparate people together to offer fresh perspectives and inspire new approaches. And, to that extent, it is relatively easy to emulate: any organisation can set up teams drawn from different departments to advise and encourage. But for an organisation to bake a truly innovatory mindset into its DNA it needs to go further. A conventional enterprise that sets up braintrust sessions may well see them degenerate quickly into being just another set of meetings. Only one that has a culture of encouraging disparate people to get together and swap ideas will truly benefit from what a braintrust can achieve.

7.

In summary, Centennials create a 'bumpy' culture where people find new things to do and new ways to do them by:

> Getting people to sit next to those who are unlike them – who have different purposes, personalities or perspectives

> Getting people to work simultaneously on at least two (normally three) different projects, in at least two (normally three) different teams

Asking outsiders to help review a project's impact and progress on a monthly basis

Changing the teams that people work in on a regular basis, at the beginning of each new project

Strategically placing cafés and meeting rooms in central areas, so that people are more likely to hang out together and benefit from chance encounters accordingly.

Habit 12

BREAK BREAD

Quality time is the best time

1.

Why are soldiers prepared to put themselves in danger? Why do they unhesitatingly accept orders that could lead to them being severely injured or even killed? Is it simply that they are, by nature, more devoted to a particular cause or country than others? Or is it something else?

These were the questions that four researchers – one academic and three soldiers – asked themselves back in 2003, as the US and its Western allies launched a full-scale attack on Iraq in a bid to topple the country's leader, Saddam Hussein.[1] While some 200,000 troops poured into the country and engaged in fierce combat over the following six weeks, the researchers put cameras on dozens of soldiers' helmets so that they could follow them wherever they went, observe their interactions with each other, and gain an understanding of day-to-day life on the front line. Later, they conducted intensive interviews with each of the soldiers so that they could better understand what they did and why. To get a different perspective, they also spoke to captured Iraqi prisoners.

Their findings were unequivocal. Soldiers, they discovered, don't fight for a leader, or a campaign, or even an individual mission. They may want to know why they are fighting and what that fighting will achieve. They certainly need to feel that they can trust the people who have sent them into battle. But at the critical moment, when they go into battle and their guns are blazing, they actually fight not for a cause but for each other – for their comrades. As one combatant in the Iraq conflict put it: 'We weren't fighting for anybody else but ourselves. We weren't fighting for some higher-up who is somebody; we were just fighting for each other.'[2] 'If he holds my back,' said another, 'then I will hold his, and nothing is going to go wrong.'[3]

Such a powerful sense of camaraderie is not the by-product of training or conflict. It's the direct outcome of the hours that soldiers spend in each other's company. Numerous soldiers in the study attested to the power of a growing sense of companionship on their behaviour and attitudes. 'In a fighting hole with somebody for so many hours, you get to know them real good because there is nothing else to talk about,' one said. 'You become real good friends.'[4] 'You are sitting in the dirt, scanning back and forth for hours,' said another, '[and] the only person you got to talk to for me is him, which is on my left right here, about eighteen inches away, sitting shoulder to shoulder. After about a month or so in the dirt like that together, you start talking about family. You start talking about everything . . . family, friends, what is going on, and your life in general pretty much, what is not right at home. Everything.'[5] According to a third soldier: 'We are together every day for the majority of the day, five days a week. You are going to start knowing what ticks people off, what makes them happy, what you need to do to work with them. Eventually a bond is going to form.'[6]

To explain this burgeoning relationship, many soldiers reached for the word 'family'. In the words of one soldier: 'It is just like a big family. Nothing can come to you without going through them first. It is kind of comforting.'[7] 'Everyone here becomes your family,' another reported. 'With my wife, for the first couple years of being with her, I had to learn to live with her – her routine in the morning and how my routine fits in with that, who uses the bathroom first and what have you. It is the same thing with a bunch of Joes walking around. You learn everybody's personality – who is grumpy in the morning, who is grumpy at night, and who is grumpy when they miss chow and let them up in front of you. It is pretty much the same deal.'[8] Another soldier concurred: 'We eat, drink, [go to the bathroom], everything – together. I think that it should be like that . . . I really consider these guys my own family, because we fight together, we have fun together . . . We are to the point where we even call the squad leader "Dad".'[9]

Friendships forged, regular routines, the constant expression of likes and dislikes, hopes and fears, bring each fighting unit together. Once they're a family, they will do anything for each other – and be prepared to risk their life in the process. Numerous soldiers in the study attested to this: 'You have got to trust them more than your mother, your father, or girlfriend, or your wife, or anybody,' said one. 'It becomes almost like your guardian angel.'[10] Another described the power of the friendship he developed with a fellow soldier named Taylor. 'I knew Taylor would personally look out for me. It was stupid little things like, "Dude, you look like you need a hug." He would come over and give me a big old bear hug. He knew that I looked out for him and vice versa . . . Knowing that there is somebody watching when I didn't have the opportunity to watch myself when I am driving – Taylor watched everywhere. When I am driving down the road, I have to watch in front of me knowing where I am driving and knowing that I am not going to drive over anything. I don't know what is behind me. I don't know what is to my side. I trusted Taylor was going to keep an eye on everything. He always did. Obviously, he did. We are still here. Thank God.'[11]

2.

Military families may represent an extreme in the way in which close professional relationships are forged, but the fundamental principle they embody applies universally – to everyone from manufacturers to service companies, and from cultural organisations to sports teams. Those that encourage a sense of family and kinship invariably thrive. Their staff are happier. They suffer less stress. They are more creative.[12] A meta-analysis of 120 previous studies found that when people feel that they are part of a family they become more committed, involved and motivated to do their work and that the performance of their team generally improves by almost 15 per cent.[13] Those organisations that fail to nurture a familial culture invariably pay the price, sooner or later.

It's tempting to ascribe the influence of an almost military sense of family to the extraordinary performance of Liverpool Football Club in the 1960s and 1970s. The manager, Bill Shankly, had served in the armed forces: he had been a corporal in the Royal Air Force during the Second World War. He had therefore experienced for himself what the building of a close sense of kinship could achieve. Looking back on his time with the RAF, Shankly recalled: 'All the time I was preparing myself for the day when I would become a football manager. I also knew I could be a leader. I had confidence in my ability. I had not been sleeping. I had been working for the future.'[14]

At Liverpool he would spend hours each day chatting to coaches and other staff, thrashing out problems, debating ideas and strategies. The tiny 'Boot Room' near the changing rooms at the club's Anfield ground – where many of these discussions took place – became a symbol of the culture Shankly sought to develop. According to Bob Paisley, Shankly's first-team trainer who managed the team after he left in 1974: 'It started initially with Joe [Fagan] and I as a place to have a drink with visiting managers and backroom staff. We tried to win every game but, no matter how hard the match was, we liked to relax afterwards and have a drink with the opposition. Just talking about the game is a most interesting aspect of football.'

'On Sunday mornings,' Paisley continued, 'we'd go [back] in [to the Boot Room] and talk about the Saturday game. There were differing opinions and disagreements and everyone put their oar in. But it was all done in the right manner. We liked everyone to air their views and you probably got a more wide-ranging discussion in the Boot Room than you would get in the boardroom. But nothing spilled out of there. What went on was within those four walls. There was a certain mystique about the place, which I also believe there should be about the dressing room. What's said in there should, by and large, be private, too.'[15]

This sense of family intimacy was enhanced by other new practices too. Paisley suggested introducing a forty-minute cooling-down period after each training session and before the players had a bath. At a practical level, this was a good way to ensure players' skin pores had time to close before they washed, so that they were less likely to catch a cold or strain a muscle. But it also ensured that the players spent more time together socially. Meanwhile, the team's reserves' coach, Joe Fagan, proposed that players should meet at their home ground (Anfield) and then travel together on a bus to and from their training ground (Melwood) each day. At a stroke the time they hung out together tripled, from one to three hours a day. Simultaneously, Liverpool developed a fluid, collaborative way of playing that secured for them first the Second Division championship in 1962, and then thirteen First Division titles in the twenty-eight years after that.

But then Graeme Souness, the club's former captain, arrived as manager in 1991, and everything changed. The Boot Room went to make space for a press office (not Souness's decision, he later said). Players stopped meeting at Anfield before they travelled on a bus together to and from Melwood to train (to save time, the new management argued). In short, the team and its coaches stopped hanging out together.

Their performance suffered. They finished sixth in the league in 1992, their worst performance in twenty-seven years. They had won the league thirteen times in twenty-six years. They wouldn't win it again for a quarter of a century.

In 2015, Jürgen Klopp took over as manager. An experienced player (fourteen years) and coach (fourteen years), the German had learnt how important relationships are if a team wants to win. 'All that we do in life,' he explained, 'how I understand it – is about relationships. Otherwise, if you only want to be responsible for the things you do and not anyone else, then live in a forest alone or on a mountain alone.'[16] Klopp was a family man, too, who became a father when he was just twenty years old. 'It was not perfect timing, let's be honest,' he recalled. 'I was playing amateur football and going to the university during the day. To pay for school, I was working in a warehouse where they stored movies for the cinema . . . I would sleep for five hours every night, go to the warehouse in the morning, and then go to class during the day. At night I would go to training, and then I'd come home and try to spend some time with my son. It was a very difficult time. But it taught me about real life.'[17] 'I was a very young father, and wasn't prepared,' he added, 'but it gave me the opportunity to handle younger people than myself. I still have that understanding, and can give the players my experiences. It's like a father role.'[18]

When Klopp arrived at Liverpool, he started to reinstate many of the rituals and values that had been lost since the Shankly era. He even reconstituted the Boot Room in the expanded stadium that was opened the year after he joined. 'When I arrived at Liverpool,' he said, 'and went first time to the stadium, they showed me the dressing room – which was not very impressive . . . [and then] went down a floor and told me, "OK, this is your little Boot Room." "What is that?" [I asked]. So they explained it to me and it was really nice, like a little pub in the stadium, only for the manager and stuff like this. And I liked it a lot. So, in the new stand . . . we did our own Boot Room. It was pretty much Ulla, my wife, [who] was responsible for the furniture, how it looks. For me, it's the best pub in Liverpool. After a game, we love going there with all my staff – with all my friends . . . and their families. And it's great. We don't have that in Germany. We go in a pub you go [to] after the game. You have maybe a corner in the public 'VIP' area – which is quite intense when you have to talk to all the people after a game, when you have not a lot of words anymore. It's better that you are together with the people you know already. And that's . . . our safe place, I would say . . . That's my Boot Room.'[19]

The team started hanging out and bonding and learning again. Three years later, in 2019, they won their first English league title in thirty years. Mark Lawrenson, a former Liverpool player and now a commentator, described the transformation that the new manager brought about. 'When Jürgen Klopp came to the football club, you . . . felt this sea change. And within months, you just knew that this was something completely different . . . I hate that thing where a player comes through – and he's small and he's Argentinian – and they say: "He's the next Lionel Messi." He's not, he's just him. So Klopp came and everyone went: "He's the next Shankly." Do you know what? He's been Shankly-esque in everything that he's done . . . all the players he's got, he's made them, all of them, better. Every single one.'[20] Pepijn Lijnders, Klopp's assistant manager, described how 'Jürgen creates a family. We always say: 30 per cent tactic, 70 per cent team-building.'[21] Goalkeeper Alisson Becker praised 'the way he makes the team feel comfortable and at the same time puts pressure on us'. 'He's a guy', said Becker, 'who is always happy, but when you go on to the pitch it's hard work, serious work and he's a top manager, so all those things contribute to a good relationship. I really love to be here and working with him. I love my life here at Liverpool.'[22]

3.

It should come as no surprise that engendering a sense of family is key to all of the Centennials. Take British Cycling. Its athletes train together the whole time. But on top of that, four times a year, the squad – its cyclists, coaches, nutritionists, psychologists and physiotherapists – all go away together for five days. During that period, they hang out with one another, endlessly discussing, experimenting, training and strategising in accordance with an intensive daily calendar:

06.00   Get up, wash, get dressed.

06.30   Eat breakfast together as prepared by the nutritionists – usually some combination of cereal, porridge and eggs.

08.00   Endurance training, with the coaches and the psychologists, consisting of a twenty-minute warm-up, followed by four twenty-minute racing sessions against a motorbike, with five-minute breaks to recuperate and rehydrate.

10.00   One-hour session with the team physiotherapist, to rest, recover, stretch, warm down, and conduct physical checks.

11.00   Review of morning's activities, with other athletes, coaches and psychologists.

12.00   Lunch, usually some combination of chicken, ham, quinoa and rice.

14.00   Speed training with the coaches and the psychologists, consisting of a twenty-minute warm-up, followed by eight five-minute sessions, working individually, in pairs and in teams, with twenty-minute breaks to recuperate and rehydrate.

17.00   One-hour session with the physiotherapist, to warm down from the day.

18.00   Review of the afternoon's activities, with the coaches and psychologists.

19.00   Dinner, usually a combination of chicken, couscous, pasta and risotto.

21.00   Relax and hang out with the other athletes.

22.00   Retire to bed.

Superficially, it's the lengthy training sessions that stand out here. But as the performance director points out, these are similar in terms of length and toughness to those undertaken in any ordinary week. What makes the transformative impact is the time people spend simply hanging out together – while they're getting ready in the morning, at mealtimes, during the regular reviews, and while they're enjoying downtime. Seven-time Olympic gold medal winner Jason Kenny has described how it was only through such periods of downtime that he really got to know Chris Hoy (six gold medals).[23] Victoria Pendleton (two gold medals) has talked about the difference that being in the living room with other athletes makes at times when she would otherwise be on her own 'in a small box, feeling lost and alone'.[24] Laura Kenny (five Olympic gold medals) has explained how eating and relaxing together allows athletes to talk through any anxieties and issues that they might be experiencing.[25] According to Dan Hunt, the endurance head coach: 'There is a physical element and a teamship one. They are going through things together, helping each other. The gold medal will be won by guys who do this, who have unity . . . [And] twenty-four hours before the race, these are the sessions you remind them about.'[26]

It might be tempting to assume that if British Cycling were in each other's company for even longer, they would do that much better. But it doesn't quite work that way. Members of the team need time away between each session, so that they have the opportunity to absorb any new ideas that come up, play with them and see whether they work. (This is, incidentally, the reason why new initiatives are not attempted in the six-month lead-up to major competitions: at such a time people need to master what they know, not attempt something new.) The bonds that time away together builds, however, are unquestionably powerful. 'People always ask me, what can I learn from cycling?' Peter Keen, the team's former performance director, said to me. 'And I tell them, take your team away for a week and live together, like a family. That's when our biggest shifts always happened.'[27]

The results of such a strategy for British Cycling speak for themselves. The team have won twice as many medals – and five times as many gold medals – as any other country in the last three Olympics.

4.

For many, the prospect of going away with colleagues for extended periods may seem the stuff of nightmares. But bonding also happens over much shorter time spans too. It occurs during the five-minute break between each All Blacks training session. It takes place during the ten-minute interval between each class at Eton, and during the quarter of an hour between meetings that Nasa allows. Above all, it takes root over a lunch or a dinner. At such times, when people are unwinding and relaxing, they can enjoy free-flowing, unplanned conversations with friends and colleagues, exploring new ideas, forming new friendships, and building those bonds that become so important when they need to perform later on – under pressure. 'My best ideas always come when I'm eating or drinking with someone,' a tutor at the Royal College of Art told me. 'Sometimes I eat with people from my programme to review the morning and plan the afternoon. But normally, I try to eat with people from other programmes, to get to know them, and see what I can learn from them.'[28]

'I work with my colleagues every day, so why do I need to eat with them too?' is a common refrain. It is, however, a misguided view. Research led by Professor Robin Dunbar, an anthropologist and psychologist at Oxford University, shows that there is a sound scientific reason why eating together should have such a powerful bonding effect. Back in 2016 he teamed up with a project called the Big Lunch – which encourages people from different communities to get together to eat, drink and chat – so that he could establish precisely what happens when people 'hang out' with others.[29] His findings were unequivocal. 'Those who eat socially more often', Dunbar explains, 'feel happier and are more satisfied with life, are more trusting of others, are more engaged with their local communities, and have more friends they can depend on for support.'[30] His conclusions have been supported by other studies that show that the act of eating together triggers the release of endorphins – hormones that not only help relieve stress, reduce pain and induce an overall sense of wellbeing, but also create a sense of bonding among humans and primates. Dunbar notes that other social activities, such as dancing, drinking, laughing, singing and storytelling, have a very similar effect.[31] When one or more of those activities is combined with eating, the beneficial effects are compounded – hence, Dunbar says, the reason why evening meals often prove so successful. 'Our most important social activities happen in the evening,' he claims. 'Doing these things at night seems to have an added "magic".'[32]

As striking as the positives are the negatives that flow from not eating together. It's been shown, for example, that children who don't eat regularly with their parents are more likely to suffer from depression, to skip school and to take drugs.[33] Shannon Robson, a nutritionist at Delaware University, reviewed more than a thousand studies on the subject. 'Family meals', she says, 'have been positively associated with healthy eating behaviours, improved dietary quality, psychosocial outcomes, and reduced engagement in high-risk behaviours. [They] play a protective role for children and are often recommended for health promotion.'[34]

Some researchers have gone so far as to say that there is a correlation in the US between the decline in meals taken together (it's estimated that a fifth of all meals, for example, are now consumed in the car) and the rise in divorce levels (currently twice the European average – and fifteen times higher than in Mexico, where families regularly eat, dance, sing and hang out together).[35] 'Every meal [in the US] is becoming a solitary affair, even dinner,' Darren Seifer, a food industry expert, explains. 'People are eating alone at home and out [too].'[36] If organisations are like families, it's not difficult to see the implications of such worrying figures and trends for workplaces where people fail to spend sufficient social time together.

One inspirational figure who very much takes the meal culture to heart is Gregg Popovich, the president and head coach of one of the

US's top basketball teams, the San Antonio Spurs. Like Bill Shankly, 'Pop' had military experience, serving five years with the United States Air Force. Like Shankly, he is obsessed with engendering team spirit. 'It's not about any one person,' he says. 'You've got to get over yourself and realise that it takes a group to get this thing done.'[37] He therefore makes sure that Spurs players spend plenty of downtime in each other's company, relaxing, chatting and, above all, eating together. He will book a restaurant and then turn up there an hour early to make sure everything is ready (the right food, the right music, the right ambience) and that he is on hand to greet everyone as they arrive – to shake their hand, thank them for coming, and guide them to their seat. Over the next three hours, he will work the room, chatting and laughing with everyone, from players to coaches to any family who accompanied them. 'The first time I saw it, it took me by surprise,' Chad Forcier, the former Spurs assistant coach, explains. 'It was one of the most amazing displays of leadership I'd ever seen.'[38] Pop even pays attention to how the restaurant is laid out, stipulating that the fifteen players should sit at four tables in the centre, with the team's five coaches distributed as evenly as possible among them and with family members sat around at tables nearby. There should, he says, be no more than six people per table. That way, everyone can hear what is being said; everyone has an opportunity to make a contribution. Occasionally, when Pop wants to increase the level of learning, bonding and team-building he will even organise two back-to-back meals over four hours.

There's nothing performative about this. Pop sees his team as his family, and he treats team members as such. Michael Mina, a chef whose restaurants have won Michelin stars and who has cooked for the Spurs, has described his surprise at how 'gentle' Pop is.[39] Will Perdue, who played for Pop for four years, talks of his ability to see players as 'a human being first and a basketball player second'.[40] Even now, Perdue says, some twenty years after he stopped playing for the Spurs, Pop will greet him warmly when they bump into each other and ask him how he is doing. 'He won't let go of your hand until he gets answers that he feels are genuine and honest.'[41] As Pop himself has said: 'Relationships with people are what it's all about. You have to make players realise you care about them. And they have to care about each other and be interested in each other. Then they start to feel a responsibility towards each other. Then they want to do for each other.[42]

Under Pop's tutelage and watchful eye, the Spurs went from a losing streak that had lasted for twenty years to become five-time NBA champions over the course of the following fifteen years. Eating together wasn't the sole determining factor here, of course. But it was a major one.

5.

As Gregg Popovich's work at the San Antonio Spurs demonstrates, there's rather more to bringing people together than simply ensuring they gather socially on a regular or occasional basis. How they gather is also crucial – in particular, the size of the groups they form. Research over the past twenty years has proved the wisdom of Pop's instinct to keep group sizes small. The ideal number for a spontaneous, interactive discussion, it has been shown, is somewhere between three and five (it's no coincidence that this is the size of the average family – and of most primate social groups).[43] Six or seven is fine, though there is a risk that any discussion that takes place won't have quite the focus or quality to be found in a smaller gathering. Once ten is reached, conversations tend to break down: there's simply too much noise; people start feeling left out; subgroups form or one person dominates.[44] Nicolas Fay, a psychologist at Western Australia University who studied how 150 undergraduate students interacted with each other, concluded: 'In small, five-person groups the communication is like dialogue and members are influenced most by those with whom they interact in the discussion. However, in large, ten-person groups, the communication is like monologue and members are influenced most by the dominant speaker.'[45] In other words, groups of 'seven plus or minus two', as the psychologist George Miller famously put it – although he was talking about the number of things people can remember, rather than group size.[46]

That's why the Centennials are so careful to keep the numbers down in any setting where personal interactions are key. Eton, typically, puts no more than five to seven pupils together in a tutorial. Seminars at the Royal Academy of Music, again, involve five to seven students. The same principle holds for crew members on a Nasa mission. Other high-performing organisations adopt a similar philosophy: a Facebook group comprises three to five engineers; a McKinsey team four to six consultants; a US Navy squad four to six personnel.

There's a practical, physical aspect to all this. Ideally, for a fruitful conversation to take place, individuals need to be somewhere between sixty and ninety centimetres away (two to three feet) from each other: far enough away that they don't feel crowded; close enough that they can really hear one another. Robert Sommer, a psychologist at the University of California, Davis, who studied how people sat at tables in a hospital café, found that when the distance across the table was less than three feet, they would take up seats opposite each other but that when the gap exceeded three and a half feet they would opt to sit side by side.[47] That's why the typical café table is so ideally suited for the social environment it's there to serve: it's typically between sixty and ninety centimetres across. And, given the relaxed nature of cafés and the fact that they serve a strong mental stimulant – coffee – that's why they have historically proved such popular places to hang out. In the Arab world they were once known as 'schools of wisdom'. In London they were described as 'penny universities'. Their convivial set-up and eagerness to provide coffee made them bastions of free thinking and free speech – hence the reason why national rulers from Stuart kings to Turkish sultans sought at one time or another to ban them.[48] Forward-thinking modern organisations recognise their benefits too – hence, in turn, the reason why Apple has seven large cafés, Facebook has one 'epic café' and Google has 170 small cafés.

6.

Of course, providing social spaces is one thing. Getting people to use them is another. Studies suggest that, far from hanging out together at work, as many as four out of five people eat lunch by themselves at their desks. And the trend is getting worse.[49] An understandable sense of time and work pressure is responsible for this. But while working through the day in this way may seem a sensibly practical approach, the fact is that, in the medium and long term, it's counterproductive. High-functioning teams need downtime to hang out together.

US firefighters, for example, invariably eat together every day. They often cook for each other too. Studies have shown that on the rare occasions they don't or can't, their performance inevitably dips. The less frequently they eat together, the deeper the dip.[50] Ken Kniffin, who oversaw the study of more than 400 fire stations that made this finding, showed that the high-performing stations made a point of being inclusive; even if people didn't like the same food, they still ate together. He described, for example, 'one vegetarian firefighter, with decades of service, who did not eat the same foods as others at meals during his regular shifts but [still] made it a practice to eat his brown bag meals at the same time and place as the rest of the crew and contributed to kitchen cleaning just as most firefighters who do not cook are expected to do'.[51]

For their part, companies as varied at Burberry and Facebook, Google and Pret A Manger, all provide free hot and cold meals in their cafés each day. The Centennials invariably ensure that their (centrally located) cafés offer constant cheap, good food and drink, and provide the space in people's daily calendars to enable them to make best use of what is on offer. When time is tight, some organisations combine work with relaxation. Just as the San Antonio Spurs review games over dinner, so at Pixar they review films over lunch.[52]

Research from Google undertaken in 2012 offers a window on the elements that go to make such occasions so powerfully effective.[53] Project Aristotle set out to examine every aspect of the members of each of Google's teams – their education, gender, hobbies, personalities and skills – along with the challenge, complexity and duration of the project they happened to be working on at any given time to establish what factors shaped successful teams. It concluded that individual ability and the nature of the task involved were surprisingly unimportant. What mattered was the nature of the social bonds that teams formed. Those who regularly ate lunch and dinner together to the point where they were happy to talk about their personal lives, successes and failures, worries and concerns, achieved a level of 'psychological safety' that brought with it optimum team performance. They took time to get to know each other. They bothered to find out how each felt and what they were up to. They didn't talk over each other; they gave everyone a chance to contribute. As a result, they didn't fall into the trap of seeking answers before they had explored the question. They became more collaborative. In some teams, the social code that members followed took the form of 'unwritten rules' that weren't openly discussed but could easily be observed. In others, they were 'defined behaviours' and 'established rules' that had been consciously developed over time. Either way, they helped people open up, so deepening the debate and broadening the discussion.

'The biggest thing that you should take away from this work,' explains Laszlo Bock, Google's head of people operations at the time, 'is that how teams work matters, in a lot of ways, more than who is on them. There's a myth we all carry inside our head. We think we all need superstars. But that's not what the research found. You can take a team of average performers, and if you teach them to interact in the right way, they'll do things no superstar could ever accomplish.'[54] In a very Google way the company even designed a checklist to help people run their meetings better: 1) Don't interrupt your teammates; 2) Summarise what people are saying to show you're listening; 3) Say when you 'don't know'; 4) Don't end a meeting before everyone has spoken; 5) Encourage people to share their frustrations with the team; 6) Call out conflict when you see it, and try to resolve it through open discussion within the team.[55]

All this is possible when a team has truly bonded.

7.

In summary, the Centennials bond – and learn – like a family by:

Having a large, central area in all of their sites, where people can come together to eat, drink and hang out

Serving high-quality cheap – or free – food and drink, at set times on set days, in these central areas

Spending at least an hour together each day, eating, drinking and hanging out

Talking openly and honestly with each other, and making sure everyone has the chance to talk, and is properly listened to, when they meet

Spending time together outside work, every two to three months, often with families in tow, in order to get to know each other better.

Conclusion

PROTECT YOUR HOME

When unsure, go back to the core

1.

If there's one central, overriding lesson that the Centennials teach us, it's that lasting success comes from maintaining an organisation's core culture while also driving change at the edge. It's a delicate balancing act, and one that so many institutions fail to acknowledge or achieve. Most fall all too easily into one camp or the other. Either they seek to build a future by solely living on past successes. Or they throw away what has made them successful in the first place and try to make a dash for the new and untested.

How, then, do you ensure that you have got the balance right? That you are what might be termed 'radically traditional'?

A good starting point is to ask yourself one central question for each of the twelve Centennial approaches I have outlined in this book.

Stable purpose
Q1. Do we positively shape society's beliefs and behaviours?
Q2. Do we engage and develop the next generation of talent?

Stable stewardship

Q3. Do we have the right stewards in place, to keep us on track?

Q4. Do we carefully manage stewardship handovers so we always stay on track?

Stable openness

Q5. Do we perform in public, to encourage everyone to perform at their best?

Q6. Do we share our stories, so others trust us and want to work with us?

Disruptive experts

Q7. Do we find brilliant people, and ask them to work with us part-time?

Q8. Do we recruit and retain the world's best talent?

Disruptive nervousness

Q9. Do we always focus on getting better, not bigger?

Q10. Do we constantly x-ray everything we do?

Disruptive accidents

Q11. Do we encourage chance encounters?

Q12. Do we eat, drink and hang out together?

Few, if any, organisations can answer 'yes' to all twelve questions. What is important is that there should be a balance of positives between stability and disruption. If you have a large number on the stability side and few in the disruptive camp, then the chances are that you are not moving forward. A large number in the disruptive camp and few on the stability side and you're in danger of veering off track.

2.

It's also vitally important that if a problem or crisis arises, you look to your stable core first and then to your disruptive edge – not the other way round. When discussing stable stewards (Habit 3) I described how the All Blacks responded to their defeat in the quarter-final of the Rugby World Cup in 2007. Faced with the choice of disruption ('fire the head coach and find someone else') or stability ('keep the head coach but analyse what went wrong'), they went for the second option. The head coach, Graham Henry, was invited to submit a report outlining why, in his view, things had not worked out better. A panel of eight experienced people (both from within New Zealand Rugby and from outside) were similarly tasked. Two months later, when all the evidence was in, Henry and four other coaches were asked to give a presentation to the expert panel explaining why they thought they should remain in post to coach the team at the next World Cup. The panel concluded – in the face of enormous pressure from fans and media alike – that the All Blacks should retain their head coach.[1]

This was not a case of simply burying their heads in the sand. The process was a very considered one, taking in more or less all the habits I have outlined above. First the senior team clarified their purpose: to win the next World Cup and make New Zealand proud. Next they stabilised their stewardship: by deciding to keep the head coach in place, while simultaneously opening themselves up: by inviting him to tell them what he thought should be done. The head coach in turn clarified his purpose, confirmed the values (such as the 'no dickheads' policy) that had been instilled over the previous few years, and stabilised the stewards who served him both by keeping his core coaching team in place and appointing a player leadership team (all of whom would go on to play in future World Cups).[2]

'We're very sorry that we couldn't bring that cup home to New Zealand,' Henry told the New Zealand people at his first press conference after he was reappointed. 'But I'm grateful to be given another chance. We have learnt lessons from this campaign, and we now look forward to being able to build on those learnings, and the experience we have.'[3]

He went on to explain how the loss against France still hurt. But he promised he'd do everything in his power to prevent such an occurrence in the future. He also opened the team up to outside scrutiny, inviting a journalist to come in to study the team for five weeks and then write a book – *Legacy* – about them.[4]

Once the core was stable, the All Blacks turned to their disruptive edge. Forty new players were brought in over the next four years, all of whom were rotated in and out of different positions in order to shake things up and move them forward.[5] Outside experts were invited in to help their players think better (a criminal psychologist), tackle better (cage fighters), lift better (ballet dancers) and lead better (the Marines). The team also spent more time in each other's company, eating, drinking and living together like a family.[6]

By the time the next World Cup came round, the All Blacks were ready for it.

Core first, edge second is a mantra to be found in the other Centennials too. Nasa, for example, didn't fire its CEO – or anyone else – when the Space Shuttle exploded in 2003, but instead undertook a vigorous investigation to find out what precisely had gone wrong and why. It clarified its purpose (to push forward the boundaries of scientific possibility), stabilised its stewardship, and opened itself up to the outside world (via a 400-page report).[7] After that it turned to its disruptive edge, inviting in psychologists to advise on creating a more open workplace culture, providing its staff with a 'stop work' card if they thought something might go wrong, and changing the command structure so that engineers had greater autonomy. This painstaking approach has since paid off handsomely.[8]

Core first, edge second.

Epilogue

CENTENNIAL TRUTHS

Will you stay great?

Having worked with hundreds of organisations over the past decade, I've found that one of the best ways to pinpoint where strengths and weaknesses lie is to complete the following questionnaire, and to invite as many colleagues – and people from outside the organisation – to do so too. Obviously, this can only be a first step, but a study of the results can help change the conversation, refocus people's attention and offer useful pointers for the future.

Remember: there are no 'right' answers here. Different people will come up with different responses. This in itself can be very revealing. If, for example, you find that people inside the organisation and those outside are coming up with very different responses, you know that there is a disconnect between what you believe you are doing and achieving and how the outside world perceives you. At this point the questions to ask become: Why do these different perspectives exist? What can one person see – or believe they see – that another person can't?

Mark each T (for 'Truth') statement that follows from 1 (strongly disagree) to 5 (strongly agree).

Part 1: Stable core

Build your north star		Strongly disagree				Strongly agree
T1.	We know which beliefs and behaviours we want to create in society.	1	2	3	4	5
T2.	We develop these beliefs and behaviours in the people who work with us.	1	2	3	4	5
T3.	Our products and services develop these beliefs and behaviours in the people who use them.	1	2	3	4	5
T4.	People regard the time they work with us as a key moment in their lives.	1	2	3	4	5
T5.	Society has a positive view of the way in which we shape its beliefs and behaviours.	1	2	3	4	5

Do it for the kids' kids		Strongly disagree				Strongly agree
T6.	We know which skills we will need in the future.	1	2	3	4	5
T7.	We look twenty-plus years ahead when seeking to create and attract the future talent we need.	1	2	3	4	5
T8.	We help children acquire the future skills we will need in our organisation.	1	2	3	4	5
T9.	Schools teach children the future skills we will need in our organisation.	1	2	3	4	5
T10.	The most talented and ambitious people want to work with us.	1	2	3	4	5

Have strong roots		Strongly disagree				Strongly agree
T11.	We know where and what the critical knowledge in our organisation is.	1	2	3	4	5
T12.	We know who our critical leaders are who possess this knowledge and have the influence to share it.	1	2	3	4	5
T13.	We keep these critical leaders in role for ten-plus years	1	2	3	4	5
T14.	We have an average seven-plus-year tenure across all our critical leaders.	1	2	3	4	5
T15.	Our critical leaders behave like stewards – more concerned about the organisation they leave behind than how it looks while they're there.	1	2	3	4	5

Mind the gap		Strongly disagree				Strongly agree
T16.	We know what knowledge and experience critical leaders possess, and so have mechanisms in place to pass these on to their successors.	1	2	3	4	5
T17.	When filling critical leadership roles, we promote 80 per cent of our leaders from within.	1	2	3	4	5
T18.	We identify a critical leader's successor four-plus years before that leader steps down.	1	2	3	4	5

T19.	We have a one-plus-year handing-over period to a new critical leader.	1	2	3	4	5
T20.	Previous critical leaders continue offering advice and support for two-plus years after handing over.	1	2	3	4	5

Perform in public		Strongly disagree				Strongly agree
T21.	We know what knowledge and perspectives we lack within our business.	1	2	3	4	5
T22.	We know the people who have that knowledge and those perspectives.	1	2	3	4	5
T23.	We ask these people to watch us in action.	1	2	3	4	5
T24.	We ask these people to challenge and question what we do and how we do it.	1	2	3	4	5
T25.	We use this challenging and questioning to continually improve what we do.	1	2	3	4	5

Give more, get more		Strongly disagree				Strongly agree
T26.	We know what caused our previous successes, failures and recoveries.	1	2	3	4	5
T27.	We share that knowledge with the people who work with us.	1	2	3	4	5
T28.	We ask others to study us and help us share what we have learnt with the world.	1	2	3	4	5
T29.	Most people outside our organisation know what we do and how we do it.	1	2	3	4	5

| T30. | Most people outside our organisation like and trust us. | 1 | 2 | 3 | 4 | 5 |

As a rule, if you scored under 100 out of 150, you need to give more attention to your stable core.

Part 2: Disruptive edge

Be porous		Strongly disagree				Strongly agree
T31.	We know who our critical experts are, and how they help us shape society.	1	2	3	4	5
T32.	We ensure our critical experts work at the cutting edge of their field.	1	2	3	4	5
T33.	Our critical experts work on their own projects 20 per cent of the time.	1	2	3	4	5
T34.	Our critical experts work with people outside our organisation 50 per cent of the time.	1	2	3	4	5
T35.	We continually redefine best practice within and outside our organisation.	1	2	3	4	5

Shake all trees		Strongly disagree				Strongly agree
T36.	We know who is the best in the world at the critical skills we need.	1	2	3	4	5
T37.	We know what the world's best is trying to do, and how they're doing it.	1	2	3	4	5
T38.	We continually share our ideas and practices with the world's best.	1	2	3	4	5

T39.	We have strong relation-ships with 50 per cent of the world's best.	1	2	3	4	5
T40.	Fifty per cent of the world's best work with us.	1	2	3	4	5

Get better, not bigger		Strongly disagree				Strongly agree
T41.	We prioritise getting better over getting bigger.	1	2	3	4	5
T42.	We know how big we need to be to shape soci-ety and be financially stable.	1	2	3	4	5
T43.	We manage ourselves like a small organisation, even though we're big.	1	2	3	4	5
T44.	We have fewer than five levels of management in our organisation.	1	2	3	4	5
T45.	We employ fewer than 300 people per site.	1	2	3	4	5

X-ray everything		Strongly disagree				Strongly agree
T46.	We unpick success and failure so that we can learn how to improve.	1	2	3	4	5
T47.	We scientifically analyse anything that might affect our performance.	1	2	3	4	5
T48.	We codify what works and continually improve what we do, and how we do it.	1	2	3	4	5
T49.	Eighty per cent of our key practices have signifi-cantly improved in the last three years.	1	2	3	4	5

T50.	Forty per cent of last year's revenue came from ideas developed in the last three years.	1	2	3	4	5

Make time for random		Strongly disagree				Strongly agree
T51.	We put people with different ideas and perspectives next to each other.	1	2	3	4	5
T52.	We design our offices so that people have to walk around.	1	2	3	4	5
T53.	We continually change the teams people work in, and who they work with.	1	2	3	4	5
T54.	We ask people to constantly review and question areas outside their core expertise.	1	2	3	4	5
T55.	We notice that people's views and practices change through the challenge they receive.	1	2	3	4	5

Break bread		Strongly disagree				Strongly agree
T56.	We create space and time at work for people to hang out together.	1	2	3	4	5
T57.	We encourage people to eat and drink together every day.	1	2	3	4	5
T58.	We are confident that people hang out together for at least an hour a day.	1	2	3	4	5

T59.	We are confident that people share problems, ideas and opportunities with one another.	1	2	3	4	5
T60.	People tell us that some of their best ideas come from hanging out, and having casual conversations with each other.	1	2	3	4	5

As a rule, if you scored under 100 out of 150, you need to give more attention to your disruptive edge. You also need to compare your score here with the score you arrived at for the first set of questions to make sure that your organisation balances its stable core with its disruptive edge.

Once you think you have identified your strengths and weaknesses it's a good idea to select one strength and one weakness in each of the stable core and disruptive edge categories and study them closely. Since, in my experience, it's easier to build on a strength than fix a weakness, put together an action plan on your strengths first, not least because an easy win here will encourage others to come on board and will reduce the risk of blanket resistance to new ideas. By picking both a traditional (stable) and radical (disruptive) area to work on, you will find that you're giving a voice to a wide range of people, which should further help minimise any early pushback. Involving different generations is often also a good idea: younger people will tend to want to shake things up; older people will tend to be more cautious. Getting them to work together will both promote better understanding between them and generate better ideas.

Acknowledgements

Centennials, like most important ventures in life, was a team effort. It has my name on the cover only because I had the time, and desire, to write it. But it is actually the work of lots of people. Twenty-six, to be precise. And a further six who were heavily involved all along the way: opening doors, gathering data and developing ideas.

There are too many people to mention who have guided my thinking and helped create the book that you now hold in your hands – but hopefully, if you're reading this book and your name isn't mentioned below, then you'll know who you are.

In particular, I would like to thank my dad, who has always supported and guided me, and from a very young age taught me how to manage, research, teach and write. Also Jules Goddard and Liz Mellon, who have been a huge support and who helped me research and write the original *Harvard Business Review* article on which this book is based. I am grateful to Sarah Green Carmichael, who edited the article and helped with its publication, and to John Bull and Steve Harrison, who guided my thinking along the way, Jonathan Harris and Rachid Ahouiyek, who helped sharpen it, and Paul Davies and Pete Wilkinson, who always offer the best advice.

I am also deeply grateful to everyone at the Centennials. They were prepared to open their doors to us at the start of the project, when we had no idea what we were doing, what we were looking for, and what we might find, and have been endlessly generous with their time – always willing to meet up and answer our questions. Particular thanks go to Peter Keen (who started so many balls rolling), Jonnie Noakes and Paul Thompson (who opened so many doors), and Andy Salmon, Catherine Mallyon, Clive Grinyer, Ian Mitchell, Lucy Skilbeck, Michael

Bourne, Shaun Fitzgerald and Tim Leunig (who were a constant source of fresh ideas).

Finally, I would like to thank the people who went before me and laid the foundations on which this book is built. In particular, Charles Handy, Jim Collins and Tom Peters (for their early work in this area), Malcolm Gladwell and Michael Lewis (for showing how to share a complex idea with a simple story), Daniel Kahneman and Robin Dunbar (whose work is a constant inspiration), and Nigel Wilcockson, my editor, who has helped shape so many of the important books in this area. Throughout this project, he has constantly challenged and questioned my thinking – helping to make this a much better book than it could have been, and make me appear a much better writer than I really am.

Endnotes

Prologue: The theory of everything

1   Bernard Pullman, *The Atom in the History of Human Thought*, Oxford University Press, 1998.

2   John Dalton, 'On the Absorption of Gases by Water and Other Liquids', *Philosophical Magazine*, 1806, series 1, vol. 24, no. 1, pp. 15–24; John Dalton, *A New System of Chemical Philosophy*, Part 1–2, S. Russell, 1808.

3   Michael Faraday, 'VIII. Experimental Researches in Electricity – Thirteenth Series', *Philosophical Transactions*, 1838, vol. 128, pp. 125–68; John Thomson, 1897, 'Cathode Rays', Weekly Evening Meeting, 30 April 1897; John Thomson, 'On Bodies Smaller than Atoms', Royal Institution lecture, 1901; John Thomson, 'On the Structure of the Atom: An Investigation of the Stability and Periods of Oscillation of a Number of Corpuscles Arranged at Equal Intervals Around the Circumference of a Circle; with Application of the Results to the Theory of Atomic Structure', *Philosophical Magazine*, 1904, series 6, vol. 7, no. 39, pp. 237–65.

4   Marie Curie, 'Nobel Lecture: Radium and the New Concepts in Chemistry', 11 December 1911; Susan Quinn, *Marie Curie: A Life*, Simon & Schuster, 1995.

5   Ernest Rutherford, 'The Scattering of Alpha and Beta Particles by Matter and the Structure of the Atom', *Philosophical Magazine*, 1911, series 6, vol. 21, no. 125, pp. 669–88; David Wilson, *Rutherford: Simple Genius*, MIT Press, 1983.

6   Author interview with Paul Thompson on 6 March 2015.

7   See, for example, Ben Branch, 'The Costs of Bankruptcy: A Review', *International Review of Financial Analysis*, 2002, vol. 11, no. 1, pp. 39–57; Joseph Bower and Stuart Gibson, 'The Social Cost of Fraud and Bankruptcy', *Harvard Business Review*, December 2003, pp. 20–2; Marco Bontje, 'Facing the Challenge of Shrinking Cities in East Germany: The Case of Leipzig', *GeoJournal*, 2004, vol. 61, no. 1, pp. 13–21; John Heilbrunn, 'Paying the

Price of Failure: Reconstructing Failed and Collapsed States in Africa and Central Asia', *Perspectives on Politics*, 2006, vol. 4, no. 1, pp. 135–50; Dominic Barton, James Manyika and Sarah Keohane Williamson, 'Finally, Evidence that Managing for the Long Term Pays Off', *Harvard Business Review*, 7 February 2017.

8   See, for example, Franco Bassanini and Edoardo Reviglio, 'Financial Stability, Fiscal Consolidation and Long Term Investment After the Crisis', *Financial Market Trends*, 2011, vol. 2011, no. 1; Daron Acemoglu and James Robinson, *Why Nations Fail: The Origins of Power, Prosperity and Poverty*, Profile Books, 2012.

9   Tom Peters and Robert Waterman, *In Search of Excellence: Lessons from America's Best-Run Companies*, Harper & Row, 1982; Jim Collins and Jerry Porras, *Built to Last: Successful Habits of Visionary Companies*, HarperCollins, 1994; Jim Collins, *Good to Great: Why Some Companies Make the Leap. . . And Others Don't*, Random House Business, 2001.

10   Christian Stadler, 'The Four Principles of Enduring Success', *Harvard Business Review*, July–August 2007, pp. 62–72; Michael Raynor and Mumtaz Ahmed, 'Three Rules for Making a Company Truly Great', *Harvard Business Review*, April 2013, pp. 108–17.

11   See, for example, Jennifer Reingold and Ryan Underwood, 'Was "Built to Last", Built to Last?', *Fast Company*, 1 November 2004; 'Good to Great to Gone', *The Economist*, 7 July 2009; Chris Bradley, 'Surprise: Those Great Companies Generally Turn Out to Be Meh . . . or Duds', MarketWatch, 31 August 2017.

12   Michael Lewis, *Moneyball: The Art of Winning an Unfair Game*, W.W. Norton & Company, 2003; Malcolm Gladwell, *Outliers: The Story of Success*, Penguin, 2008; Matthew Syed, *Rebel Ideas: The Power of Diverse Thinking*, John Murray, 2019.

13   The Royal Shakespeare Company was originally the Shakespeare Memorial Theatre, Nasa was originally part of the US army, and the first British Olympic cyclists competed at the first summer Games in 1896.

Habit 1: Build your north star

1   This is described in more detail in Hamish McDougall, '"The Whole World's Watching": New Zealand, International Opinion, and the 1981 Springbok Rugby Tour', *Journal of Sport History*, 2018, vol. 45, no. 2, pp. 202–23; Geoff Chapple, *1981: The Tour*, Reed Publishing, 1984. A video of

the protest can be seen at: https://teara.govt.nz/en/video/27165/
the-game-that-never-was

2   A diary of the tour, with various articles and videos, can be seen on the
New Zealand History website: https://nzhistory.govt.nz/
culture/1981-springbok-tour

3   This is described in more detail in John Minto, 'Rugby, Racism and the
Battle for the Soul of Aotearoa New Zealand', *Guardian*, 15 August 2021.

4   Neil Reid, '1981 Springbok Tour: Nelson Mandela's Salute to NZ Protest
Movement', *New Zealand Herald*, 15 July 2021.

5   This is described in more detail in John McCrystal, *The Originals: 1905 All
Black Rugby Odyssey*, Random House, 2005; Ron Palenski, *All Blacks:
Myths and Legends*, Hodder Moa, 2008.

6   See, for example, Shane Gilchrist, 'Game on, the "Ki" is Back in Court',
Otago Daily Times, 5 October 2007, and the New Zealand History website:
https://nzhistory.govt.nz/culture/the-new-zealand-natives-rugby-tour/
nz-natives-rugby-tour

7   Peter Bills, *The Jersey: The All Blacks – The Secrets Behind the World's Most
Successful Team*, Macmillan, 2018, p. 26.

8   This is explained in more detail in Peter Bills, *The Jersey*, and in the 'Political Milestones' section of the New Zealand History website: https://
nzhistory.govt.nz

9   Why New Zealand's Other All Blacks Matter', *The Economist*, 18 July 2019.

10   Rugby New Zealand, 'Record Number Playing Rugby in NZ', 6 November
2016.

11   Author interview with Catherine Mallyon on 26 August 2014.

12   This is described in more detail in each of the Centennials' annual reports,
mission statements and strategic plans that are available on their
websites.

13   See, for example, Andrew Haldane and Richard Davies, 'The Short Long',
Bank of England, 9 May 2011; Bassanini and Reviglio, 'Financial Stability,
Fiscal Consolidation and Long Term Investment After the Crisis.

14   See, for example, Caroline Valetkevitch, 'Key Dates and Milestones in
the S&P 500's History', Reuters, 10 April 2013; Scott Anthony, Patrick
Viguerie, Evan Schwartz and John Van Landeghem, '2018 Corporate
Longevity Forecast: Creative Destruction is Accelerating', Innosight,
February 2018.

15   This is described in more detail on their websites and in their annual
reports.

16   Dan Schawbel, 'Chip Bergh: Why Levi Strauss Cares About Sustainability', *Forbes*, 29 April 2015.

17   David Goodman, 'Kellogg Foundation Keeps a Low Philanthropic Profile', *Los Angeles Times*, 6 June 1998.

18   This is described in more detail in their annual reports and on their websites.

19   I completed this analysis myself by looking at the ages of the S&P 500 companies in 2021 and comparing them with the annual sales and profits they made in the previous five years.

20   Barton, Manyika and Williamson, 'Finally, Evidence that Managing for the Long Term Pays Off'.

21   See, for example, 'The Founding Prospectus' on Sony's website: www.sony. com en/SonyInfo/CorporateInfo/History/prospectus.html; Sea-Jin Chang, *Sony vs Samsung: The Inside Story of the Electronics Giants' Battle for Global Supremacy*, Wiley, 2008.

22   Akio Morita, *Made in Japan: Akio Morita and Sony*, Collins, 1987, p. 37.

23   Akio Morita, *Made in Japan*, p. 138.

24   See, for example, Michael Kamins and Akira Nagashima, 'Perceptions of Products Made in Japan Versus Those Made in the United States Among Japanese and American Executives: A Longitudinal Perspective', *Asia Pacific Journal of Management*, 1995, vol. 12, no. 1, pp. 49–68; Angus Maddison, *Contours of the World Economy 1–2030 AD: Essays in Macro-Economic History*, Oxford University Press, 2007; Sébastien Lechevalier, *The Great Transformation of Japanese Capitalism*, Routledge, 2014; and the figures in the World Economic Outlook Database: www.imf.org

25   Brent Schlender, 'Inside: The Shakeup at Sony', *Fortune*, 4 April 2005.

26   Peter Temin, *Engines of Enterprise: An Economic History of New England*, Harvard University Press, 2000.

27   This is described in more detail in Acemoglu and Robinson, *Why Nations Fail*; Roger Crowley, *City of Fortune: How Venice Won and Lost a Naval Empire*, Faber & Faber, 2012.

28   This is described in more detail in David Western, *Booms, Bubbles and Busts in the US Stock Market*, Routledge, 2004; Scott Nations, *A History of the United States in Five Crashes: Stock Market Meltdowns That Defined a Nation*, William Morrow, 2017; Somer Anderson, 'Stocks Then and Now: The 1950s and 1970s', Investopedia, 26 January 2021; Saikat Chatterjee and Thyagaraju Adinarayan, 'Buy, Sell, Repeat! No Room for "Hold" in Whip-sawing Markets', Reuters, 3 August 2020.

29 See, for example, Franco Modigliani and Merton Miller, 'The Cost of Capital, Corporate Finance, and the Theory of Investment', *American Economic Review*, 1958, vol. 48, no. 3, pp. 261–97; Milton Friedman, 'The Social Responsibility of Business Is to Increase Its Profits', *New York Times*, 13 September 1970, p. 17.

30 See for example, Caroline Valetkevitch, 'Key Dates and Milestones in the S&P 500's History'; Scott Anthony et al., 'Corporate Longevity Forecast'.

31 This is described in more detail in Walter Isaacson, *Steve Jobs*, Abacus, 2015.

32 This is described in more detail in John Sculley and John Byrne, *Odyssey: Pepsi to Apple*, Collins, 1988; Owen Linzmayer, *Apple Confidential 2.0: The Definitive History of the World's Most Colorful Company – The Real Story of Apple Computer, Inc*, No Starch Press, 2004.

33 This is described in more detail in Owen Linzmayer, *Apple Confidential 2.0*.

34 This is explained in more detail in Walter Isaacson, *Steve Jobs*.

35 Steve Jobs' full presentation can be seen on YouTube at: https://www.youtube.com/watch?v=VQKMoT-6XSg

36 This is explained in more detail in Walter Isaacson, *Steve Jobs*; Brian Merchant, *The One Device: The Secret History of the iPhone*, Little, Brown, 2018.

37 See, for example, Jacob Kastrenakes, 'Apple Says There Are Now Over 1 Billion Active iPhones', The Verge, 27 January 2021.

38 This process is described in more detail on the Korn Ferry website, who conduct the research for *Fortune* magazine: www.kornferry.com

39 See, for example, Howard Schultz, *Pour Your Heart Into It: How Starbucks Built a Company One Cup at a Time*, Hyperion, 1997; Owen Linzmayer, *Apple Confidential 2.0*; Eric Schmidt and Jonathan Rosenberg, *How Google Works*, John Murray, 2014; Jeff Bezos and Walter Isaacson, *Invent and Wander: The Collected Writings of Jeff Bezos, with an Introduction by Walter Isaacson*, Harvard Business Review Press, 2020.

40 This is described in more detail in the 'About Us' section on the Starbucks website: www.starbucksathome.com/gb/story/about-starbucks; Howard Schultz, *Pour Your Heart Into It*.

41 Herman Melville, *Moby-Dick*, Richard Bentley, 1851.

42 This is explained in more detail on the company history section of its website: https://stories.starbucks.com

43 Corporate Design Foundation, 'Starbucks: A Visual Cup o' Joe', *Journal of Business and Design*, 1995, vol. 1, no. 1, p. 18.

44 Joseph Michelli, *The Starbucks Experience: 5 Principles for Turning Ordinary into Extraordinary*, McGraw Hill, 2007, p. 48.

45 Howard Schultz, *Onward: How Starbucks Fought for Its Life Without Losing Its Soul*, John Wiley & Sons, 2012, p. 10.

46 See, for example, Henry Brean, 'UNLV Professor Targets "Wasteful" Dipper Wells', *Las Vegas Review-Journal*, 8 June 2009; Melanie Warner, 'Starbucks Will Use Cups with 10% Recycled Paper', *New York Times*, 17 November 2004; Tiffany May, 'Starbucks Will Stop Using Disposable Coffee Cups in South Korea by 2025', *New York Times*, 6 April 2021.

47 Howard Schultz, *Onward*, p. 10.

48 Howard Schultz, *Onward*, p. 19.

49 See, for example, Henry Brean, 'UNLV Professor Targets "Wasteful" Dipper Wells'; Melanie Warner, 'Starbucks Will Use Cups with 10% Recycled Paper'; Tiffany May, 'Starbucks Will Stop Using Disposable Coffee Cups in South Korea by 2025. More examples of what it has done can be seen on its website: https://stories.starbucks.com

50 Author interview with Steve Tew on 16 August 2017 (this is described in more detail in: Graham Henry, *Final Word*, HarperCollins, 2013); Gregor Paul, *The Reign of King Henry: How Graham Henry Transformed the All Blacks*, Exisle Publishing, 2015; Richie McCaw, *The Real McCaw: The Autobiography*, Aurum Press, 2015.

51 This is described in more detail in New Zealand Rugby, 'Annual Report', 2020.

52 See, for example, Royal College of Art, 'Redesigning the Ambulance' and 'Design for Dementia' research projects; Dalya Alberge, 'This is Another Crack in the Glass Ceiling: RSC Casts Disabled Actors in New Season', *Guardian*, 26 January 2019.

53 This is described in more detail in Tesla's annual impact reports and annual reports, available on its website: www.tesla.com

54 See, for example, Tesla's mission statement: www.tesla.com

55 As explained in Facebook's mission statement: www.facebook.com

56 See, for example, Natasha Singer, 'How Big Tech Is Going After Your Health Care', *New York Times*, 26 December 2017; Natasha Singer, 'How Google Took Over the Classroom', *New York Times*, 13 May 2017; Andy Ihnatko, 'Apple's New Approach to Education Is Humbler, but Stronger', *Fast Company*, 29 March 2018.

57 This is described in more detail on Double the Donation's website: www.doublethedonation.com

Habit 2: Do it for the kids' kids

1   This is explained in more detail in Robert Mueller, 'Lunabotics Mining Competition: Inspiration Through Accomplishment', Nasa, 2019, and at www.nasa.gov/lunabotics/

2   This is explained in more detail in Nasa, 'STEM Education Strategic Plan', 2018; Nasa, 'Nasa Strategy for STEM Engagement', 2020; Jeremy Engle, 'Lesson of the Day: Nasa's Perseverance Rover Lands on Mars to Renew Search for Extinct Life', *New York Times*, 24 February 2021.

3   See, for example, *Nasa Astronaut Fact Book* and the current astronaut biographies at www.nasa.gov

4   Author interview with Catherine Mallyon on 7 April 2014. This is explained more on the Royal Shakespeare Company's education website: www.rsc.org.uk/education

5   This is explained in more detail in 'Next Generation: Talent Development Programme', Royal Shakespeare Company, 2020; and the apprenticeships page on its website: www.rsc.org.uk

6   See, for example, David Maurice Smith, 'Raised on Rugby', *New York Times*, 5 August 2018; Peter Bills, *The Jersey*; and the 'participation framework' page of the New Zealand Rugby website: www.nzrugby.co.nz; the 'Small Blacks' website: www.smallblacks.com; and the coach education website: www.rugbytoolbox.co.nz

7   Author interview with Dave Brailsford on 17 April 2019.

8   Viv Richards, *Hitting Across the Line: An Autobiography*, Headline, 1992, p. 9.

9   See, for example, Frank Birbalsingh, *The Rise of West Indian Cricket: From Colony to Nation*, Hansib Publishing, 1996; Ray Goble and Keith Sandiford, *75 Years of West Indies Cricket: 1928–2003*, Hansib Publishing, 2004.

10 See, for example, Associated Press, 'Overseas Players Courted by N.B.A.', *New York Times*, 26 June 2005; Professional Cricketers' Association, 'PCA Report into Overseas Players in Domestic Professional Cricket', 2 October 2013; Orlando Patterson, 'The Secret of Jamaica's Runners', *New York Times*, 13 August 2016; Gregor Aisch, Kevin Quealy and Rory Smith, 'Where Athletes in the Premier League, the N.B.A., and Other Sports Leagues Come From, in 15 Charts', *New York Times*, 29 December 2017; Major League Baseball, 'MLB Rosters Feature 251 International Players', 29 March 2019.

11 This is described on the MVP website: https://mvptrackclub.com; and the Racers Track Club website: http://racerstrackclub.com

12 This is described in more detail in Benjamin Bloom, *Developing Talent in Young People*, Ballantine Books, 1985.

13 This is described in more detail in David Epstein, *Range: How Generalists Triumph in a Specialized World*, Riverhead Books, 2019.

14 Much fuller and more detailed descriptions of the stages of development of the different artists, athletes and scientists are given in Benjamin Bloom, *Developing Talent in Young People*.

15 See, for example, Harry Chugani, 'A Critical Period of Brain Development: Studies of Cerebral Glucose Utilization with PET', *Preventive Medicine*, 1998, vol. 27, no. 2, pp. 184–8; Suzana Herculano-Houzel, 'The Human Brain in Numbers: A Linearly Scaled-up Primate Brain', *Frontiers in Human Neuroscience*, 2009, vol. 3, article 31; Timothy Brown and Terry Jernigan, 'Brain Development During the Preschool Years', *Neuropsychology Review*, 2012, vol. 22, no. 4, pp. 313–33; Patrice Voss, Maryse Thomas, Miguel Cisneros-Franco and Etienne de Villers-Sidani, 'Dynamic Brains and the Changing Rules of Neuroplasticity: Implications for Learning and Recovery', *Frontiers in Psychology*, 2017, vol. 8, article 1657.

16 See, for example, Andreja Bubic, Ella Striem-Amit and Amir Amedi, 'Large-Scale Brain Plasticity Following Blindness and the Use of Sensory Substitution Devices', in *Multisensory Object Perception in the Primate Brain*, ed. Jochen Kaiser and Marcus Johannes Naumer, Springer, 2010, pp. 351–380; Lotfi Merabet and Alvaro Pascual-Leone, 'Neural Reorganization Following Sensory Loss: The Opportunity of Change', *Nature Reviews Neuroscience*, 2010, vol. 11, pp. 44–52; Katherine Woollett and Eleanor Maguire, 'Acquiring "the Knowledge" of London's Layout Drives Structural Brain Changes', *Current Biology*, 2011, vol. 21, no. 24, pp. 2109–14; Karen Barrett, Richard Ashley, Dana Strait and Nina Kraus, 'Art and Science: How Musical Training Shapes the Brain', *Frontiers in Psychology*, 2013, vol. 4, article 713.

17 See, for example, 'Future of Work and Skills', OECD, 2017; 'The Future of Jobs Report', World Economic Forum, 2020.

18 This is described in more detail in Caroline Criado Perez, *Invisible Women: Exposing Data Bias in a World Designed for Men*, Vintage, 2020.

19 This is described in more detail in Jane Margolis, Allan Fisher and Faye Miller, 'The Anatomy of Interest: Women in Undergraduate Computer Science', *Women's Studies Quarterly*, 2000, vol. 28, no. 1, pp. 104–27; Jane Margolis, *Unlocking the Clubhouse: Women in Computing*, MIT Press, 2002; Allan Fisher and Jane Margolis, 'Unlocking the Clubhouse: The Carnegie Mellon Experience', *ACM SIGCSE Bulletin*, 2002, vol. 34, no. 2, pp. 79–83.

20   This is described in more detail in Sara Kiesler, Lee Sproull and Jacque-
      lynne Eccles, 'Pool Halls, Chips, and War Games: Women in the Culture
      of Computing', *Psychology of Women Quarterly*, 1985, vol. 9, no. 4, pp.
      451–62.

21   See, for example, 'Degrees in Computer and Information Sciences Con-
      ferred by Degree-Granting Institutions by Level of Degree and Sex of Stu-
      dent: 1970–71 through 2010–11', National Center for Education Statistics,
      2012; Katharine Sanderson, 'More Women than Ever Are Starting Careers
      in Science', *Nature*, 5 August 2021.

22   See for example, 'Closing the STEM Gap: Why STEM Classes and Careers
      Still Lack Girls and What We Can Do About It', Microsoft, 2019; 'Crack-
      ing the Gender Code: Get 3X More Women in Computing', Accenture and
      Girls Who Code, 2016.

23   See, for example, 'Nasa Equal Employment Opportunity Strategic Plan:
      FY 2017–19', Nasa, 2019; and the biographies of their current astronauts at
      www.nasa.gov

24   See, for example, 'Employed Persons by Detailed Occupation, Sex, Race,
      and Hispanic or Latino Ethnicity', US Bureau of Labor Statistics, 2020.

25   See, for example, 'Future of Work and Skills', OECD; 'The Future of Jobs
      Report', World Economic Forum.

26   See, for example, Robert Atkinson and John Wu, 'False Alarmism: Techno-
      logical Disruption and the U.S. Labor Market, 1850–2015', Information
      Technology & Innovation Foundation, 8 May 2017; 'Current Labor Stat-
      istics: December 2000', US Bureau of Labor Statistics, 2000; 'Employment
      Projections', US Bureau of Labor Statistics, 2021.

27   See, for example, 'Future of Work and Skills', OECD; 'The Future of Jobs
      Report', World Economic Forum.

28   See, for example, Malcolm Mulholland, 'Rugby World Cup: All Blacks,
      New Zealand Maori and the Politics of the Pitch', *The Conversation*,
      6 September 2011; 'All Blacks Stars Make Powerful Statement About
      Cultural Diversity in New Zealand', *Stuff*, 26 March 2021; British
      Cycling's athlete biographies at www.britishcycling.org.uk; Nasa astro-
      naut biographies at www.nasa.gov; 'Annual Equality Report', Royal
      College of Art, 2019.

29   See, for example, Jasper Hamill, 'Apple Brings Life-changing "Everyone
      Can Code" Curriculum to Thousands of Students Across the UK and
      Europe', *Metro*, 19 January 2018; '500 Words Final 2020', BBC Radio 2;
      'World of Stories', Puffin, Penguin Random House.

30   See, for example, 'Kellogg's Apprentice Scheme Hunts for Talent', Kellogg's, 13 March 2017; 'Internship Questions', Nordstrom; 'Future Leaders Start Here', Starbucks.

31   This is described in more detail in Kevin Badgett, 'School–Business Partnerships: Understanding Business Perspectives', *School Community Journal*, 2016, vol. 26, no. 2, pp. 83–105.

32   See, for example, Nye Cominetti, Paul Sissons and Katy Jones, 'Beyond the Business Case: The Employer's Role in Tackling Youth Unemployment', The Work Foundation, July 2013; Anthony Mann and Prue Huddleston, 'How Should Our Schools Respond to the Demands of the Twenty-First Century Labour Market? Eight Perspectives', Education and Employers Research, 2015; 'School Ties: Transforming Small Business Engagement with Schools', Rocket Science, 15 February 2016.

33   Author interview on 1 April 2022.

34   This is described in more detail in Kevin Badgett, 'School–Business Partnerships: Understanding Business Perspectives'; Peter Crush, 'Why Small Business Owners Should Be Building Relationships with Local Schools', First Voice, 9 January 2017.

35   See, for example, Ciara Byrne, 'The Loneliness of the Female Coder', *Fast Company*, 11 September 2013; Sylvia Ann Hewlett, 'What's Holding Women Back in Science and Technology Industries', *Harvard Business Review*, 13 March 2014; 'Women in Technology Survey 2019', Women in Tech, September 2019; Sarah White, 'Women in Tech Statistics: The Hard Truths of an Uphill Battle', CIO, 8 March 2021.

36   See the research on https://girlswhocode.com for more detail.

37   See, for example, 'Inclusion & Diversity', Apple; 'Annual Diversity Report', Facebook, 2021; 'Diversity Annual Report', Google, 2021.

Habit 3: Have strong roots

1   A typical day at Eton is described in more detail in Nick Fraser, *The Importance of Being Eton*, Short Books, 2006; John Corbin, *School Boy Life in England: An American View*, Leopold Classic Library, 2015; Musa Okwonga, 2021, *One of Them: An Eton College Memoir*, Unbound, 2021.

2   Author interview with Jonnie Noakes on 18 November 2018, at Leaders in Sport, see: Alex Hill, 'Summit Session: Are You Radically Traditional?', Radically Traditional, 14 February 2019.

3   This is described in more detail in Paul Moss, 'Why Has Eton Produced So Many Prime Ministers?', *The World Tonight*, BBC Radio 4, 12 May 2010; Tony Little, *An Intelligent Person's Guide to Education*, Bloomsbury Continuum, 2015; Christopher de Bellaigue, 'Eton and the Making of a Modern Elite', *1843*, 16 August 2016.

4   See, for example, Graeme Patton, 'Eton College to Admit Pupils Irrespective of Family Income', *Daily Telegraph*, 5 February 2014; 'Annual Report', Eton College, 2020.

5   Author interview on 4 December 2018, which is included in Lisa Mainwaring, 'Eton College', *How to Outperform*, 2019, Audible Original podcast.

6   This is described in more detail in Julian Barnes, Megan Barnett, Christopher Schmitt and Marianne Lavelle, 'Investigative Report: How a Titan Came Undone', *U.S. News and World Report*, 18 March 2002; Bethany McLean and Peter Elkins, 2003, *The Smartest Guys in the Room: The Amazing Rise and Scandalous Fall of Enron*, Viking, 2003; Malcolm Salter, *Innovation Corrupted: The Origins and Legacy of Enron's Collapse*, Harvard University Press, 2008.

7   This is described in more detail in Bethany McLean and Peter Elkins, *The Smartest Guys in the Room*; Malcolm Salter, *Innovation Corrupted*.

8   See, for example: Ed Michaels, Helen Handfield-Jones and Beth Axelrod, *The War for Talent*, Harvard Business Review Press, 2001.

9   See, for example, 'Annual Report', Enron, 2000; Paul Healy and Krishna Palepu, 'The Fall of Enron', *Journal of Economic Perspectives*, 2003, vol. 17, no. 2, pp. 3–26.

10 Brian O'Reilly, 'Once a Dull-As-Methane Utility, Enron Has Grown Rich Making Markets Where Markets Were Never Made Before', *Fortune*, 17 April 2000.

11 This is explained in more detail in Malcolm Salter, *Innovation Corrupted*.

12 Author interview with Catherine Mallyon on 26 August 2014.

13 See, for example, Lawrence Mishel and Jori Kandra, 'CEO Pay Has Skyrocketed 1,322% Since 1978', Economic Policy Institute, 10 August 2021.

14 See, for example, Maggie Fitzgerald, '2019 Had the Most CEO Departures on Record with More than 1,600', CNBC, 8 January 2020; '2021 CEO Turnover Report', Challenger, Gray & Christmas, Inc., 2022.

15 See, for example, Tyler Cowen, 'Why CEOs Actually Deserve Their Gazillion-Dollar Salaries', *Time*, 11 April 2019.

16 This is explained in more detail in 'The Best-Performing CEOs in the World 2019', *Harvard Business Review*, November–December 2019.

17 See, for example, Chuck Lucier, Eric Spiegle and Rob Schuyt, 'Why CEOs Fall: The Causes and Consequences of Turnover at the Top', *Strategy + Business*, 15 July 2002; 'CEO Turnover Report', Challenger, Gray and Christmas Inc., 2017; 'CEO Success Study', Strategy&, PwC, 2018; Dan Marcec, 'CEO Tenure Rates', Harvard Law School Forum on Corporate Governance, 12 February 2018.

18 This is described in more detail in Graham Henry, *Final Word*; Gregor Paul, *The Reign of King Henry*; David Long, 'Cardiff 2007: The All Blacks' Loss to France Through the Eyes of the Media', *Stuff*, 16 October 2015; Richie McCaw, *The Real McCaw*.

19 See, for example, Gregor Paul, 'The Contentious Decision That Led to Unprecedented All Blacks Success', *New Zealand Herald*, 26 April 2019.

20 See, for example, 'All Blacks: The Most Experienced Rugby World Cup Squad', *New Zealand Herald*, 1 September 2015.

21 See, for example, John Mahon and Romana Danysh, *Infantry, Part I: Regular Army*, Army Lineage Series, Office of the Chief of Military History United States Army, 1972; Rod Powers, 2019, 'How the US Army Is Organized', Liveabout.com, 26 April 2019; the 'Rank Progression' section of the British Army website: www.army.mod.uk

22 See, for example, Dr Paul Thompson's biography on the Royal College of Art website: www.rca.ac.uk

23 Author interview with Paul Thompson on 5 January 2017.

24 Author interview with Zowie Broach on 3 July 2015.

25 Author interview on 21 January 2019.

Habit 4: Mind the gap

1 This is described in more detail in Dan Carter, *The Autobiography of an All Blacks Legend*, Headline, 2015; Tony Johnson and Lynn McConnell, *Behind the Silver Fern: The All Blacks in Their Own Words*, Polaris, 2016; Kieran Read, *Straight 8: The Autobiography*, Headline, 2019.

2 See for example, 'CEO Turnover Report', Challenger, Gray & Christmas, 2017; 'CEO Success Study', Strategy&; Dan Marcec, 'CEO Tenure Rates'; 'CEO Succession Practices in the Russell 3000 and S&P 500: 2021 Edition', The Conference Board, 2021.

3 This is described in more detail in Jim White, *Manchester United: The Biography*, Sphere, 2008.

4 This is described in more detail in Alex Ferguson, *My Autobiography*, Hodder & Stoughton, 2013.

5 I completed this analysis myself using the football squad information on transfermarkt.com and wikipedia.com.

6 This is described in more detail in, for example, Mr X, 'Has David Moyes Made a Mistake with His Coaching Team at Manchester United?', *Bleacher Report*, 5 July 2013; Daniel Taylor, 'David Moyes Ignored Manchester United Staff's Advice, Says Meulensteen', *Guardian*, 24 April 2014.

7 This is based on my own analysis.

8 Author interview with Jonnie Noakes on 13 May 2016.

9 This is based on my own analysis of the collective experience within the Centennials at any point in time.

10 See, for example, Anders Ericsson, Ralf Krampe and Clemens Tesch-Römer, 'The Role of Deliberate Practice in the Acquisition of Expert Performance', *Psychological Review*, 1993, vol. 100, no. 3, pp. 363–406; Anders Ericsson, Michael Prietula and Edward Cokely, 'The Making of an Expert', *Harvard Business Review*, July–August 2007, pp. 7–8; Anders Ericsson and Robert Pool, *Peak: How All of Us Can Achieve Extraordinary Things*, Vintage Books, 2016.

11 See, for example, Pam Hruska, Kent Hecker, Sylvain Coderre, Kevin McLaughlin, Filomeno Cortese, Christopher Doig, Tanya Beran, Bruce Wright and Olav Krigolson, 'Hemispheric Activation Differences in Novice and Expert Clinicians During Clinical Decision Making', *Advances in Health Sciences Education*, 2010, vol. 21, no. 5, pp. 921–33.

12 See, for example, Martin Hill Ortiz, 'New York Times Bestsellers: Ages of Authors', *It's Harder Not To* blog, May 2015; 'Nobel Laureates by Age', Nobel Prize, 2021; Pierre Azoulay, Benjamin Jones, Daniel Kim and Javier Miranda, 'Age and High-Growth Entrepreneurship', *American Economic Review: Insights*, 2020, vol. 2, no. 1, pp. 65–82; Statista, 'Average Age at Hire of CEOs and CFOs in the United States from 2005 to 2018', Statista, 2019.

13 This is described in more detail in Pie Hobu, Henk Schmidt, Henny Boshuizen and Vimla Patel, 'Contextual Factors in the Activation of First Diagnostic Hypotheses: Expert–Novice Differences', *Medical Education*, 1987, vol. 21, no. 6, pp. 471–6.

14 See, for example, Marie-France Pochna, *Christian Dior: The Man Who Made the World Look New*, Arcade Publishing, 1994; Statista, 'Most Valuable French Brands 2020', Statista, 2021.

15 See, for example, 'CEO Turnover Report', Challenger, Gray and Christmas, 2017; 'CEO Success Study', Strategy&; Dan Marcec, 'CEO Tenure Rates'; 'CEO Succession Practices in the Russell 3000 and S&P 500', The Conference Board.

16 Author interview on 4 May 2018.

17 See for example, 'CEO Turnover Report', Challenger, Gray and Christmas, 2017; 'CEO Success Study', Strategy&; Dan Marcec, 'CEO Tenure Rates'; 'CEO Succession Practices in the Russell 3000 and S&P 500', The Conference Board.

Habit 5: Perform in public

1 As described in Katherine Phillips, Katie Liljenquist and Margaret Neale, 'Is the Pain Worth the Gain? The Advantages and Liabilities of Agreeing with Socially Distinct Newcomers', *Personality and Social Psychology Bulletin*, 2009, vol. 35, no. 3, pp. 336–50.

2 Phillips, Liljenquist and Neale, 'Is the Pain Worth the Gain?'.

3 Phillips, Liljenquist and Neale, 'Is the Pain Worth the Gain?'.

4 Phillips, Liljenquist and Neale, 'Is the Pain Worth the Gain?'.

5 See, for example, Robert Lount and Katherine Phillips, 'Working Harder with the Out-Group: The Impact of Social Category Diversity on Motivation Gains', *Organizational Behavior and Human Decision Processes*, 2007, vol. 103, no. 2, pp. 214–24; Katherine Phillips and Evan Apfelbaum, 'Delusions of Homogeneity? Reinterpreting the Effects of Group Diversity', in *Looking Back, Moving Forward: A Review of Group and Team-Based Research*, ed. Margaret Neale and Elizabeth Mannix, Emerald Publishing, 2012; Denise Lewin Loyd, Cynthia Wang, Katherine Phillips and Robert Lount, 'Social Category Diversity Promotes Premeeting Elaboration: The Role of Relationship Focus', *Organization Science*, 2013, vol. 24, no. 3, pp. 757–72; Hong Bui, Vinh Sum Chau, Marta Degl'Innocenti, Ludovica Leone and Francesca Vicentini, 'The Resilient Organisation: A Meta-analysis of the Effect of Communication on Team Diversity and Team Performance', *Applied Psychology*, 2019, vol. 68, no. 4, pp. 621–57.

6 Bui, Chau, Degl'Innocenti, Leone and Vicentini, 'The Resilient Organisation'.

7   Samuel Sommers, 'On Racial Diversity and Group Decision Making: Iden-
     tifying Multiple Effects of Racial Composition on Jury Deliberations', *Jour-
     nal of Personality and Social Psychology*, 2006, vol. 90, no. 4, pp.
     597–612.

8   Charles Bond and Linda Titus, 'Social Facilitation: A Meta-analysis of 241
     Studies', *Psychological Bulletin*, 1983, vol. 94, no. 2, pp. 265–92.

9   See, for example, Mihaly Csikszentmihalyi, *Flow: The Psychology of Opti-
     mal Experience*, Ingram International, 2002; Jeanne Nakamura and Mihaly
     Csikszentmihalyi, 'The Concept of Flow', in *The Oxford Handbook of Posi-
     tive Psychology*, ed. Rick Snyder and Shane Lopez, Oxford University Press,
     2002.

10   Kristin Elwood, Danah Henriksen and Punya Mishra, 'Finding Meaning
     in Flow: A Conversation with Susan K. Perry on Writing Creatively', *Tech-
     Trends*, 2017, vol. 61, no. 1, pp. 212–17.

11   Melissa Warr, Danah Henriksen and Punya Mishra, 'Creativity and Flow
     in Surgery, Music, and Cooking: An Interview with Neuroscientist Charles
     Limb', *Tech Trends*, 2018, vol. 62, no. 42, pp. 137–42.

12   'Final Report of the Investigation into the Accident with the Collision of
     KLM Flight 4805, Boeing 747-206B, PH-BUF and Pan American Flight
     1736, Boeing 747–121, N736PA at Tenerife Airport, Spain on 27 March 1977',
     Netherlands Aviation Safety Board, 1978.

13   As described in 'Final Report of the Investigation into the Accident with
     the Collision of. . .', Netherlands Aviation Safety Board; 'Joint Report: Pro-
     ject Tenerife', KLM and PAA, 1978.

14   'Final Report of the Investigation into the Accident with the Collision of
     . . .', Netherlands Aviation Safety Board.

15   'Resource Management on the Flight Deck: Proceedings of a Nasa/Indus-
     try Workshop Held at San Francisco, California June 26–28, 1979', Nasa
     Conference Publication, 1980.

16   'Resource Management on the Flight Deck', Nasa Conference
     Publication.

17   As described in Rex Hardy, *Callback: NASA's Aviation Safety Reporting
     System*, Smithsonian Institution, 1990; 'Resource Management on the
     Flight Deck', Nasa Conference Publication.

18   'Resource Management on the Flight Deck', Nasa Conference
     Publication.

19   See, for example, 'Report on the Workshop on Aviation Safety/Automa-
     tion Program', Nasa Conference Publication, 1980; 'Pilot Judgement in

TCA-Related Flight Planning', Nasa, 1989; 'General Aviation Weather Encounters', Nasa, 2007.

20 'Fatal Accidents Per Year: 1946–2019', Aviation Safety Network, 2020.

21 Henry Beecher and Donald Todd, 'A Study of the Deaths Associated with Anesthesia and Surgery: Based on a Study of 599,548 Anesthesias in Ten Institutions 1948–1952, Inclusive', *Annals of Surgery*, 1954, vol. 140, no. 1, pp. 2–34.

22 Henry Beecher and Donald Todd, 'A Study of the Deaths Associated with Anesthesia and Surgery'.

23 See, for example, B.S. Clifton and W. Hotten, 'Deaths Associated with Anesthesia', *British Journal of Anaesthesia*, 1963, vol. 35, no. 4, pp. 250–9; O.C. Phillips and L.S. Capizzi, 'Anesthesia Mortality', *Clinical Anesthesia*, 1974, vol. 10, no. 3, pp. 220–44.

24 Jeffrey Cooper, Ronald Newbower, Charlene Long and Bucknam McPeek, 'Preventable Anesthesia Mishaps: A Study of Human Factors', *Anesthesiology*, 1978, vol. 49, pp. 399–406.

25 Cooper, Newbower, Long and McPeek, 'Preventable Anesthesia Mishaps'.

26 Frederick Cheney, 'The American Society of Anesthesiologists Closed Claims Project', *Anesthesiology*, 1999, vol. 91, pp. 552–6.

27 Frederick Cheney, 'The American Society of Anesthesiologists Closed Claims Project'.

28 Joy Steadman, Blas Catalani, Christopher Sharp and Lebron Cooper, 'Life-threatening Perioperative Anesthetic Complications: Major Issues Surrounding Perioperative Morbidity and Mortality', *Trauma Surgery Acute Care Open*, 2017, vol. 2, no. 1, article 113.

29 Bernie Liban, 'Innovations, Inventions and Dr Archie Brain', *Anaesthesia*, 2012, vol. 67, no. 12, pp. 1309–13.

30 Alan Aitkenhead and M. Irwin, 'Deaths Associated with Anaesthesia – 65 Years On', *Anaesthesia*, 2021, vol. 76, no. 2, pp. 277–80.

31 Guohua Li, Margaret Warner, Barbara Lang, Lin Huang and Lena Sun, 'Epidemiology of Anesthesia-Related Mortality in the United States, 1999–2005', *Anesthesiology*, 2009, vol. 110, no. 4, pp. 759–65.

32 Ann Bonner and Gerda Tolhurst, 'Insider–Outsider Perspectives of Participant Observation', *Nurse Researcher*, 2002, vol. 9, no. 4, pp. 7–19.

33 Robert Sapolsky, 'Why Your Brain Hates Other People', *Nautilus*, 16 June 2017.

34 See, for example, Lasana Harris and Susan Fiske, 'Dehumanizing the Lowest of the Low: Neuroimaging Responses to Extreme Out-Groups',

Psychological Science, 2006, vol. 17, no. 10, pp. 847–53; Adam Chekroud, Jim Everett, Holly Bridge and Miles Hewstone, 'A Review of Neuroimaging Studies of Race-Related Prejudice: Does Amygdala Response Reflect Threat?', *Frontiers in Human Neuroscience*, 2014, vol. 8, article 179.

35   Robert Sapolsky, 'Why Your Brain Hates Other People'.

36   Robert Sapolsky, 'Why Your Brain Hates Other People'.

37   See, for example, Henri Tajfel, 'Experiments in Intergroup Discrimination', *Scientific American*, 1970, vol. 223, no. 5, pp. 96–103; Henri Tajfel, 'Social Psychology of Intergroup Relations', *Annual Review of Psychology*, 1982, vol. 33, pp. 1–39; Feng Sheng and Shihui Han, 'Manipulations of Cognitive Strategies and Intergroup Relationships Reduce the Racial Bias in Empathic Neural Responses', *Neuroimage*, 2012, vol. 61, no. 4, pp. 786–97.

38   Laura Babbitt and Samuel Sommers, 'Framing Matters: Contextual Influences on Interracial Interaction Outcomes', *Personality and Social Psychology Bulletin*, 2011, vol. 37, no. 9, pp. 1233–44.

39   Robert Sapolsky, 'Why Your Brain Hates Other People'.

40   See, for example, Bonner and Tolhurst, 'Insider–Outsider Perspectives of Participant Observation'.

41   Harry Wolcott, *Ethnography: A Way of Seeing*, AltaMira Press, 2008.

42   See, for example, 'Policy and Guidance for Examiners and Others Involved in University Examinations', University of Oxford, 2018; Barbara Whitaker, 'Yes, There Is a Job That Pays You to Shop', *New York Times*, 13 March 2005; 'Visualizing Apple Product Release Patterns', InfoNewt, 8 September 2021.

43   See, for example, a review of the Land Rover Experience on the Trip Advisor website: www.tripadvisor.co.uk; the Harley-Davidson factory tour on www.harley-davidson.com; the Toyota tour on www.toyotauk.com; and Southwest Airlines stores on its blog at https://community.southwest.com

44   Author interview on 10 September 2020.

45   Evan Hoopfer, 'Social Media LUV: How Southwest Airlines Connects with Customers Online', *Dallas Business Journal*, 3 March 2019.

46   Richie McCaw, *The Real McCaw*, p. 122.

47   Author interview with Felicity Aylieff on 7 December 2015.

48   Author interview with Peter Keen on 20 November 2012.

49   *All or Nothing: New Zealand All Blacks*, Amazon Prime, 2018.

50   Alan Light, *The Holy or the Broken*, Atria, 2012.

51   Guy Garvey, *The Fourth, the Fifth, the Minor Fall*, BBC Radio 2, 13 June 2009.

52　Alan Light, *The Holy or the Broken*.

53　Alan Light, *The Holy or the Broken*.

54　Alan Light, *The Holy or the Broken*.

55　Jack Whatley, 'Without John Cale, Leonard Cohen's "Hallelujah" Would've Been Forgotten', *Far Out*, 9 March 2020.

56　Alan Light, *The Holy or the Broken*.

57　Alan Light, *The Holy or the Broken*.

58　Alan Light, *The Holy or the Broken*.

59　Alan Light, *The Holy or the Broken*.

60　Wes Phillips, 'Jeff Buckley: Amazing Grace', Schwann Spectrum, Spring 1995.

61　Alan Light, *The Holy or the Broken*.

62　Daphne Brooks, *Grace*, Bloomsbury, 2005.

63　'The 10 Most Perfect Songs Ever', Q, 30 August 2007.

Habit 6: Give more, get more

1　See, for example, John Carreyrou, *Bad Blood: Secrets and Lies in a Silicon Valley Startup*, Picador, 2018; Peter Cohan, '4 Startling Insights into Elizabeth Holmes from Psychiatrist Who's Known Her Since Childhood', *Forbes*, 17 February 2019.

2　The level of venture capital investment, and number of deals made, from 1995 to 2019, are shown in 'MoneyTree', PwC, 2020.

3　This is described in more detail in John Carreyrou, *Bad Blood*; Norah O'Donnell, 'The Theranos Deception: How a Company with a Blood-testing Machine That Could Never Perform as Touted Went from Billion-Dollar Baby to Complete Bust', *60 Minutes*, 4 January 2018.

4　Elizabeth Holmes, 'TEDMED: Healthcare the Leading Cause of Bankruptcy', TEDMED, 2014.

5　See, for example, Mariella Moon, 'Walgreens to Offer Affordable and Needle-Free Blood Tests in More Stores', Engadget, 18 November 2014; Roger Parloff, 'A Singular Board at Theranos', *Fortune*, 12 June 2014.

6　Ludmila Leiva, 'Here Are the Theranos Investors Who Lost Millions', Yahoo! Finance, 5 March 2019.

7　See, for example, 'Forbes Announces Its 33rd Annual Forbes 400 Ranking of the Richest Americans', *Forbes*, 29 September 2014.

8　This is described in more detail in John Carreyrou, *Bad Blood*; Norah O'Donnell, 'The Theranos Deception'.

9 John Carreyrou, 'Hot Startup Theranos Has Struggled with Its Blood-Test Technology; Silicon Valley Lab, Led by Elizabeth Holmes, Is Valued at $9 Billion but Isn't Using Its Technology for All the Tests It Offers', *Wall Street Journal*, 16 October 2015.

10 Christopher Weaver, John Carreyrou and Michael Siconolfi, 'Theranos Is Subject of Criminal Probe by US', *Wall Street Journal*, 18 April 2016; Sheelah Kolhatkar and Caroline Chen, 'Theranos Under Investigation by SEC, US Attorney's Office', *Bloomberg Business*, 18 April 2016.

11 See, for example, John Carreyrou, 'U.S. Files Criminal Charges Against Theranos's Elizabeth Holmes, Ramesh Balwani', *Wall Street Journal*, 15 June 2018; 'US vs Elizabeth Holmes, et al.', United States Attorney's Office, 2020.

12 This is described in more detail in John Carreyrou, *Bad Blood*.

13 It is estimated that typically, more than a million fans watch each All Blacks game, either in person or on TV, as described in 'Annual Report', New Zealand Rugby, 2019.

14 See, for example, John McCrystal, *The Originals*; Richie McCaw, *The Real McCaw*; Dan Carter, *The Autobiography of an All Blacks Legend*; Peter Bills, *The Jersey*; Kieran Read, *Straight 8*.

15 These datasets can be downloaded for free from the Nasa Open Data Portal at https://data.nasa.gov

16 'Edelman Trust Barometer 2020', Edelman, 2020.

17 See for example, Naomi Oreskes, *Why Trust Science?*, Princeton University Press, 2019; Cary Funk, Alec Tyson, Brian Kennedy and Courtney Johnson, 'Science and Scientists Held in High Esteem Across Global Publics', Pew Research Center, 29 September 2020.

18 Rebecca Johannsen and Paul Zak, 'The Neuroscience of Organisational Trust and Business Performance: Findings from United States Working Adults and an Intervention at an Online Retailer', *Frontiers in Psychology*, 11 January 2021.

19 See, for example, Paul Zak and Stephen Knack, 'Trust and Growth', *Economic Journal*, 2001, vol. 111, no. 470, pp. 295–321; Joel Slemrod and Peter Katuščák, 'Do Trust and Trustworthiness Pay Off?', *Journal of Human Resources*, 2005, vol. 40, no. 3, pp. 621–46; Paul Zak, *Trust Factor: The Science of Creating High-Performance Companies*, Amacom, 2018.

20 See, for example, Michael Kosfeld, Marcus Heinrichs, Paul Zak, Urs Fischbacher and Ernst Fehr, 'Oxytocin Increases Trust in Humans', *Nature*, 2005, vol. 435, pp. 673–76; Paul Zak, Robert Kurzban and William Matzner, 'Oxytocin Is Associated with Human Trustworthiness', *Hormones and Behavior*, 2005, vol. 48, no. 5, pp. 522–7; Paul Zak, Angela Stanton and

Sheila Ahmadi, 'Oxytocin Increases Generosity in Humans', *PLOS One*, 2007, vol. 2, no. 11, article 1128.

21 See, for example, Aleeca Bell, Elise Erickson and Sue Carter, 'Beyond Labor: The Role of Natural and Synthetic Oxytocin in the Transition to Motherhood', *Journal of Midwifery and Women's Health*, 2014, vol. 59, no. 1, pp. 35–42; James Rilling and Larry Young, 'The Biology of Mammalian Parenting and Its Effect on Offspring Social Development', *Science*, 2014, vol. 345, no. 6198, pp. 771–6; Francis McGlone and Susannah Walker, 'Four Health Benefits of Hugs – And Why They Feel So Good', *The Conversation*, 17 May 2021.

22 See, for example, Christina Grape, Maria Sandgren, Lars-Olof Hansson, Mats Ericson and Töres Theorell, 'Does Singing Promote Well-Being?: An Empirical Study of Professional and Amateur Singers During a Singing Lesson', *Integrative Psychological and Behavioral Science*, 2003, vol. 38, no. 1, pp. 65–74; Roman Wittig, Catherine Crockford, Tobias Deschner, Kevin Langergraber, Toni Ziegler and Klaus Zuberbühler, 'Food Sharing Is Linked to Urinary Oxytocin Levels and Bonding in Related and Unrelated Wild Chimpanzees', *Proceedings of the Royal Society B: Biological Sciences*, 2014, vol. 281, no. 1778, article 20133096; Alan Harvey, 'Links Between the Neurobiology of Oxytocin and Human Musicality', *Frontiers in Human Neuroscience*, 2020, vol. 14, article 350; Courtney King, Anny Gano and Howard Becker, 'The Role of Oxytocin in Alcohol and Drug Abuse', *Brain Research*, 2020, vol. 1736, article 146761.

23 See, for example, Philippe Richard, Françoise Moos and Marie-José Freund-Mercier, 'Central Effects of Oxytocin', *Physiological Reviews*, 1991, vol. 71, no. 2, pp. 331–70; Thomas Baumgartner, Markus Heinrichs, Aline Vonlanthen, Urs Fischbacher and Ernst Fehr, 'Oxytocin Shapes the Neural Circuitry of Trust and Trust Adaptation in Humans', *Neuron*, 2008, vol. 58, no. 4, pp. 639–50; Waguih IsHak, Maria Kahloon and Hala Fakhry, 'Oxytocin Role in Enhancing Well-Being: A Literature Review', *Journal of Affective Disorders*, 2011, vol. 130, no. 1–2, pp. 1–9; Liran Samuni, Anna Preis, Roger Mundry, Tobias Deschner, Catherine Crockford and Roman Wittig, 'Oxytocin Reactivity During Intergroup Conflict in Wild Chimpanzees', *PNAS*, 2017, vol. 114, no. 2, pp. 268–73; Guilherme Brockington, Ana Gomes Moreira, Maria Buso, Sérgio Gomes da Silva, Edgar Altszyler, Ronald Fischer and Jorge Moll, 'Storytelling Increases Oxytocin and Positive Emotions and Decreases Cortisol and Pain in Hospitalized Children', *PNAS*, 2021, vol. 118, no. 22, article 2018409118.

24 Author interview with Peter Keen on 20 November 2012.

25 See, for example: Matt Slater, 'Olympics Cycling: Marginal Gains Underpin Team GB Dominance', BBC Sport, 8 August 2012; 'Annual Report', British Cycling, 2019.

26 See, for example, Matt Lawton, 'British Cycling and UK Anti-Doping Face Questions Over Traces of Steroid in Prominent Rider's 2010 Test', *The Times*, 27 March 2021; 'List of Doping Cases in Cycling', Wikipedia.

27 A description of the programme can be found at 'Character Animation', School of Film/Video, CalArts.

28 See, for example, Jim Korkis, 'The Birth of Animation Training', Animation World Network, 23 September 2004; Sam Kashner, 'The Class That Roared', *Vanity Fair*, March 2014.

29 Peter Hartlaub, 'The Secret of Pixar's Magic Can Be Found at CalArts, Where Legendary Old-School Animators from Disney's Golden Era Passed on Their Knowledge – and Passion – to Younger Generations', SF Gate, 17 September 2003.

30 Peter Hartlaub, 'The Secret of Pixar's Magic Can Be Found at CalArts'.

31 Frank Thomas and Ollie Johnston, *Disney Animation: The Illusion of Life*, Abbeville Press, 1981.

32 Susan King, 'Walt Disney Animation Studios Turns 90 in Colorful Fashion', *Los Angeles Times*, 10 December 2013.

33 Sam Kashner, 'The Class That Roared'.

34 This is described in more detail in Leslie Iwerks, *The Pixar Story*, Buena Vista Pictures Distribution, 2007; David Price, 2009, *The Pixar Touch: The Making of a Company*, Alfred A. Knopf, 2008; Ed Catmull, *Creativity Inc.: Overcoming the Unseen Forces That Stand in the Way of True Inspiration*, Bantam Press, 2014.

35 This is described in more detail in Leslie Iwerks, *The Pixar Story*; David Price, *The Pixar Touch*; Ed Catmull, *Creativity Inc*.

36 These figures are taken from 'Toy Story (1995)', The Numbers.

37 Associated Press, 'Disney to Buy Pixar for $7.4 Billion', *New York Times*, 24 January 2006.

38 Author interview with Catherine Mallyon on 26 August 2014.

39 See, for example, Yael Lapidot, Ronit Kark and Boas Shamir, 'The Impact of Situational Vulnerability on the Development and Erosion of Followers' Trust in Their Leader', *Leadership Quarterly*, 2007, vol. 18, no. 1, pp. 16–34; Ann-Marie Nienaber, Marcel Hofeditz and Philipp Daniel Romeike,

'Vulnerability and Trust in Leader–Follower Relationships', *Personnel Review*, 2015, vol. 44, no. 4, pp. 567–91.

40   See, for example, Gene Kranz, *Failure Is Not an Option: Mission Control from Mercury to Apollo 13 and Beyond*, Simon & Schuster, 2000; Paul Sean Hill, *Mission Control Management: The Principles of High Performance and Perfect Decision-Making Learned from Leading at NASA*, Nicholas Brealey Publishing, 2018.

41   See, for example, Steve Peters, *The Chimp Paradox: The Mind Management Programme for Confidence, Success and Happiness*, Vermilion, 2011; Joe Friel, *The Cyclist's Training Bible: The World's Most Comprehensive Training Guide*, VeloPress, 2018; Alan Murchison, *The Cycling Chef: Recipes for Getting Lean and Fuelling the Machine*, Bloomsbury, 2021.

42   See, for example, Tomoki Kitawaki, 'The Synergy of EMG Waveform During Bicycle Pedaling Is Related to Elemental Force Vector Waveform', *Journal of Science and Cycling*, 2019, vol. 8, no. 2, pp. 3–4; Borja Martinez-Gonzalez, 'The Sleep of Professional Cyclists During a 5-Day UCI Europe Tour Road Cycling Race', *Journal of Science and Cycling*, 2019, vol. 8, no. 2, pp. 20–1; Masahiro Fukuda, 'Easy to Use Accurate Measuring System for Cycling Pedaling Motion Using a Small LED and a Smartphone', *Journal of Science and Cycling*, 2019, vol. 8, no. 2, pp. 59–60.

43   See, for example, John Massie and Martin Delatycki, 'Cystic Fibrosis Carrier Screening', *Paediatric Respiratory Reviews*, 2013, vol. 14, no. 4, pp. 270–5; Stuart Elborn, 'Cystic Fibrosis', *Lancet*, 2016, vol. 388, no. 10059, pp. 2519–31.

44   See, for example, Warren Warwick, 'Cystic Fibrosis Sweat Test for Newborns', *JAMA*, 1966, vol. 198, no. 1, pp. 59–62; Warren Warwick and Leland Hansen, 'The Silver Electrode Method for Rapid Analysis of Sweat Chloride', *Pediatrics*, 1965, vol. 36, pp. 261–4; Leland Hansen, Mary Buechele, Joann Koroshec and Warren Warwick, 'Sweat Chloride Analysis by Chloride Ion-Specific Electrode Method Using Heat Stimulation', *American Journal of Clinical Pathology*, 1968, vol. 49, no. 6, pp. 834–41.

45   This is described in more detail in Preston Campbell, 'Warren Warwick: A Pioneer in CF Care and Research', Cystic Fibrosis Foundation, 19 February 2016; 'Research – What the CF?', Cystic Fibrosis Trust.

46   This is described in more detail in 'CF Basic Research Centers', Cystic Fibrosis Foundation.

47   See, for example, 'Patient Registry Annual Data Report', Cystic Fibrosis Foundation, 2019.

48 See, for example, Michael Boyle, Kathryn Sabadosa, Hebe Quinton, Bruce Marshall and Michael Schechter, 'Key Findings of the US Cystic Fibrosis Foundation's Clinical Practice Benchmarking Project', *BMJ Quality and Safety*, 2014, vol. 23, no. S1, pp. i15– i22; Bruce Marshall and Eugene Nelson, 'Accelerating Implementation of Biomedical Research Advances: Critical Elements of a Successful 10 Year Cystic Fibrosis Foundation Healthcare Delivery Improvement Initiative', *BMJ Quality and Safety*, 2014, vol. 23, no. S1, pp. i95–i103; Bruce Marshall, 'Survival Trending Upward but What Does This Really Mean?', Cystic Fibrosis Foundation, 16 November 2017.

49 This is explained in more detail in Bruce Fallick, Charles Fleischman and James Rebitzer, 'Job-Hopping in Silicon Valley: Some Evidence Concerning the Microfoundations of a High-Technology Cluster', *Review of Economics and Statistics*, 2006, vol. 88, no. 3, pp. 472–81; Eric Taub, 'US High Tech Said to Slip', *New York Times*, 25 June 2008.

50 See, for example, 'Explosive Growth', Britannica; 'Silicon Valley Employment Trends Through 2016', Silicon Valley Institute for Regional Studies, 2017; George Avalos, 'Silicon Valley Job Market Bounces Back Strongly, Inflation Soars: Report', *Mercury News*, 15 February 2022.

51 This is explained in more detail in Conner Forrest, 'How Buck's of Woodside Became the "Cheers" of Silicon Valley', TechRepublic, 4 July 2014; Jamis MacNiven, *Breakfast at Buck's: Tales from the Pancake Guy*, Liverwurst Press, 2004; Adam Fisher, *Valley of Genius: The Uncensored History of Silicon Valley*, Twelve, 2018.

52 This is explained in more detail in Michael Lewis, *The New New Thing: A Silicon Valley Story*, Coronet, 2000; Adam Fisher, *Valley of Genius*.

53 See, for example, John Sandelin, 'Co-Evolution of Stanford University & the Silicon Valley: 1950 to Today', presentation, 2004; Jeff Chu, 'Stanford University's Unique Economic Engine', *Fast Company*, 1 October 2010.

54 See, for example, Melanie Warner, 'Inside the Silicon Valley Money Machine', *Fortune*, 26 October 1998; Bruce Schulman, *Making the American Century: Essays on the Political Culture of Twentieth Century America*, Oxford University Press, 2014; Tom Nicholas, *VC: An American History*, Harvard University Press, 2020.

55 As described in more detail in Michael Hiltzik, *Dealers of Lightning: Xerox PARC and the Dawn of the Computer Age*, HarperBusiness, 1999; Tom Nicholas, *VC: An American History*.

56 Michael Malone, *The Big Score: The Billion Dollar Story of Silicon Valley*, Doubleday, 1985.

57 See, for example, Mohamed Atalla, Emmanuel Tannenbaum and E. Scheibner, 'Stabilization of Silicon Surfaces by Thermally Grown Oxides', *Bell System Technical Journal*, 1959, vol. 38, no. 3, pp. 749–83; Marcian Hoff, Stanley Mazor and Federico Faggin, 'Memory System for a Multi-Chip Digital Computer', *IEEE Solid-State Circuits Magazine*, 1974, vol. 1, no. 1, pp. 46–54; Thomas Wadlow, 'The Xerox Alto Computer', *BYTE*, September 1981, pp. 58–68; John Markoff, 'Searching for Silicon Valley', *New York Times*, 16 April 2009.

58 'Top 30 US Companies in the S&P 500 Index', Disfold, 2021.

59 This is described in more detail in Adam Fisher, *Valley of Genius*; Michael Malone, 'The Twitter Revolution: The Brains Behind the Web's Hottest Networking Tool', *Wall Street Journal*, 18 April 2009.

60 Adam Fisher, *Valley of Genius*.

Habit 7: Be porous

1 Dylan Jones, *David Bowie: A Life*, Windmill Books, 2017.

2 See, for example, 'The 500 Greatest Albums of All Time', *NME*, 25 October 2013; Joe Lynch, 'David Bowie Influenced More Musical Genres than Any Other Rock Star', *Billboard*, 14 January 2016; Nolan Feeney, 'Four Ways David Bowie Influenced Musicians Today', *Time*, 11 January 2016; Robin Reiser, 'One Year Gone, David Bowie Is Still the Most Influential Musician Ever', *Observer*, 10 January 2017; '500 Greatest Albums of All Time', *Rolling Stone*, 22 September 2020; Rob Sheffield, 'Thanks, Starman: Why David Bowie Was the Greatest Rock Star Ever', *Rolling Stone*, 11 January 2016.

3 BBC Radio 2, *David Bowie's "Heroes" 40th Anniversary*, 2017.

4 BBC Radio 2, *David Bowie's "Heroes" 40th Anniversary*.

5 BBC Radio 2, *David Bowie's "Heroes" 40th Anniversary*.

6 You can buy a set of these cards from Brian Eno's website: https://enoshop.co.uk

7 BBC Radio 2, *David Bowie's "Heroes" 40th Anniversary*.

8 Dylan Jones, *David Bowie: A Life*.

9 Jon Fingas, 'RIM: A Brief History from Budgie to BlackBerry 10', Engadget, 28 January 2013.

10 As shown in Research in Motion's annual reports from 2001 to 2007.

11   Juliette Garside, 'BlackBerry: How Business Went Sour', *Guardian*, 13 August 2013.

12   'App-Centric iPhone Model Is Overrated: RIM CEO', *Independent*, 17 November 2010; Jay Yarow, 'All the Dumb Things RIM's CEOs Said While Apple and Android Ate Their Lunch', *Business Insider*, 16 September 2011.

13   Jacquie McNish and Sean Silcoff, *Losing the Signal: The Untold Story Behind the Extraordinary Rise and Spectacular Fall of BlackBerry*, Flatiron Books, 2015.

14   This is described in more detail in Jacquie McNish and Sean Silcoff, *Losing the Signal*; and the story of Monitor Group's eventual demise is described in Steve Denning, 'What Killed Michael Porter's Monitor Group? The One Force That Really Matters', *Forbes*, 20 November 2012.

15   Brian Chen, 'Apple Registers Trademark for: There's an App for That', *Wired*, 11 October 2010; Jonathan Geller, 'Open Letter to BlackBerry Bosses: Senior RIM Exec Tells All as Company Crumbles Around Him', BGR, 30 January 2011; Xavier Lanier, 'Developers Face Challenges Gearing Up for Playbook', GottaBe Mobile, 27 February 2011.

16   David Crow, 'BlackBerry Hangs Up on Handset Business', *Financial Times*, 28 September 2016; Lisa Eadicicco, 'The Company Keeping BlackBerry Phones Alive Will Stop Selling Them Later This Year, Marking the Final Nail in the Coffin for the Once-Dominant Phone Brand', *Business Insider*, 4 February 2020.

17   Caroline Valetkevitch, 'Key Dates and Milestones in the S&P 500's History'.

18   Scott Anthony, Patrick Viguerie and Andrew Waldeck, 'Corporate Longevity: Turbulence Ahead for Large Organisations', Innosight, spring 2016.

19   See, for example, 'Strategic Readiness and Transformation Survey: Are Business Leaders Caught in a Confidence Bubble?', Innosight, June 2017; Mark Bertolini, David Duncan and Andrew Waldeck, 'Knowing When to Reinvent: Detecting Marketplace "Fault Lines" Is the Key to Build the Case for Preemptive Change', *Harvard Business Review*, December 2015, pp. 90–101; Anthony, Viguerie, Schwartz and Van Landeghem, '2018 Corporate Longevity Forecast'.

20   'Strategic Readiness and Transformation Survey: Are Business Leaders Caught in a Confidence Bubble?', Innosight.

21   See, for example, Thucydides, *History of the Peloponnesian War*, Guild Publishing, 1990; Dante Alighieri, 'Divine Comedy', Foligno, 11 April 1472; Francis Bacon, *Novum Organum*, 1620; Arthur Schopenhauer, *Die Welt*

als Wille und Vorstellung, Routledge, 1844; Leo Tolstoy, *What Is Art?*, Macmillan, 1897; Peter Wason, 'On the Failure to Eliminate Hypotheses in a Conceptual Task', *Quarterly Journal of Experimental Psychology*, 1960, vol. 12, no. 3, pp. 129–40; Peter Wason, 'Reasoning About a Rule', *Quarterly Journal of Experimental Psychology*, 1968, vol. 20, no. 3, pp. 273–81; Peter Wason and Diana Shapiro, 'Natural and Contrived Experience in a Reasoning Problem', *Quarterly Journal of Experimental Psychology*, 1971, vol. 23, no. 1, pp. 63–71.

22 See, for example, William Hart, Dolores Albarracín, Alice Eagly, Inge Brechan, Matthew Lindberg and Lisa Merrill, 'Feeling Validated Versus Being Correct: A Meta-analysis of Selective Exposure to Information', *Psychological Bulletin*, 2009, vol. 135, no. 4, pp. 555–88; Glinda Cooper and Vanessa Meterko, 'Cognitive Bias Research in Forensic Science: A Systematic Review', *Forensic Science International*, 2019, vol. 297, pp. 35–46; Kajornvut Ounjai, Shunsuke Kobayashi, Muneyoshi Takahashi, Tetsuya Matsuda and Johan Lauwereyns, 'Active Confirmation Bias in the Evaluative Processing of Food Images', *Scientific Reports*, 2018, vol. 8, article 16864.

23 See, for example, 'Dick Cheney's Suite Demands', Smoking Gun, 22 March 2006; Jason Wiles, 'The Missing Link: Scientist Discovers That Evolution Is Missing from Arkansas Classrooms', *Arkansas Times*, 24 March 2006.

24 This is described in more detail in Joyce Ehrlinger, Wilson Readinger and Bora Kim, 'Decision-Making and Cognitive Biases', in *Encyclopaedia of Mental Health*, ed. Howard Friedman, Academic Press, 2016; Uwe Peters, 'What Is the Function of Confirmation Bias?', *Erkenntnis*, 2022, vol. 87, no. 3, pp. 1351–76.

25 Author interview with Peter Keen on 20 November 2012.

26 Chris Boardman, *Triumphs and Turbulence: My Autobiography*, Ebury Press, 2016.

27 Author interview with Timothy Jones on 3 February 2014.

28 The changes made are described in more detail in Graham Henry, *Final Word*; Peter Bills, *The Jersey*.

29 Dan Carter, *The Autobiography of an All Blacks Legend*.

30 Johnson and McConnell, *Behind the Silver Fern*.

31 Richie McCaw, *The Real McCaw*.

32 Richie McCaw, *The Real McCaw*.

33 See, for example, 'Football: Barca Coach Likes What He Sees with All Blacks', *New Zealand Herald*, 1 February 2016; Gregor Paul, 'Rugby: All Blacks Learn from Marines', *New Zealand Herald*, 26 May 2017; Ben Smith,

'How an NBA GM Inspired the All Blacks Lethal Counter Attack', Rugby-Pass, 30 August 2018; 'All Blacks Try Life in Fast Lane at McLaren's F1 Garage', *Stuff*, 8 November 2018.

34   See 'List of New Zealand National Rugby Union Players', Wikipedia; and '2015 Rugby World Cup Final', Wikipedia, to see how New Zealand moved experienced and inexperienced players in and out of a match.

35   See, for example, James Laylin, *Nobel Laureates in Chemistry: 1901–1992*, American Chemical Society / Chemical Heritage Foundation, 1993; Robert Root-Bernstein, Maurine Bernstein and Helen Garnier, 'Correlations Between Avocations, Scientific Style, Work Habits, and Professional Impact of Scientists', *Creativity Research Journal*, 1995, vol. 8, no. 2, pp. 115–37; Robert Root-Bernstein and Maurine Bernstein, 'Artistic Scientists and Scientific Artists: The Link Between Polymathy and Creativity', in *Creativity: From Potential to Realization*, ed. Robert Sternberg, E. Grigorenko and J. Singer, Ringgold, 2004; Albert Rothenberg, 'Family Background and Genius II: Nobel Laureates in Science', *Canadian Journal of Psychiatry*, 2005, vol. 50, no. 14, pp. 918–25; Robert Root-Bernstein, 'Arts and Crafts as Adjuncts to STEM Education to Foster Creativity in Gifted and Talented Students', *Asia Pacific Education Review*, 2015, vol. 16, no. 2, pp. 203–12.

36   Michael Bond, 'Clever Fools: Why a High IQ Doesn't Mean You're Smart', *New Scientist*, 28 October 2009; New Scientist, *The Brain: Everything You Need to Know*, John Murray, 2018.

37   See, for example, Lewis Terman, *Mental and Physical Traits of a Thousand Gifted Children: Genetic Studies of Genius, Volume 1*, Stanford University Press, 1925; Reva Jenkins-Friedman, 'Myth: Cosmetic Use of Multiple Selection Criteria!', *Gifted Child Quarterly*, 1982, vol. 26, no. 1, pp. 24–6; Carole Holahan and Robert Sears, *The Gifted Group in Later Maturity*, Stanford University Press, 1995; Daniel Goleman, '75 Years Later, Study Still Tracking Geniuses', *New York Times*, 7 March 1995.

38   Robert Root-Bernstein, 'Arts Foster Scientific Success: Avocations of Nobel, National Academy, Royal Society, and Sigma Xi Members', *Journal of Psychology of Science and Technology*, 2008, vol. 1, no. 2, pp. 51–63.

39   See, for example, Bernard Schlessinger and June Schlessinger, *The Who's Who of Nobel Prize Winners, 1901–1990*, Oryx Press, 1991; Paul Feltovich, Rand Spiro and Richard Coulson, 'Issues of Expert Flexibility in Contexts Characterized by Complexity and Change', in *Expertise in Context: Human and Machine*, ed. Paul Feltovich, Kenneth Ford and Robert Hoffman,

American Association for Artificial Intelligence, 1997; Fernand Gobet, *Understanding Expertise: A Multi-disciplinary Approach*, Red Globe Press, 2016.

40 This is described in more detail in their profiles at www.nobelprize.org

41 Sheldon Richmond, 'The Aesthetic Dimension of Science: The Sixteenth *Nobel Conference* ed. by Dean W. Curtin (review)', *Leonardo*, 1984, vol. 17, no. 2, p. 129.

42 Dorothy Hodgkin and Guy Dodson, *The Collected Works of Dorothy Crowfoot Hodgkin*, Interline, 1994.

43 Santiago Ramón y Cajal, *Precepts and Counsels on Scientific Investigation: Stimulants of the Spirit*, Pacific Press, 1951.

44 Robert Root-Bernstein, Maurine Bernstein and Helen Garnier, 'Identification of Scientists Making Long-Term, High-Impact Contributions, with Notes on Their Methods of Working', *Creativity Research Journal*, 1993, vol. 6, no. 4, pp. 329–43.

45 See, for example, Tim Harford, 'A Powerful Way to Unleash Your Natural Creativity', TED Talk, 2018; Kep Kee Loh and Stephen Wee Hun Lim, 'Positive Associations Between Media Multitasking and Creativity', *Computers in Human Behavior Reports*, 2020, vol. 1, article 100015.

46 See, for example, David Archibald, *Charles Darwin: A Reference Guide to His Life and Works*, Rowman and Littlefield, 2018; Eva Amsen, 'Leonardo da Vinci's Scientific Studies, 500 Years Later', *Forbes*, 2 May 2019.

47 Root-Bernstein, Bernstein and Gernier, 'Correlations Between Avocations, Scientific Style, Work Habits, and Professional Impact of Scientists'.

48 See, for example, Will Dahlgreen, 'Why Are Nobel Prize Winners Getting Older?', BBC, 7 October 2016; 'List of Nobel Laureates by University Affiliation', Wikipedia.

Habit 8: Shake all trees

1 See, for example, *Astronaut Fact Book*, Nasa, 2013; 'Astronaut Selection Timeline', Nasa, 23 September 2021.

2 'Human Exploration of Mars Design Reference Architecture 5.0', Nasa, July 2009.

3 See 'Building a Winning Team for Missions to Mars', opening speech at the American Association for the Advancement of Science Annual Meeting, 2019, which is on YouTube.

4   This is explained in more detail in 'Critical Team Composition Issues for Long-Distance and Long-Duration Space Exploration: A Literature Review, an Operational Assessment, and Recommendations for Practice and Research', Nasa, 1 February 2015; 'Training "The Right Stuff": An Assessment of Team Training Needs for Long-Duration Spaceflight Crews', Nasa Johnson Space Center Technical Manuscript 2015-218589, 2015.

5   Adam Hadhazy, 'How NASA Selected the 2013 Class of Astronauts: What Is "The Right Stuff" for a Trip to Mars?', *Popular Science*, 31 January 2013.

6   Biographies of the current Nasa astronauts are at www.nasa.gov

7   Adam Hadhazy, 'How NASA Selected the 2013 Class of Astronauts'.

8   See, for example, Kelly Slack, Al Holland and Walter Sipes, 'Selecting Astronauts: The Role of Psychologists', presentation at the 122nd Annual Convention of the American Psychological Association, 8 August 2014; 'An Astronaut's Guide to Applying to Be an Astronaut', Nasa, 2 March 2020.

9   See, for example, Henry Dethloff, *Suddenly, Tomorrow Came: The NASA History of the Johnson Space Center*, Dover Publications, 2012; J.D. Barrett, A.W. Holland and W.B. Vessey, 'Identifying the "Right Stuff": An Exploration-Focused Astronaut Job Analysis', Annual Conference of the Society for Industrial and Organizational Psychology, 2015; Lauren Blackwell Landon, Kelly Slack and Jamie Barrett, 'Teamwork and Collaboration in Long-Duration Space Missions: Going to Extremes', *American Psychologist*, 2018, vol. 73, no. 4, pp. 563–75.

10   See, for example, the Conference Board annual CEO surveys over the last fifty years at https://conference-board.org; and PwC annual CEO surveys over the last twenty years at www.ceosurvey.pwc

11   See, for example, Peter Cappelli, 'Your Approach to Hiring Is All Wrong: Outsourcing and Algorithms Won't Get You the People You Need', *Harvard Business Review*, May–June 2019, pp. 49–58; 'Employee Tenure in 2018', US Bureau of Labor Statistics, 2018; 'Companies with the Most and Least Loyal Employees', PayScale.

12   Shane McFeely and Ben Wigert, 'This Fixable Problem Costs U.S. Businesses $1 Trillion', Gallup, 13 March 2019.

13   See, for example, Fay Hansen, 'What Is the Cost of Employee Turnover?', *Compensation and Benefits Review*, 1997, vol. 29, no. 5, pp. 17–18; Matthew O'Connell and Mei-Chuan Kung, 'The Cost of Employee Turnover', *Industrial Management*, 2007, vol. 49, no. 1, pp. 14–19.

14 See, for example, Elizabeth Chambers, Mark Foulon, Helen Handfield-Jones, Steven Hankin and Edward Michaels, 'The War for Talent', *McKinsey Quarterly*, 1998, no. 3, pp. 44–57; 'This Year in Employee Engagement', Jiordan Castle, 2016; Jim Clifton, 'The World's Broken Workplace', Gallup, 13 June 2017; Scott Keller and Mary Meaney, 'Attracting and Retaining the Right Talent', McKinsey and Company, 24 November 2017.

15 See, for example, 'Recruiting and Selection Procedures: Personnel Policies Forum Survey No. 146', Bureau of National Affairs, May 1988; Robert Dipboye, *Selection Interviews: Process Perspectives*, South-Western, 1992; Laura Graves and Ronald Karren, 'The Employee Selection Interview: A Fresh Look at an Old Problem', *Human Resource Management*, 1996, vol. 35, no. 2, pp. 163–80; Frank Schmidt, 'The Role of General Cognitive Ability and Job Performance: Why There Cannot Be a Debate', *Human Performance*, 2002, vol. 15, no. 1–2, pp. 187–210.

16 See, for example, 'Recruiting and Selection Procedures', Bureau of National Affairs.

17 See, for example, Akhil Amar, 'Lottery Voting: A Thought Experiment', *University of Chicago Legal Forum*, 1995, vol. 1995, no. 1, pp. 193–204; Frank Schmidt and John Hunter, 'The Validity and Utility of Selection Methods in Personnel Psychology: Practical and Theoretical Implications of 85 Years of Research Findings', *Psychological Bulletin*, 1998, vol. 124, no. 2, pp. 262–74; Frank Schmidt, 'The Role of General Cognitive Ability and Job Performance'; Alia Wong, 'Lotteries May Be the Fairest Way to Fix Elite-College Admissions', *Atlantic*, 1 August 2018.

18 Andrew Jebb, Louis Tay, Ed Diener and Shigehiro Oishi, 'Happiness, Income Satiation and Turning Points Around the World', *Nature Human Behaviour*, 2018, vol. 2, pp. 33–8.

19 See, for example, Ryan Howell and Colleen Howell, 'The Relation of Economic Status to Subjective Well-Being in Developing Countries: A Meta-analysis', *Psychological Bulletin*, 2008, vol. 134, no. 4, pp. 536–60; Timothy Judge, Ronald Piccolo, Nathan Podsakoff, John Shaw and Bruce Rich, 'The Relationship Between Pay and Job Satisfaction: A Meta-analysis of the Literature', *Journal of Vocational Behavior*, 2010, vol. 77, no. 2, pp. 157–67; Lori Goler, Janelle Gale, Brynn Harrington and Adam Grant, 'Why People Really Quit Their Jobs', *Harvard Business Review*, 11 January 2018; Peakon, 'The 9-Month Warning: Understanding Why People Quit – Before It's Too Late', Heartbeat, 2019.

20 'Usual Weekly Earnings of Wage and Salary Workers', US Bureau of Labor Statistics, 19 July 2020; Lawrence Mishel and Jessica Schieder, 'CEO Compensation Surged in 2017', Economic Policy Institute, 16 August 2018.

21 Frank Schmidt and John Hunter, 'The Validity and Utility of Selection Methods in Personnel Psychology'.

22 See, for example, Peter Bills, *The Jersey*; Robert van Royen, 'Black Fern Kendra Cocksedge the First Woman to Win NZ Rugby's Top Player Award', *Stuff*, 14 December 2018; Thomas Airey, 'Eight Samoans in All Blacks World Cup Squad', *Samoa Observer*, 28 August 2019.

23 See, for example, Mark Brown, 'RSC to Reflect Diversity of Britain with Summer 2019 Season', *Guardian*, 10 September 2018; 'Diversity Data Report', Royal Shakespeare Company, 2019.

24 This is described in more detail in Graham Henry, *Final Word*; Adam Hadazy, 'How NASA Selected the 2013 Class of Astronauts'.

25 See, for example, 'Pret A Manger Staff Help Choose the New Recruits', *Personnel Today*, 23 April 2002; Peter Moore, 'Pret A Manger – Behind the Scenes at the "Happy Factory"', *Guardian*, 14 April 2015; Jody Hoffer Gittell, *The Southwest Airlines Way: Using the Power of Relationships to Achieve High Performance*, McGraw Hill, 2003; Julie Weber, 'How Southwest Airlines Hires Such Dedicated People', *Harvard Business Review*, 2 December 2015; Julian Richer, *The Richer Way: How to Get the Best out of People*, Random House Business, 2020.

26 This is explained in more detail in Laszlo Bock, *Work Rules! Insights from Inside Google That Will Transform How You Live and Lead*, John Murray, 2015.

27 See 'Annual Equality Report 2019', Royal College of Art.

28 This is explained in more detail in Andrew Hodges, *Alan Turing: The Enigma*, Vintage, 2014.

29 The full interview with Joan Joslin can be found at https://bletchleypark.org.uk; the tests and recruitment processes used are described in more detail in Sinclair McKay, *Bletchley Park Brainteasers: Over 100 Puzzles, Riddles and Enigmas Inspired by the Greatest Minds of World War II*, Headline, 2017.

30 Gordon Welchman, *The Hut Six Story: Breaking the Enigma Codes*, M. & M. Baldwin, 1982.

31 Sinclair McKay, *Bletchley Park Brainteasers*.

32 Christopher Smith, *The Hidden History of Bletchley Park: A Social and Organisational History, 1939–1945*, Palgrave Macmillan, 2015; a full list of

everyone who worked at Bletchley Park can be found at https://bletchleypark.org.uk/roll-of-honour

33   See, for example, Tom Chivers, 'Could You Have Been a Codebreaker at Bletchley?', *Daily Telegraph*, 10 October 2014.

34   Sinclair McKay, *Bletchley Park Brainteasers*.

35   Harry Hinsley and Alan Stripp, *Codebreakers: The Inside Story of Bletchley Park*, Oxford University Press, 1993.

36   Sinclair McKay, *Bletchley Park Brainteasers*.

37   Hinsley and Stripp, *Codebreakers*.

38   Ralph Erskine and Michael Smith, *The Bletchley Park Codebreakers: How Ultra Shortened the War and Led to the Birth of the Computer*, Biteback, 2011.

39   See, for example, 'College Strategic Plan 2016–21', Royal College of Art; 'Societies Programme', Eton College.

40   Eton's last one was John Gurdon in 1951.

41   A number of books have later been written by some of the people who've worked with them. See, for example, Dr Charles Pellerin, *How NASA Builds Teams: Mission Critical Soft Skills for Scientists, Engineers, and Project Teams*, Wiley, 2009; Dr Steve Peters, *The Chimp Paradox*; Dr Ceri Evans, *Perform Under Pressure: Change the Way You Feel, Think and Act Under Pressure*, Thorsons, 2019.

42   See, for example, 'Building a Winning Team for Missions to Mars'; 'The Problems of Flying to Mars', *The Economist*, 23 February 2019; Rhys Blakely, 'Class Clowns Find Their Calling on Eight-Month Journey to Mars', *The Times*, 16 February 2019.

43   See, for example, Philip Norman, *Shout! The True Story of the Beatles*, Pan, 2011; Khoi Tu, *Superteams: The Secrets of Stellar Performance of Seven Legendary Teams*, Portfolio Penguin, 2012.

44   See, for example, Hunaid Hasan and Tasneem Fatema Hasan, 'Laugh Yourself Into a Healthier Person: A Cross Cultural Analysis of the Effects of Varying Levels of Laughter on Health', *International Journal of Medical Sciences*, 2009, vol. 6, no. 4, pp. 200–11; Ramon Mora-Ripoll, 'Potential Health Benefits of Simulated Laugher: A Narrative Review of the Literature and Recommendations for Future Research', *Complementary Therapies in Medicine*, 2011, vol. 19, no. 3, pp. 170–7.

45   Michael Seth Starr, *Ringo: With a Little Help*, Backbeat, 2016.

46   Michael Seth Starr, *Ringo*.

47   Clive Thompson, 'If You Liked This, You're Sure to Love That', *New York Times*, 21 November 2008.

48 See, for example, James Bennett and Stan Lanning, 'The Netflix Prize', Proceedings of KDD Cup and Workshop, San Jose, 12 August 2007; Eliot Van Buskirk, 'How the Netflix Prize Was Won', *Wired*, 22 September 2009; Blake Hallinan and Ted Striphas, 2014, 'Recommended for You: The Netflix Prize and the Production of Algorithmic Culture', *New Media and Society*, 2016, vol. 18, no. 1, pp. 117–37.

49 Clive Thompson, 'If You Liked This, You're Sure to Love That'; Dan Jackson, 'The Netflix Prize: How a $1 Million Contest Changed Binge-Watching Forever', Thrillist, 7 July 2017.

50 Eliot Van Buskirk, 'How the Netflix Prize Was Won'.

51 See, for example, James Surowiecki, *The Wisdom of Crowds: Why the Many Are Smarter than the Few*, Abacus, 2005; Scott Page, *The Diversity Bonus: How Great Teams Pay Off in the Knowledge Economy*, Princeton University Press, 2017; David Shenk, *The Genius in All of Us: Why Everything You've Been Told About Genetics, Talent, and IQ Is Wrong*, Icon Books, 2010; Professor Tim Spector, *Identically Different: Why You Can Change Your Genes*, Weidenfeld & Nicolson, 2013.

52 Author interview with Paul Thompson on 18 November 2018, at Leaders in Sport, see: Alex Hill, 'Summit Session: Are You Radically Traditional?', Radically Traditional, 14 February 2019.

53 See, for example, Laszlo Bock, 'Here's Google's Secret to Hiring the Best People', *Wired*, 7 April 2015; Laszlo Bock, *Work Rules!*.

54 Jillian D'Onfro, 'The Unconventional Way Google Snagged a Team of Engineers Microsoft Desperately Wanted', *Business Insider India*, 6 April 2015; Rob Minto, 'The Genius Behind Google's Browser', *Financial Times*, 27 March 2009.

55 'Number of Full-Time Alphabet Employees from 2007 to 2021', Statista, 27 July 2011.

Habit 9: Get better, not bigger

1 Chris Boardman, *Triumphs and Turbulence*; Donald McRae, 'London 2012 Olympics: Peter Keen Ruthless in Pursuit of British Medals', *Guardian*, 27 July 2010.

2 Chris Boardman, *Triumphs and Turbulence*.

3 Chris Boardman, *Triumphs and Turbulence*.

4 'Annual Report', British Cycling, 2019; 'Great Britain Cycling Team Squad', British Cycling.

5   Matt Slater, 'Olympics Cycling: Marginal Gains Underpin Team GB Dominance'.

6   Angela Monaghan, 'Nokia: The Rise and Fall of a Mobile Phone Giant', *Guardian*, 3 September 2013; Jorma Ollila and Harri Saukkomaa, *Against All Odds: Leading Nokia from Near Catastrophe to Global Success*, Maven House, 2016.

7   Timo Vuori and Quy Huy, 'Distributed Attention and Shared Emotions in the Innovation Process: How Nokia Lost the Smartphone Battle', *Administrative Science Quarterly*, 2016, vol. 61, no. 1, pp. 9–51.

8   Vuori and Huy, 'Distributed Attention and Shared Emotions in the Innovation Process'.

9   Yves Doz and Keeley Wilson, *Ringtone: Exploring the Rise and Fall of Nokia in Mobile Phones*, Oxford University Press, 2017.

10 Juha-Antti Lamberg, Sandra Lubinaitė, Jari Ojala and Henrikki Tikkanen, 'The Curse of Agility: The Nokia Corporation and the Loss of Market Dominance in Mobile Phones, 2003–2013', *Business History*, 2021, vol. 63, no. 4, pp. 574–605.

11 Doz and Wilson, *Ringtone*.

12 These figures were calculated using Nokia's annual reports, and a full list of its products is at 'List of Nokia Products', Wikipedia.

13 See, for example, Juliette Garside and Charles Arthur, 'Microsoft Buys Nokia Handset Business for €5.4bn', *Guardian*, 3 September 2013; Alex Hern, 'Nokia Returns to the Phone Market as Microsoft Sells Brand', *Guardian*, 18 May 2016.

14 Author interview with Timothy Jones on 3 February 2014.

15 'Main Points of Longevity for Japanese Companies', Bank of Korea, 2008; Takashi Shimizu, 'The Longevity of the Japanese Big Businesses', *Annals of Business Administrative Science*, 2002, vol. 1, no. 3, pp. 39–46; Bryan Lufkin, 'Why So Many of the World's Oldest Companies Are in Japan', BBC, 12 February 2020.

16 Nasa has 155 facilities in total, which it has either inherited from the US Air Force, the US Army, or has built itself, 'NASA Facilities', Wikipedia.

17 This is described in more detail in Doz and Wilson, *Ringtone*.

18 Doz and Wilson, *Ringtone*.

19 Doz and Wilson, *Ringtone*.

20 Cyrus Ramezani, Luc Soenen and Alan Jung, 'Growth, Corporate Profitability, and Value Creation', *Financial Analysts Journal*, 2002, vol. 58, no. 6, pp. 56–67.

21 Ramezani, Soenen and Jung, 'Growth, Corporate Profitability, and Value Creation'; Leigh Buchanan, 'Life After the Inc. 500: Fortune, Flameout, and Self Discovery', *Inc.*, September 2012.

22 Max Marner, Bjoern Lasse Herrmann, Ertan Dogrultan and Ron Berman, 'The Startup Genome Report Extra on Premature Scaling: A Deep Dive Into Why Most High Growth Startups Fail', Startup Genome, 2012.

23 Marner, Herrmann, Dogrultan and Berman, 'The Startup Genome Report Extra on Premature Scaling'.

24 Marner, Herrmann, Dogrultan and Berman, 'The Startup Genome Report Extra on Premature Scaling'.

25 Marner, Herrmann, Dogrultan and Berman, 'The Startup Genome Report Extra on Premature Scaling'.

26 See, for example, Robin Dunbar, *Grooming, Gossip, and the Evolution of Language*, Faber & Faber, 1996; Hirotani Kudo and Robin Dunbar, 'Neocortex Size and Social Network Size in Primates', *Animal Behaviour*, 2001, vol. 62, no. 4, pp. 711–22; Robin Dunbar, 'Why Humans Aren't Just Great Apes', *Issues in Ethnology and Anthropology*, 2008, vol. 3, no. 3, pp. 15–33; Robin Dunbar, Pádraig Mac Carron and Susanne Shultz, 'Primate Social Group Sizes Exhibit a Regular Scaling Pattern with Natural Attractors', *Biology Letters*, 2018, vol. 14, no. 1, article 20170490; Robin Dunbar and Richard Sosis, 'Optimising Human Community Sizes', *Evolution and Human Behavior*, 2018, vol. 39, no. 1, pp. 106–11.

27 Robin Dunbar, 'Coevolution of Neocortical Size, Group Size and Language in Humans', *Behavioral and Brain Sciences*, 1993, vol. 16, no. 4, pp. 681–94.

28 This process is explained in more detail on www.hutterites.org; Gianmarco Alberti, 'Modeling Group Size and Scalar Stress by Logistic Regression from an Archaeological Perspective', *PLOS One*, 2014, vol. 9, no. 3, article 91510.

29 Robin Dunbar, *Grooming, Gossip, and the Evolution of Language*.

30 See, for example, Kudo and Dunbar, 'Neocortex Size and Social Network Size in Primates'; Catherine Markham and Laurence Gesquiere, 'Costs and Benefits of Group Living in Primates: An Energetic Perspective', *Philosophical Transactions of the Royal Society B: Biological Sciences*, 2017, vol. 372, no. 1727, article 20160239 ; Ethan Pride, 'Optimal Group Size and Seasonal Stress in Ring-Tailed Lemurs (*Lemur catta*)', *Behavioral Ecology*, 2005, vol. 16, no. 3, pp. 550–60; Katja Rudolph, Claudia Fichtel, Dominic Schneider, Michael Heistermann, Flavia Koch and Rolf Daniel, 'One Size Fits All? Relationships Among Group Size, Health, and Ecology Indicate

a Lack of an Optimal Group Size in a Wild Lemur Population', *Behavioral Ecology and Sociobiology*, 2019, vol. 73, article 132.

31 See, for example, 'The Future of Jobs: Employment, Skills and Workforce Strategy for the Fourth Industrial Revolution', World Economic Forum, January 2016; Gary Hamel and Michele Zanini, 'The $3 Trillion Prize for Busting Bureaucracy (and How to Claim It)', Humanistic Management Network, 2016, Research Paper Series, no. 28/16; Gary Hamel and Michele Zanini, 'The End of Bureaucracy: How a Chinese Appliance Maker Is Reinventing Management for the Digital Age', *Harvard Business Review*, November–December 2018, pp. 50–9.

32 David Hounshell and John Kenly-Smith, *Science and Corporate Strategy: DuPont R and D, 1902–1980*, Cambridge University Press, 1988.

33 A more detailed description of Gore's journey is given in 'Culture Press Kit', Gore.

34 Douglas McGregor, *The Human Side of Enterprise*, McGraw Hill, 1960.

35 Alan Deutschman, 'The Fabric of Creativity: At W.L. Gore, Innovation Is More than Skin Deep: The Culture Is as Imaginative as the Products', *Fast Company*, 4 January 2004.

36 Gary Hamel, 'W.L. Gore: Lessons from a Management Revolutionary', *Wall Street Journal*, 18 March 2010; Gary Hamel, 'W.L. Gore: Lessons from a Management Revolutionary, Part 2', *Wall Street Journal*, 2 April 2010.

37 Gary Hamel, 'W.L. Gore: Lessons from a Management Revolutionary'; Gary Hamel, 'W.L. Gore: Lessons from a Management Revolutionary, Part 2'.

38 Gary Hamel, 'W.L. Gore: Lessons from a Management Revolutionary'.

39 Gary Hamel, 'W.L. Gore: Lessons from a Management Revolutionary'; Gary Hamel, 'W.L. Gore: Lessons from a Management Revolutionary, Part 2'.

40 Simon Caulkin, 'Gore-Tex Gets Made Without Managers', *Guardian*, 2 November 2008.

41 Gary Hamel, 'W.L. Gore: Lessons from a Management Revolutionary'; Gary Hamel, 'W.L. Gore: Lessons from a Management Revolutionary, Part 2'.

42 'America's Largest Private Companies', *Forbes*.

43 'Best Workplaces for Innovators,' *Fast Company*, 2021.

44 See, for example, 'Annual Report and Consolidated Financial Statements', Eton College, 2020; 'Annual Report', Royal Academy of Music, 2020; 'Annual Accounts', Royal College of Art, 2020.

45 See, for example, Matt Trueman, 'RSC's Matilda: The Musical a Hit on Broadway', *Guardian*, 12 April 2013; 'Spinoff 2022', Nasa, 2022; 'NASA Spinoff Technologies', Wikipedia.

46 'List of Fatal Accidents and Incidents Involving Commercial Aircraft in the United States', Wikipedia.

47 'Resource Management on the Flight Deck', Nasa Conference Publication.

48 See, for example, Robert Helmreich and John Wilhelm, 'Outcomes of Crew Resource Management Training', *International Journal of Aviation Psychology*, 1991, vol. 1, no. 4, pp. 287–300; Paul O'Connor, Justin Campbell, Jennifer Newon, John Melton, Eduardo Salas and Katherine Wilson, 'Crew Resource Management Training Effectiveness: A Meta-analysis and Some Critical Needs', *International Journal of Aviation Psychology*, 2008, vol. 18, no. 4, pp. 353–68.

49 Graham Henry, *Final Word*; Thomas Johnson, Andrew Martin, Farah Palmer, Geoffrey Watson and Phil Ramsey, 'Collective Leadership: A Case Study of the All Blacks', *Asia-Pacific Management and Business Application*, 2012, vol. 1, no. 1, pp. 53–67.

50 See, for example, Maria Krysan, Kristin Moore and Nicholas Zill, 'Identifying Successful Families: An Overview of Constructs and Selected Measures', US Department of Health and Human Services, 9 May 1990.

51 See, for example, Jane Jacobs, *The Death and Life of Great American Cities*, Random House, 1961; Hildebrand Frey, *Designing the City: Towards a More Sustainable Urban Form*, E. & F.N. Spon, 1999; Brian Edwards, *The European Perimeter Block: The Scottish Experience of Courtyard Housing*, Taylor & Francis, 2004; Barrie Shelton, *Learning from the Japanese City: Looking East in Urban Design*, Routledge, 2012.

52 'Why Eton Is So Special', *Country Life*, 20 September 2007.

53 See, for example, Gregor Timlin and Nic Rysenbry, 'Design for Dementia', Royal College of Art, 2010; 'Redesigning the Emergency Ambulance: Improving Mobile Emergency Healthcare', Helen Hamlyn Centre for Design, Royal College of Art, 2011.

Habit 10: X-ray everything

1 Robert May, 'How Many Species Are There on Earth?' *Science*, 1988, vol. 241, no. 4872, pp. 1441–9; Leslie Hannah, 'Marshall's Trees and the Global Forest: Were Giant Redwoods Different?', LSE Research Online Documents on Economics 20363, 1997.

2 Howard McCurdy, *Inside NASA: High Technology and Organizational Change in the U.S. Space Program*, Johns Hopkins University Press, 1993.

3 Howard McCurdy, *Inside NASA*.

4   'NASA Pocket Statistics: 1990 Edition', Nasa, 1990.

5   Howard McCurdy, *Inside NASA*.

6   Howard McCurdy, *Inside NASA*.

7   Andrew Dunar and Stephen Waring, *Power to Explore: A History of the Marshall Space Flight Center*, CreateSpace, 1999.

8   Edward Tufte, *Visual Explanations: Images and Quantities, Evidence and Narrative*, Graphics Press, 1997; Joseph Hall, '*Columbia* and *Challenger*: Organizational Failure at NASA', *Space Policy*, 2016, vol. 37, part 3, pp. 127–33.

9   Joseph Hall, 'Columbia and Challenger'.

10   Diane Vaughan, *The Challenger Launch Decision: Risky Technology, Culture, and Deviance at NASA*, University of Chicago Press, 1996.

11   'Report to the President by the Presidential Commission on the Space Shuttle Challenger Accident', Nasa, 6 June 1986.

12   Howard McCurdy, *Faster, Better, Cheaper: Low-Cost Innovation in the U.S. Space Program*, Johns Hopkins University Press, 2001; Ariana Eunjung Cha, 'At NASA, Concerns on Contractors', *Washington Post*, 17 February 2003.

13   Julianne Mahler, *Organizational Learning at NASA: The Challenger and Columbia Accidents*, Georgetown University Press, 2009.

14   Julianne Mahler, *Organizational Learning at NASA*.

15   'Culture Change at NASA', Wayne Hale's Blog, 22 January 2010.

16   Stephen Johnson, 'Success, Failure, and NASA Culture', *ASK*, 1 September 2008; Behavioral Safety Technology, 'Interim Assessment of the NASA Culture Change Effort', Nasa, 16 February 2005.

17   Keith Darce, 'Ground Control: NASA Attempts a Cultural Shift', *Seattle Times*, 24 April 2005.

18   Dunar and Waring, *Power to Explore*.

19   Anna Haislip, 'Failure Leads to Success', *Colorado Daily*, 21 February 2007.

20   The work done by the Standish Group can be seen at www.standishgroup.com; Jorge Dominguez, 'The Curious Case of the CHAOS Report 2009', July 2009, Project Smart.

21   Peter Bills, *The Jersey*.

22   See, for example, Shane Lopez and Michelle Louis, 'The Principles of Strengths-Based Education', *Journal of College and Character*, 2009, vol. 10, no. 4; Janis Birkeland, 'Positive Development and Assessment', *Smart and Sustainable Built Environment*, 2014, vol. 3, no. 1, pp. 4–22; Mette

Jacobsgaard and Irene Nørlund, 'The Impact of Appreciative Inquiry on International Development', *AI Practitioner*, 2001, vol. 13, no. 3, pp.4–8.

23 Geoffrey Murray, *Vietnam Dawn of a New Market*, Palgrave Macmillan, 1997; Spencer Tucker, *The Encyclopedia of the Vietnam War: A Political, Social, and Military History*, ABC-CLIO, 1998.

24 Richard Pascale, Jerry Sternin and Monique Sternin, *The Power of Positive Deviance: How Unlikely Innovators Solve the World's Toughest Problems*, Harvard Business Review, 2010.

25 Marian Zeitlin, Hossein Ghassemi and Mohamed Mansour, *Positive Deviance in Child Nutrition: With Emphasis on Psychological and Behavioural Aspects and Implications for Development*, United Nations University Press, 1990.

26 Pascale, Sternin and Sternin, *The Power of Positive Deviance*.

27 Dennis Sparks, 'From Hunger Aid to School Reform: An Interview with Jerry Sternin', *Journal of Staff Development*, 2004, vol. 25, no. 1, pp. 46–51.

28 Olga Wollinka, Erin Keeley, Barton Burkhalter and Naheed Bashir, 'Hearth Nutrition Model: Applications in Haiti, Vietnam and Bangladesh', published for the US Agency for International Development and World Relief Corporation by the Basic Support for Institutionalizing Child Survival (BASICS) Project, 1997; Monique Sternin, Jerry Sternin and David Marsh, 'Designing a Community-Based Nutrition Program Using the Hearth Model and the Positive Deviance Approach – A Field Guide', Save the Children, 1998; Monique Sternin, Jerry Sternin and David Marsh, *Scaling Up Poverty Alleviation and Nutrition Program in Vietnam*, Routledge, 1999.

29 Sternin, Sternin and Marsh, 'Designing a Community-Based Nutrition Program'.

30 Richard Pascale and Jerry Sternin, 'Your Company's Secret Change Agents', *Harvard Business Review*, May 2005, pp. 72–81.

31 Pascale, Sternin and Sternin, *The Power of Positive Deviance*.

32 Pascale, Sternin and Sternin, *The Power of Positive Deviance*.

33 Dennis Sparks, 'From Hunger Aid to School Reform'.

34 Monique Sternin, Jerry Sternin and David Marsh, 'Rapid, Sustained Childhood Malnutrition Alleviation Through a Positive Deviance Approach in Rural Vietnam: Preliminary Findings', in 'Hearth Nutrition Model', ed. Wollinka, Keeley, Burkhalter and Bashir, 1997; Agnes Mackintosh, David Marsh and Dirk Schroeder, 'Sustained Positive Deviant Child

Care Practices and Their Effects on Child Growth in Vietnam', *Food and Nutrition Bulletin*, 2002, vol. 23, no. 4, pp. 16–25.

35   Dennis Sparks, 'From Hunger Aid to School Reform'.

36   Daniel Kahneman and Amos Tversky, 'Choices, Values, and Frames', *American Psychologist*, 1984, vol. 39, no. 4, pp. 341–50; Irwin Levin, Sandra Schneider and Gary Gaeth, 'All Frames Are Not Created Equal: A Typology and Critical Analysis of Framing Effects', *Organizational Behavior and Human Decision Processes*, 1998, vol. 76, no. 2, pp. 149–88; Nathan Novemsky and Daniel Kahneman, 'The Boundaries of Loss Aversion', *Journal of Marketing Research*, 2005, vol. 42, no. 2, pp. 119–28; Eldad Yechiam and Guy Hochman, 'Losses as Modulators of Attention: Review and Analysis of the Unique Effects of Losses Over Gains', *Psychological Bulletin*, 2013, vol. 139, no. 2, pp. 497–518.

37   Marcel Detienne and Jean-Pierre Vernant, *Cunning Intelligence in Greek Culture and Society*, University of Chicago Press, 1991; James Scott, *Seeing Like a State: How Certain Schemes to Improve the Human Condition Have Failed*, Yale University Press, 1998; Cheryl De Ciantis, 'Gods and Myths in the Information Age', *Agir*, 2005, no. 20–21, pp. 179–86.

38   Peter Frisk, 'Marginal Gains: Alcohol on Bike Tyres, and Electrically Heated Shorts', peterfrisk.com, 20 March 2019.

39   Peter Lovatt, 'Dance Psychology: The Science of Dance and Dancers', Dr Dance Presents: Norfolk, 2018; Marily Oppezzo and Daniel Schwartz, 'Give Your Ideas Some Legs: The Positive Effect of Walking on Creative Thinking', *Journal of Experimental Psychology: Learning, Memory, and Cognition*, 2014, vol. 40, no. 4, pp. 1142–52.

40   Nicholas Kohn, Paul Paulus and YunHee Choi, 'Building on the Ideas of Others: An Examination of the Idea Combination Process', *Journal of Experimental Social Psychology*, 2011, vol. 47, no. 3, pp. 554–61; Runa Korde and Paul Paulus, 'Alternating Individual and Group Idea Generation: Finding the Elusive Synergy', *Journal of Experimental Social Psychology*, 2017, vol. 70, pp. 177–90; Simone Ritter and Nel Mostert, 'How to Facilitate a Brainstorming Session: The Effect of Idea Generation Techniques and of Group Brainstorm After Individual Brainstorm', *Creative Industries Journal*, 2018, vol. 11, no. 3, pp. 263–77.

41   Author interview with Clive Grinyer on 27 March 2019.

42   Sara Kraemer, Pascale Carayon and Ruth Duggan, 'Red Team Performance for Improved Computer Security', *Proceedings of the Human Factors and Ergonomics Society Annual Meeting*, 2004, vol. 48, no. 14,

pp. 1605–9; *Red Teaming Handbook*, 3rd Edition, UK Ministry of Defence, 2021.

43 Colin Powell, *My American Journey*, Ballantine Books, 1995; Oren Harari, 'Quotations from Chairman Powell: A Leadership Primer', *Management Review*, 1996, vol. 85, no. 12, pp. 34–7.

44 Daniel Kahneman, *Thinking Fast and Slow*, Penguin, 2011.

45 Adrian Furnham and Hua Chu Boo, 'A Literature Review of the Anchoring Effect', *Journal of Socio-Economics*, 2011, vol. 40, no. 1, pp. 35–42.

46 See, for example, Nicholas Epley and Thomas Gilovich, 'Putting Adjustment Back in the Anchoring and Adjustment Heuristic: Differential Processing of Self-Generated and Experimenter-Provided Anchors', *Psychological Science*, 2001, vol. 12, no. 5, pp. 391–6; Adam Galinsky and Thomas Mussweiler, 'First Offers as Anchors: The Role of Perspective-Taking and Negotiator Focus', *Journal of Personality and Social Psychology*, 2001, vol. 81, no. 4, pp. 657–69.

47 Andrew Gelman and Deborah Nolan, *Teaching Statistics: A Bag of Tricks*, 2nd Edition, Oxford University Press, 2017.

48 Jerry Markham, *A Financial History of the United States*, M.E. Sharpe, 2002; Claudio Feser, *Serial Innovators: Firms That Change the World*, Wiley, 2011; Gavin Braithwaite-Smith, 'The Cost of a Car in the Year You Were Born', Motoring Research, 13 May 2020.

49 Robert McNamara, *In Retrospect: The Tragedy and Lessons of Vietnam*, Vintage, 1996; Keir Martin, 'Robert McNamara and the Limits of "Bean Counting"', *Anthropology Today*, 2010, vol. 26, no. 3, pp. 16–19.

50 Colin Powell, *My American Journey*; Ralph White, 'Misperception of Aggression in Vietnam', *Journal of International Affairs*, 1967, vol. 21, no. 1, pp. 123–40; 'NLF and PAVN Battle Tactics', Wikipedia.

51 Andrew Natsios, 'The Clash of the Counter-Bureaucracy and Development', Center for Global Development, 1 July 2010.

52 Colin Powell, *My American Journey*.

53 'Vietnam War U.S. Military Fatal Casualty Statistics', US National Archives, 2019; Douglas Dacy, *Foreign Aid, War and Economic Development: South Vietnam 1955–1975*, Cambridge University Press, 1986.

54 Amos Tversky and Daniel Kahneman, 'Belief in the Law of Small Numbers', *Psychological Bulletin*, 1971, vol. 76, no. 2, pp. 105–10; Richard Nisbett and Eugene Borgida, 'Attribution and the Psychology of Prediction', *Journal of Personality and Social Psychology*, 1975, vol. 32, no. 5, pp. 932–43; Gelman and Nolan, *Teaching Statistics: A Bag of Tricks*; Howard Wainer

and Harris Zwerling, 'Evidence That Smaller Schools Do Not Improve Student Achievement', *Phi Delta Kappan*, 2006, vol. 88, no. 4, pp. 300–3.

55 Such as 'Sample Size Calculator', Calculator.net

56 Jack Hopkins, 'The Eradication of Smallpox: Organizational Learning and Innovation in International Health Administration', *Journal of Developing Areas*, 1988, vol. 22, no. 3, pp. 321–32.

57 Jack Hopkins, 'The Eradication of Smallpox'; Donald Henderson, 'How Smallpox Showed the Way', *World Health*, December 1989, pp. 19–21.

58 Molecular Interventions, 'Interview with D.A. Henderson: Acting Globally, Thinking Locally', *Molecular Interventions*, 2003, vol. 3, no. 5, pp. 242–7.

59 Donald Henderson and Petra Klepac, 'Lessons from the Eradication of Smallpox: An Interview with D.A. Henderson', *Philosophical Transactions of the Royal Society B: Biological Sciences*, 2013, vol. 368, mo. 1623, article 20130113.

60 Robert Coram, *Boyd: The Fighter Pilot Who Changed the Art of War*, Back Bay, 2004; Tim Brown, *Change by Design: How Design Thinking Transforms Organizations and Inspires Innovation*, Harper Business, 2009.

Habit 11: Make time for random

1 Mikel Harry and Richard Schroeder, *Six Sigma: The Breakthrough Management Strategy Revolutionizing the World's Top Companies*, Bantam, 2000.

2 Bill Smith, 'Making War on Defects', *IEEE Spectrum*, 1993, vol. 30, no. 9, pp. 43–50.

3 Peter Pande, Robert Neuman and Roland Cavanagh, *The Six Sigma Way: How GE, Motorola and Other Top Companies Are Honing Their Performance*, McGraw Hill, 2000.

4 Pande, Neuman and Cavanagh, *The Six Sigma Way*.

5 Associated Press, 'Motorola Suspends Dividend Amid $3.6 Billion Loss', *New York Times*, 3 February 2009.

6 Michael Raynor and Mumtaz Ahmed, *The Three Rules: How Exceptional Companies Think*, Penguin, 2013; Michael Raynor and Mumtaz Ahmed, 'Three Rules for Making a Company Truly Great', *Harvard Business Review*, April 2013.

7 Raynor and Ahmed, 'Three Rules for Making a Company Truly Great'.

8 Raynor and Ahmed, 'Three Rules for Making a Company Truly Great'.

9 Stated in General Electric's annual report, 2001.

10 Raynor and Ahmed, *The Three Rules*.

11 'Innovation and Growth: Rationale for an Innovation Strategy', OECD, 2007; this view is supported by other research such as: Nathan Rosenberg, 'Innovation and Economic Growth', OECD, 27 September 2004; Rana Maradana, Rudra Pradhan, Saurav Dash, Kunal Gaurav, Manu Jayakumar and Debaleena Chatterjee, 'Does Innovation Promote Economic Growth? Evidence from European Countries', *Journal of Innovation and Entrepreneurship*, 2017, vol. 6, article 1; James Broughel and Adam Thierer, 'Technological Innovation and Economic Growth: A Brief Report on the Evidence', Mercatus Research Center, George Mason University, 2019.

12 'Innovation and Growth', OECD.

13 Robert Slater, *Jack Welch and the GE Way: Management Insights and Leadership Secrets of the Legendary CEO*, McGraw Hill Education, 1998.

14 Brian Hindo, 'At 3M, a Struggle Between Efficiency and Creativity', Bloomberg, 11 June 2007.

15 Dennis Carey, Brian Dumaine, Michael Useem and Rodney Zemmel, *Go Long: Why Long-Term Thinking Is Your Best Short-Term Strategy*, Wharton School Press, 2018.

16 Carey, Dumaine, Useem and Zemmel, *Go Long*.

17 Brian Hindo, 'At 3M, a Struggle Between Efficiency and Creativity'.

18 '3M Shelves Six Sigma in R&D', *Design News*, 10 December 2007.

19 Brian Hindo, 'At 3M, a Struggle Between Efficiency and Creativity'.

20 David Gelles, Natalie Kitroeff, Jack Nicas and Rebecca Ruiz, 'Boeing Was "Go, Go, Go" to Beat Airbus with the 737 Max', *New York Times*, 23 March 2019.

21 Gelles, Kitroeff, Nicas and Ruiz, 2019, 'Boeing Was "Go, Go, Go" to Beat Airbus'.

22 'Final Committee Report: The Design, Development and Certification of the Boeing 737 Max', The House Committee on Transportation and Infrastructure, September 2020.

23 Dominic Gates and Mike Baker, 'Engineers Say Boeing Pushed to Limit Safety Testing in Race to Certify Planes, Including 737 MAX', *Seattle Times*, 5 May 2019; 'Boeing's Troubles Cost the Aerospace Industry $4bn a Quarter', *The Economist*, 22 August 2019.

24 Raynor and Ahmed, *The Three Rules*; Raynor and Ahmed, 'Three Rules for Making a Company Truly Great'.

25 As shown in their annual reports.

26 Yasuhiro Monden, *Toyota Management System: Linking the Seven Key Functional Areas*, Routledge, 2019.

27 Author interview with Timothy Jones on 3 February 2014.

28   Jeffrey Miller and Thomas Vollmann, 'The Hidden Factory', *Harvard Business Review*, September 1985; Sadi Assaf, Abdulaziz Bubshait, Sulaiman Atiyah and Mohammed Al-Shahri, 'The Management of Construction Company Overhead Costs', *International Journal of Project Management*, 2001, vol. 19, no. 5, pp. 295–303; Mary Ellen Biery, 'A Sure-Fire Way to Boost the Bottom Line', *Forbes*, 12 January 2014; Hamel and Zanini, 'The $3 Trillion Prize for Busting Bureaucracy'.

29   As shown in their annual reports.

30   For a more detailed list of the RCA's recent student projects, see 'Research Projects', Royal College of Art.

31   Some examples of the Helen Hamlin Centre's collaborative projects, and other AcrossRCA projects can be seen at 'Research Projects', Royal College of Art and the AcrossRCA website.

32   Author interview with Paul Thompson on 18 November 2018, at Leaders in Sport, see: Alex Hill, 'Summit Session: Are You Radically Traditional?'.

33   'Start-up Companies', Royal College of Art.

34   United Nations Development Programme, 'Human Development Indices and Indicators: A Statistical Update', Human Development Reports, 1 January 2018; 'GDP and Its Breakdown at Current Prices in US Dollars', United Nations, 2019; 'World Economic Outlook Database', International Monetary Fund, 2022.

35   'What Next for the Start-Up Nation?', *The Economist*, 21 January 2012; David Yin, 'Secrets to Israel's Innovative Edge: Part I', *Forbes*, 5 June 2016; 'Main Science and Technology Indicators', OECD, March 2022.

36   David Yin, 'Secrets to Israel's Innovative Edge'.

37   A full list of all the companies can be found at 'Israeli-Founded Unicorns', TechAviv.

38   Dan Senor and Saul Singer, *Start-Up Nation: The Story of Israel's Economic Miracle*, Twelve, 2009.

39   'International Migration Database', OECD Statistics, 2022.

40   Senor and Singer, *Start-Up Nation*.

41   Richard Behar, 'Inside Israel's Secret Startup Machine', *Forbes*, 11 May 2016; Reed Miller, 'Intuition Robotics Is Trying to Build a Market for Robotic Companions, Launches ElliQ in US', Medtech Insight, 14 April 2022.

42   Senor and Singer, *Start-Up Nation*.

43   Dominic Rushe, 'Google Buys Waze Map App for $1.3bn', *Guardian*, 11 June 2013.

44 Parmy Olson, 'Why Google's Waze Is Trading User Data with Local Governments', *Forbes*, 7 July 2014; Nicole Kobie, 'How Your Phone Data Saves London's Transport from Chaos', *Wired*, 10 December 2018.

45 Rebecca Greenfield, 'Google Won the War for Waze by Letting It Stay out of Silicon Valley', *Atlantic*, 11 June 2013.

46 This is described in more detail at 'History Timeline: Post-it Notes', Post-it.

47 Don Peppers, 'The Downside of Six Sigma', LinkedIn, 5 May 2016.

48 Brian Hindo, 'At 3M, a Struggle Between Efficiency and Creativity'.

49 Ekaterina Olshannikova, Thomas Olsson, Jukka Huhtamäki, Susanna Paasovaara and Hannu Kärkkäinen, 'From Chance to Serendipity: Knowledge Workers' Experiences of Serendipitous Social Encounters', *Advances in Human-Computer Interaction*, 2020, vol. 2020, article 1827107; Yuki Noguchi, 'How a Bigger Lunch Table at Work Can Boost Productivity', NPR, 20 May 2015; Claire Cain Miller, 'When Chance Encounters at the Water Cooler Are Most Useful', *New York Times*, 4 September 2021.

50 Walter Isaacson, *Steve Jobs*.

51 'Pixar Headquarters and the Legacy of Steve Jobs', Office Snapshots, 16 July 2019.

52 Ed Catmull, *Creativity Inc.*

53 Author interview with Timothy Jones on 3 February 2014.

54 Ed Catmull, *Creativity Inc.*

55 Ed Catmull, *Creativity Inc.*

Habit 12: Break bread

1 Leonard Wong, Thomas Kolditz, Raymond Millen and Terence Potter, 'Why They Fight: Combat Motivation in the Iraq War', US Army War College, Strategic Studies Institute, 2003.

2 Wong, Kolditz, Millen and Potter, 'Why They Fight'.

3 Wong, Kolditz, Millen and Potter, 'Why They Fight'.

4 Wong, Kolditz, Millen and Potter, 'Why They Fight'.

5 Wong, Kolditz, Millen and Potter, 'Why They Fight'.

6 Wong, Kolditz, Millen and Potter, 'Why They Fight'.

7 Wong, Kolditz, Millen and Potter, 'Why They Fight'.

8 Wong, Kolditz, Millen and Potter, 'Why They Fight'.

9 Wong, Kolditz, Millen and Potter, 'Why They Fight'.

10 Wong, Kolditz, Millen and Potter, 'Why They Fight'.

11 Wong, Kolditz, Millen and Potter, 'Why They Fight'.

12   See, for example: Stanley Gully, Aparna Joshi, Kara Incalcaterra, Matthew Beaubien, 'Meta-analysis of Team-Efficacy, Potency, and Performance: Interdependence and Level of Analysis as Moderators of Observed Relationships', *Journal of Applied Psychology*, 2002, vol. 87, no. 5, pp. 819–32; Christopher Parker, Boris Baltes, Scott Young, Joseph Huff, Robert Altmann, Heather LaCost and Joanne Roberts, 'Relationships Between Psychological Climate Perceptions and Work Outcomes: A Meta-analytic Review', *Journal of Organizational Behavior*, 2003, vol. 24, no. 4, pp. 389–416; Khoa Tran, Phuong Nguyen, Thao Dang and Tran Ton, 'The Impacts of the High-Quality Workplace Relationships on Job Performance: A Perspective on Staff Nurses in Vietnam', *Behavioral Sciences*, 2018, vol. 8, no. 12, article 109.

13   Parker, Baltes, Young, Huff, Altmann, Lacost and Roberts, 'Relationships between Psychological Climate Perceptions And Work Outcomes'.

14   Bill Shankly, *Shankly: My Story*, Arthur Barker, 1976.

15   John Keith, *Paisley: Smile on Me and Guide My Hand*, Trinity Mirror Sport Media, 2014.

16   Harry Harris, *The Boss: Jurgen Klopp, Liverpool and the New Anfield Boot Room*, Empire Publications, 2020.

17   Andrey Chegodaev, 'Klopp Opens Up on How Being Young Dad Taught Him Most Important Thing About Football', *Tribuna*, 24 September 2019.

18   James Marshment, 'Becoming a Young Father Has Helped My Career, Says Jurgen Klopp', *TEAMTalk*, 24 May 2017.

19   Jack Lusby, 'Klopp Reveals New Anfield "Boot Room" – "It's the Best Pub in Liverpool!"', This Is Anfield, 31 March 2022.

20   'Mark Lawrenson Compares Liverpool Manager Jurgen Klopp to the Legendary Bill Shankly', BBC Sport, 27 June 2020.

21   Harry Harris, *The Boss*.

22   Gursher Chabba, '"He's Like a Father to Me": Alisson Opens Up About His Relationship with Klopp', *Tribuna*, 23 March 2022.

23   Laura Trott and Jason Kenny, *The Inside Track*, Michael O'Mara, 2016.

24   Victoria Pendleton, *Between the Lines: The Autobiography*, HarperSport, 2012.

25   Trott and Kenny, *The Inside Track*.

26   William Fotheringham, 'Behind the Scenes of British Cycling's Olympic Boot Camp', *Guardian*, 24 December 2011.

27   Author interview with Peter Keen on 20 November 2012.

28   Interview on 17 June 2015.

29   Robin Dunbar, 'Breaking Bread: The Functions of Social Eating', *Adaptive Human Behavior and Physiology*, 2017, vol. 3, pp. 198–211.

30   Robin Dunbar, 'Breaking Bread'.

31   See, for example, James Curley and Eric Kenerne, 'Genes, Brains and Mammalian Social Bonds', *Trends in Ecology & Evolution*, 2005, vol. 20, no. 10, pp. 561–7; Richard Depue and Jeannine Morrone-Strupinsky, 'A Neurobehavioral Model of Affiliative Bonding: Implications for Concept-ualizing a Human Trait of Affiliation', *Behavioral and Brain Sciences*, 2005, vol. 28, no. 3, pp. 313–50; Anna Machin and Robin Dunbar, 'The Brain Opioid Theory of Social Attachment: A Review of the Evidence', *Behaviour*, 2011, vol. 148, no. 9–10, pp. 985–1025.

32   Robin Dunbar, 'Breaking Bread'.

33   Cody Delistraty, 'The Importance of Eating Together', *Atlantic*, 18 July 2014; 'Who Are the School Truants?', OECD, Pisa in Focus, no. 35, 2014.

34   Shannon Robson, Mary Beth McCullough, Samantha Rez, Marcus Munafò and Gemma Taylor, 'Family Meal Frequency, Diet, and Family Function-ing: A Systematic Review with Meta-analyses', *Journal of Nutrition Educa-tion and Behavior*, 2020, vol. 52, no. 5, pp. 553–64.

35   See, for example, Roberto Ferdman, 'The Most American Thing There Is: Eating Alone', *Washington Post*, 18 August 2015; Harry Benson and Steve McKay, 'Happy Eaters', Marriage Foundation: Marriage Week UK, 13–19 May 2019; Esteban Ortiz-Ospina and Max Roser, 'Marriages and Divorces', Our World in Data, 2020; Robson, McCullough, Rez, Munafò and Taylor, 'Family Meal Frequency, Diet, and Family Functioning'.

36   Roberto Ferdman, 'The Most American Thing There Is: Eating Alone'.

37   Steve Serby, 'Defensive Coordinator Patrick Graham Has Been Giants' MVP Thus Far', *New York Post*, 11 November 2020.

38   Baxter Holmes, 'Michelin Restaurants and Fabulous Wines: Inside the Secret Team Dinners That Have Built the Spurs' Dynasty', ESPN, 25 July 2020.

39   Baxter Holmes, 'Michelin Restaurants and Fabulous Wines'.

40   Ira Boudway, 'The Five Pillars of Popovich', Bloomberg, 10 January 2018.

41   Ira Boudway, 'The Five Pillars of Popovich'.

42   Jack McCallum, 'Pop Art', *Sports Illustrated*, 29 April 2013.

43   Dunbar, MacCarron and Shultz, 'Primate Social Group Sizes Exhibit a Regular Scaling Pattern with Natural Attractors'; Robin Dunbar and Matt Spoors, 'Social Networks, Support Cliques, and Kinship', *Human Nature*,

1995, vol. 6, no. 3, pp. 273–90; Alistair Sutcliffe, Robin Dunbar, Jens Binder and Holly Arrow, 'Relationships and the Social Brain: Integrating Psychological and Evolutionary Perspectives', *British Journal of Psychology*, 2012, vol. 103, no. 2, pp. 149–68; Maxwell Burton-Chellew and Robin Dunbar, 'Romance and Reproduction Are Socially Costly', *Evolutionary Behavioral Sciences*, 2015, vol. 9, no. 4, pp. 229–41; Kudo and Dunbar, 'Neocortex Size and Social Network Size in Primates'.

44 George Miller, 'The Magical Number Seven, Plus or Minus Two: Some Limits on Our Capacity for Processing Information', *Psychological Review*, 1956, vol. 63, no. 2, pp. 81–97; Richard Hackman, *Leading Teams: Setting the Stage for Great Performances*, Harvard Business Review Press, 2002; Nicolas Fay, Simon Garrod and Jean Carletta, 'Group Discussion as Interactive Dialogue or as Serial Monologue: The Influence of Group Size', *Psychological Science*, 2000, vol. 11, no. 6, pp. 481–6.

45 Fay, Garrod and Carletta, 'Group Discussion as Interactive Dialogue or as Serial Monologue'.

46 George Miller, 'The Magical Number Seven, Plus or Minus Two'.

47 Robert Sommer, 'Leadership and Group Geography', *Sociometry*, 1961, vol. 24, no. 1, pp. 99–110.

48 Antony Clayton, *London's Coffee Houses: A Stimulating Story*, Historical Publications, 2003; 'The Internet in a Cup: Coffee Fuelled the Information Exchanges of the 17th and 18th Centuries', *The Economist*, 18 December 2003.

49 'We're Not Taking Enough Lunch Breaks. Why That's Bad for Business', NPR, 5 March 2015.

50 Ken Kniffin, Brian Wansink, Carol Devine and Jeffery Sobal, 'Eating Together at the Firehouse: How Workplace Commensality Relates to the Performance of Firefighters', *Human Performance*, 2015, vol. 28, no. 4, pp. 281–306.

51 Kniffin, Wansick, Devine and Sobal, 'Eating Together at the Firehouse'.

52 Ed Catmull, *Creativity Inc.*

53 Charles Duhigg, 'What Google Learned from Its Quest to Build the Perfect Team', *New York Times*, 25 February 2016.

54 Charles Duhigg, *Smarter, Faster, Better: The Secrets of Being Productive*, William Heinemann, 2016.

55 Charles Duhigg, *Smarter, Faster, Better*.

Conclusion: Protect your home

1   This is described in more detail in John Alexander, 'Mark Peters Always Confident Henry Was the Right Man for the Job', *Stuff*, 19 October 2011; Graham Henry, *Final Word*.

2   This is described in more detail in Graham Henry, *Final Word*.

3   'Reconditioning a Mistake – Henry', *New Zealand Herald*, 6 December 2007.

4   James Kerr, *Legacy: What the All Blacks Can Teach Us About the Business of Life*, Constable, 2013.

5   'List of New Zealand National Rugby Union Players', Wikipedia.

6   See, for example, 'Football: Barca Coach Likes What He Sees with All Blacks'; Gregor Paul, 'Rugby: All Blacks Learn from Marines'; Ben Smith, 'How an NBA GM Inspired the All Blacks Lethal Counter Attack'; 'All Blacks Try Life in Fast Lane at McLaren's F1 Garage.

7   'Columbia Crew Survival Investigation Report', Nasa, 2008.

8   Behavioral Safety Technology Report, 'Interim Assessment of the NASA Culture Change Effort'; Stephen Johnson, 'Success, Failure, and NASA Culture'.

Index